D0079626

DATE DUE

APR 0 6 1999	
APR 1 1 2000	
MAY 0 6 2005	
11-5-09	
GAYLORD	PRINTED IN U.S.A.

The Caribbean Challenge

Also of Interest

†*The New Cuban Presence in the Caribbean,* edited by Barry B. Levine

Revolutionary Cuba: Economic Growth, Income Distribution, and Basic Needs, Claes Brundenius

Political Change in Central America: Internal and External Dimensions, edited by Wolf-Grabendorff, Heinrich-W. Krumwiede, and Jeorg Todt

Controlling Latin American Conflicts: Ten Approaches, edited by Michael A. Morris and Victor Millán

†*Latin America and the U.S. National Interest: A Basis for U.S. Foreign Policy,* Margaret Daly Hayes

†*Revolution in Central America,* edited by Stanford Central America Action Network, Stanford University

Mexico's Oil: Catalyst for a New Relationship with the U.S.?, Manuel R. Millor

†*The End and the Beginning: The Nicaraguan Revolution,* John A. Booth

Colossus Challenged: The Struggle for Caribbean Influence, edited by H. Michael Erisman and John D. Martz

†*Revolution in El Salvador: Origins and Evolution,* Tommie Sue Montgomery, with a Foreword by Román Mayorga Quiroz

†*Latin American Foreign Policies: Global and Regional Dimensions,* edited by Elizabeth G. Ferris and Jennie K. Lincoln

Dependency and Intervention: The Case of Guatemala in 1954, José M. Aybar de Soto, with a Foreword by Fred Warner Neal

Development Strategies and Basic Needs in Latin America, edited by Claes Brundenius and Mats Lundahl, with a Foreword by Jon Sigurdson

PROFILES OF CONTEMPORARY LATIN AMERICA

†*Nicaragua: The Land of Sandino,* Thomas W. Walker

†*The Dominican Republic: A Caribbean Crucible,* Howard J. Wiarda and Michael J. Kryzanek

Colombia: Portrait of Unity and Diversity, Harvey F. Kline

†*Mexico: Paradoxes of Stability and Change,* Daniel Levy and Gabriel Székely

†Available in hardcover and paperback.

Westview Special Studies on Latin America and the Caribbean

The Caribbean Challenge:
U.S. Policy in a Volatile Region
edited by H. Michael Erisman

The revolutionary dramas unfolding in Grenada and Nicaragua, the violence-scarred Manley/Seaga electoral confrontation in Jamaica, and especially the guerrilla wars raging in El Salvador and to a lesser extent in Guatemala have thrust the Caribbean Basin into the public's consciousness throughout the world. In the United States, Caribbean affairs have become a top priority item on the Reagan administration's foreign policy agenda.

This book comprehensively examines U.S. policy toward the Caribbean Basin. The authors pinpoint the major challenges posed by the region, analyze the main variables influencing Washington's policies for responding to those challenges, evaluate the viability of the Reagan administration's specific responses, and propose a blueprint for future directions in U.S. Caribbean Basin policy.

The book combines macroanalyses of U.S. policy with case studies of contemporary U.S. relations with selected countries. The case studies investigate the translation of the general trends into specific policies for dealing with countries whose bilateral relations with the United States bring into sharp focus the crucial challenges confronting the United States in the Caribbean Basin.

H. Michael Erisman is associate professor of political science at Mercyhurst College. He has contributed a chapter to *The New Cuban Presence in the Caribbean* (Westview, 1983) and edited *Colossus Challenged* (with John Martz, Westview, 1982).

The Caribbean Challenge: U.S. Policy in a Volatile Region

edited by H. Michael Erisman

Westview Press / Boulder, Colorado

Barry University Library

A   FL 33161

To my wife

MARGE

and my daughter

TAMMY

Westview Special Studies on Latin America and the Caribbean

All rights reserved. No part of this publication may be reproduced or transmitted in any form or by any means, electronic or mechanical, including photocopy, recording, or any information storage and retrieval system, without permission in writing from the publisher.

Copyright © 1984 by Westview Press, Inc.

Published in 1984 in the United States of America by
Westview Press, Inc.
5500 Central Avenue
Boulder, Colorado 80301
Frederick A. Praeger, President and Publisher

Library of Congress Cataloging in Publication Data
Main entry under title:
The Caribbean challenge.
  Includes index.
    1. Caribbean Area—Foreign relations—United States—Addresses, essays, lectures. 2. United States—Foreign relations—Caribbean Area—Addresses, essays, lectures. 3. United States—Foreign relations—1981—Addresses, essays, lectures. I. Erisman, H. Michael.
E2178.U6C37 1984   327.729073   83-10515
ISBN 0-86531-527-2
ISBN 0-86531-528-0 (pbk.)

Printed and bound in the United States of America

10   9   8   7   6   5   4   3   2

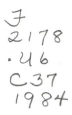

J
2178
.46
C37
1984

152943

Contents

INTRODUCTION

MACROANALYSES

CASE STUDIES

Tables

Preface

Trouble, especially revolutionary upheavals, invariably attracts attention. Consequently the Caribbean Basin—an area that geopolitically encompasses all the island nations as well as the South American littoral states, Central America, and Mexico—has lately become a hot story for the U.S. media and a top priority item on Washington's international agenda. For most of the 1970s the Basin had projected an aura of tranquility and had therefore been largely ignored by the outside world. But by decade's end this facade had begun to crumble, and political radicalism became much more pronounced, as evidenced by the New Jewel Movement's coup in Grenada, the victory of the Sandinista-led rebels in Nicaragua, the approximately 600 deaths in the violence surrounding Jamaica's 1980 general elections, and the intensified guerrilla wars in El Salvador and Guatemala. The economic situation was likewise unsettled as recession roared through the region, driving both governments and the general populace deeper into desperation. Indeed, Costa Rica, once considered the Switzerland of the Western Hemisphere, announced in 1981 that it could not meet its foreign debts, and even oil-rich Mexico tottered on the brink of default. Galvanized by such instability, the Reagan administration devoted much of its foreign-policy energy during its first eighteen months in office to Central American affairs and to developing its Caribbean Basin Initiative.

It is not, however, merely the Caribbean's recent notoriety that makes it noteworthy, but also the fact that the area frequently serves as a rather sensitive barometer for Washington's broader Third World policies for two reasons. Its proximity to the United States usually elicits a swift response to shifts in the area's economic and political winds; and the problems causing these shifts are similar to those facing many developing countries. Admittedly Washington's tradition of treating the region as its special sphere of influence makes U.S.-Caribbean relations in some respects unique, but nevertheless the Basin often is, as Abraham

Lowenthal stresses in his concluding chapter, used by Washington as a testing ground. Theories, attitudes, and strategies that first surface there may subsequently be applied elsewhere in the Third World.

Despite the region's current high visibility and intrinsic importance, no book has been published for at least the last five (extremely eventful) years that probes in depth U.S. policy toward the Caribbean Basin as a whole. This deficiency is perhaps partially due to the position taken by some specialists that the Basin conceptualization is artificial because it assumes a degree of cultural and political comparability among the region's nations that simply does not exist, and therefore it is necessary to operate in terms of more discrete analytical units such as Central America, the Hispanic islands, or the English-speaking archipelago along with its mainland extensions of Guyana, Suriname, and Belize. Although there is some validity to this viewpoint, Washington has been treating the Basin as a policy entity for the past few years (with, of course, some subregional variations), and hence this volume does likewise.

Basically this book, which grew out of a panel at the 1982 Caribbean Studies Association convention in Kingston, Jamaica, seeks to pinpoint the main challenges confronting the United States in the Basin, to uncover and explain the primary variables affecting Washington's reactions, and to evaluate the viability of U.S. Caribbean policy, paying particular attention to the Reagan administration's initiatives. To achieve these goals, the authors present both macroanalyses of U.S. policy and case studies of U.S. relations with selected countries. The macroanalyses concentrate on broad trends in Washington's behavior and project their future directions. As such, these selections not only provide insights into the contemporary dynamics of U.S. policy but also should contribute to understanding developments for quite some time to come. The case studies, on the other hand, delve into the translation of general tendencies into specific scenarios for dealing with certain situations that bring into sharp focus the most crucial problems confronting Washington in the Basin, with Cuba representing the Marxist ideological and perhaps security challenge; El Salvador, the complexities of (nationalistic?) insurgency; Mexico, the competition from emerging middle powers for regional influence; and Jamaica, the difficulties involved in implementing a successful developmental aid program. All the chapters here, with the exception of Lowenthal's, are original works prepared specifically for this volume, which we hope will fill the serious gap in the literature on U.S. policy in the Basin.

One of the unavoidable injustices of publishing is that editors and authors reap most of the credit and rewards for producing books while others whose contributions have been invaluable receive at best passing notice. The normal procedure for recognizing the latter individuals, which is totally inadequate given the services or support they have rendered, is at this point to briefly express gratitude for their help. Apologizing that it is so little for so much, I especially thank Lynne Rienner of Westview Press, whose prompt decisions on project proposals continue to amaze me and to make my professional life much simpler; to Lisa Huffman and Sue Balogh, two indispensable student assistants who typed most of the manuscript, graciously handled correspondence, proofread, and did whatever other obnoxious jobs I gave them; to Tom Kaliszak III and Dr. Detmar Straub for technical advice regarding computer problems; to Mercyhurst College for financial aid; and most important, to Marge and Tammy Erisman for tolerating my frequent absences and my occasional grouchiness.

H. Michael Erisman

Introduction

1
Contemporary Challenges Confronting U.S. Caribbean Policy

H. Michael Erisman

Introduction

Describing what he called "pygmy wars" in the Third World, Ronald Steel wrote:

> Somewhere along the banks of a muddy river in Central Africa a young postal clerk harangues his fellow workers to burn the mail sacks, steal the stamps, and take to the bush with the money orders. Deep in the Latin American rain forest a landless farmer hands out homemade machetes to the peasants for an assault on the local hacienda. . . . And in the windblown wastes of the Arabian desert sheiks on white ponies capture a mud-hut village and promptly proclaim it the capital of a rebel government.
> What do these isolated acts have in common? They are all forms of rebellion against a government in power.[1]

As the 1980s dawned, such instability began to sweep through the Caribbean Basin.[2] In March 1979 a band of young radicals led by Maurice Bishop staged the English-speaking Caribbean's first successful armed coup in Grenada. Four months later (July), the Sandinistas marched triumphantly into Managua, thus breaking the Somoza dynasty's stranglehold over Nicaragua. The October 1980 Jamaican elections, in which conservative Edward Seaga defeated incumbent socialist Prime Minister Michael Manley, were unusually bloody—over 500 people died in campaign-related violence. Finally, both El Salvador and Guatemala plunged deeper into chaos as leftist-led insurgents escalated their guerrilla wars against the two countries' generally pro-U.S. regimes.

3

The size of the individual Caribbean nations might have led Steel to characterize their political violence as pygmy wars, but Washington certainly has not considered such developments pygmy-like in importance, insisting instead that vital U.S. interests are involved and must be protected.[3] For example, U.S. officials frequently stress the Basin's pivotal role in America's petroleum picture. Venezuelan and Mexican oil shipments are, of course, already substantial, and reserves are suspected in Guatemala and offshore Puerto Rico that could allow them to become significant exporters.[4] Beyond the question of access to these supplies, which will become increasingly important as the Gulf oil fields are depleted,[5] 75 percent of current oil imports into the United States are shipped through the area. Approximately 30 percent of the oil is processed en route, with the largest refineries operating in Curaçao, Aruba, Trinidad, the U.S. Virgin Islands, and the Bahamas. In fact, over one-half of all the strategic minerals imported by the United States traverse the Caribbean and/or the nearby Gulf of Mexico. Anything might endanger this resource flow (e.g., regional instability or a leftist takeover in a producer country) would, in Washington's opinion, represent a serious threat to U.S. security.

Perceiving the spread of leftist influence as endangering the United States' traditional preeminence in the Basin and hence its ability to defend its vital interests, the Reagan administration has given the region top priority. The president himself unequivocally reaffirmed this commitment in a major speech given in February 1982 before the Organization of American States (OAS): "Let our friends and our adversaries understand that we will do whatever is prudent and necessary to insure the peace and security of the Caribbean area."[6]

Usually Washington has presented the challenges confronting U.S. Basin policy in somewhat simplistic terms, the most common being that the primary, if not *the only* serious, issue is Cuban-backed subversion inspired and directed by Moscow. But in reality the list is much longer and more complex, encompassing such crucial components as: the region's staggering developmental requirements and the related demands by many for a New International Economic Order (NIEO); the frequent unwillingness of conservative, often virulently anticommunistic elites to remedy socioeconomic inequities in their countries, the result being polarized, violence-prone political systems; Caribbean nationalism and nonaligned Third Worldism, tendencies that are fueled by the legacy of U.S. interventionism and fears of contemporary U.S. neocolonialism; and, finally, the emergence of increasingly assertive regional middle powers like Mexico.

The above scenario has been further complicated by the linkages involved. The variables mentioned do not exist in isolation from one another, but rather they can interact—a response to one might aggravate another (e.g., attempting to generate economic development by encouraging private U.S. investment in the Basin could inflame Caribbean nationalism and thereby intensify anti-American sentiment). Consequently the United States cannot operate in a piecemeal fashion. Instead it must recognize *all* the problems, must be sensitive to their relative importance and to the connections between them, and must address them with a comprehensive package that serves both U.S. interests and the inhabitants' needs. The question, of course, is, Has it?

In answering we will: (1) pinpoint and analyze the main dimensions of the Basin challenge to U.S. policy; and (2) explain and briefly evaluate the Reagan administration's responses. One must recognize, however, that the area's problems are not unique. Many similar problems can be found elsewhere in the Western Hemisphere as well as in Africa and Asia. Hence, to probe Washington's Caribbean relations is to do more than simply examine its dealings with one corner of the world. Rather, it is to begin to define the place of the United States in today's rapidly changing global mosaic, particularly in reference to the developing countries where most of humanity lives.

Reagan's Caribbean Policy

In discussing the main threads of Reagan's Central American policy, Richard Feinberg contended in 1981:

> Although differences exist within the Administration on . . . some issues, the emerging approach appears to be centering around the following attitudes and policies:
>
> 1) Security forces are the most reliable allies in the current environment of unrest. While the incorporation of Christian Democrats and moderate Social Democrats can sometimes strengthen political institutions, political solutions involving broad-based power-sharing schemes are too risky.
>
> 2) Social tension can best be addressed through rising levels of external economic assistance to existing governments, possibly reinforced by trade preferences.
>
> 3) Leftist forces are heavily influenced by Cuba, cannot easily be co-opted or accommodated and therefore should be isolated or liquidated.
>
> 4) Other external powers, including friendly ones, should be discouraged from taking initiatives not congruent with Washington's own policies, and from attempting to build bridges to leftist forces.[7]

Excluding the Commonwealth Caribbean from his first point, Feinberg's policy summary is applicable not only to Central America, but to the Basin as a whole.

That such postures evoke memories of the confrontation psychology that permeated U.S. diplomatic circles following World War II should not be surprising, for Reagan and his associates have been dedicated practitioners of Cold War politics. Their highly ideological world view, dominated by a strong aversion to communism, has generated a foreign policy whose basic operating principles have been bipolarity (i.e., the United States and the Soviet Union represent the earth's only significant power centers), macrolinkage (i.e., all important international questions are integral to the bipolar struggle for power and must be handled accordingly), and vigilant containment of Moscow. Washington has, of course, pursued containment ever since the late 1940s when George Kennan's famous "Mr. X" article[8] and NSC-68[9] laid the intellectual foundation for it. But Reagan has been much more enamored with the idea than some of his predecessors (e.g., President Carter) and quite prone to rely on military means to achieve it.

This Cold War perspective has very much colored the administration's view of developments in the Basin; the Caribbean has been seen as simply another arena in the bipolar struggle for power where, as elsewhere, the United States' main problem is Communist expansionism orches-trated by the Kremlin. Secretary of State Alexander Haig, for example, insisted that the Russians have a "hit list" that includes targets of opportunity throughout the area, the ultimate goal being Mexico and its massive oil reserves.[10] Given these assumptions, Reagan, unlike some previous presidents who, in the spirit of détente, at least gave lip service to the notion of tolerating ideological pluralism, has tended to equate any leftist challenge (especially those employing violence) to the Caribbean status quo with challenges to global containment of Communism, which then justifies bringing U.S. power to bear to restore stability and Western political orthodoxy.

Within this general framework, extreme concern has focused on Cuba. This is partially attributable to an almost visceral hatred of Havana among Reaganites and an obsession with cutting Castro down to size. Indeed, "long before Ronald Reagan entered office, he and his close political associates and his ideological allies rejected any notion of seeking accommodation with Cuba."[11] More important, however, has been the conviction that a relationship exists between Havana's alleged attempts to foment serious political instability on a regional level in the Caribbean[12] and the larger East-West battle. The conceptual vehicle used to make the connection has been the Surrogate Thesis.

Stated simply, the Surrogate Thesis holds that the Soviets have capitalized on Cuba's economic/strategic vulnerabilities to penetrate the island and create a dependency relationship giving them a predominant role in Havana's decision-making processes.[13] Thus the roots of Castro's foreign policy are seen as lying in the Kremlin—the Russians hand down the marching orders and the Fidelistas, recognizing that their country's economy and ultimately the Revolution itself would collapse without ongoing massive Soviet aid, have little choice but to cooperate.

The surrogate idea first began to acquire widespread publicity in the United States during the mid-1970s as a result of Havana's growing military involvement in Africa, particularly in Angola and Ethiopia. Soon it became almost standard procedure to portray any Cuban initiatives in surrogate terms; whether in Africa, the Nonaligned Movement, or the Caribbean and Central America, Havana was labeled a Russian stalking horse and its international activities seen within the rubric of superpower rivalry. For example, the main theme in the Reagan administration's controversial White Paper on El Salvador was that "the insurgency in El Salvador has been progressively transformed into another case of indirect armed aggression against a small Third World country by Communist powers acting through Cuba."[14] In short, Havana's foreign policy has been deemed indistinguishable from Moscow's, and hence any expansion of Cuba's influence has been considered an increase in the Soviet Union's global power (a development which, according to the containment doctrine, is a threat to U.S. security and cannot be permitted).

Operating on the surrogate assumption, the Reagan administration has adopted a tough stance not only in its relations with Cuba, but also with Nicaragua's Sandinista government (which it sees as Havana's puppet) and toward political instability in the Basin (which it believes results from Cuban/Soviet interventionism). In February 1981, for instance, following State Department accusations in its White Paper that the Cubans were providing large amounts of arms to El Salvador's leftist guerrillas, the White House warned that it might take direct action against Cuba, possibly including a military blockade, to stop the flow. Similar threats were made against Managua in December 1981, and then in March 1982 it was revealed that Reagan had approved a $19-million Central Intelligence Agency (CIA) plan to form a 500-man paramilitary force composed of Nicaraguan exiles and Latin American (particularly Argentinian) mercenaries to attack and disrupt the Sandinista government.[15]

There is nothing intrinsically wrong in employing a macroperspective, as the Reagan administration has done, to make foreign policy. In fact, doing so will probably produce more consistency than would otherwise be the case. The problem is that Reagan's Cold War paradigm appears to have generated some serious misperceptions about the Caribbean.

The first assumption to be questioned is whether the Basin actually is an arena of superpower competition where the United States is being tested by the Russians with global containment at stake. Actually the Kremlin's efforts to expand its direct presence beyond Cuba have at best been lackluster, Nicaragua being a case in point. As Feinberg notes, "The very low level of Soviet aid to Nicaragua confirms Moscow's reluctance, as demonstrated with Allende in Chile and Manley in Jamaica, to invest heavily in a 'second Cuba.'"[16] Like other great powers, the USSR will capitalize on opportunities to gain increased influence. But Reagan's charge that it has been engaged in a major campaign to establish itself in the Basin seems highly exaggerated. Rather than being on the offensive, the Soviets have not made any *bilateral* military or economic investments of any great consequence to enlarge their Caribbean beachhead beyond Cuba, nor have they displayed any inclination to risk a confrontation with the United States in the region.[17]

With overt Russian expansionism basically eliminated from the equation, the Reagan scenario then becomes heavily dependent on the Surrogate Thesis to sustain its contention that a Cold War crisis exists in the Basin. But most Cuban specialists in the academic community, including well-established critics of the revolution, feel that the surrogate approach is a simplistic and ultimately untenable view of Havana's overseas initiatives and the complexities of its relations with the USSR. While recognizing that the Kremlin has encouraged and materially supported Cuba's exploits abroad, thereby allowing it to take on more ambitious tasks and to carry them out more effectively than it could have done alone, they feel that Havana nevertheless controls its own foreign policy.

Such skepticism about the Fidelistas' satellite status has been reinforced by several instances in Africa where their policies have diverged significantly from those of the Soviet Union. Perhaps the most serious involved a situation that developed in Angola following the victory of the Cuban-backed MPLA (Popular Movement for the Liberation of Angola), which in effect pitted Moscow against Havana. In May 1977 a faction within the MPLA, feeling that its leader, Angolan president Agostinho Neto, was not sufficiently pro-Russian, organized a coup to topple him. There is no strong evidence that the Kremlin was directly involved in the plot, although it was reported that the Soviets knew about it beforehand and failed to warn Neto,[18] which obviously implies that they were not adverse to his downfall. Havana, on the other hand, stood firmly behind him. When the conspirators made their move, Cuban troops joined MPLA forces loyal to the government in putting down the uprising. According to the surrogate analysis, such rank noncooperation should never occur because Moscow supposedly sets the parameters for Havana's policies. Thus this and other similar incidents suggest that the thesis is seriously flawed.[19]

The second dubious assumption is that heavy Cuban intervention, regardless of whether Havana has undertaken it as a surrogate or on its own, has been the primary cause of instability and political violence in the Basin. This is a theme to which the United States has repeatedly returned, charging that Havana has been systematically attempting to destabilize and subvert Caribbean governments by expanding its military presence and activities in the region.

The Fidelistas have, of course, always been sympathetic to Latin American revolutionaries and have periodically extended assistance to them.[20] In the mid-1960s, for example, the Cubans became convinced that the area was ripe for insurrection and that what was required to speed up the process was a spark to light the conflagration. Drawing on their own experiences in fighting Batista, they looked to rural insurgents as the catalyst to unify the masses and to galvanize them into action. Thus the cult of the guerrilla foco was born,[21] and the keystone of Havana's hemispheric policy became its ties to radical groups that believed violence was the only possible way to achieve power. In every case, however, the rebels were defeated.

These guerrilla failures, plus serious domestic economic problems that necessitated a closer association with Moscow (which was not enthusiastic about encouraging armed struggle in Latin America) and growing Cuban involvement in Third World/African affairs, led Cuba to adopt a much lower Caribbean profile throughout much of the 1970s. Consequently it concentrated on normalizing its relations with what it called "progressive" hemispheric regimes, by which it meant those that were strongly committed to socioeconomic reform and especially were independent from (and ideally antagonistic toward) Washington's foreign policies. Thus, while not abandoning its long-standing position of solidarity with Caribbean revolutionary and national liberation movements, Havana became much more cautious and discriminating in giving them material aid.

Grenada's radicalization and, most important, the Sandinista victory in Nicaragua rekindled the Cubans' faith in the Basin's revolutionary potential, and substantial aid was quickly dispatched to help consolidate the new political order in both nations. Havana supplied security assistance, doctors, teachers, and fishing trawlers to Maurice Bishop's government and agreed to build and pay one-half the cost of a new $50-million airport on the tiny island. The commitment in personnel and material to Nicaragua was Cuba's largest ever in the Western Hemisphere; by mid-1982 the Fidelistas had approximately 2,000 military advisors and 4,000 technicians involved in various developmental projects there.

Nevertheless, Havana's dealings with insurgent movements in the Basin during the 1980s have been somewhat circumspect. Admittedly the Cubans have empathized with those fighting "nonprogressive" regimes (i.e., in El Salvador and Guatemala), and Castro has personally brokered several cooperative agreements between guerrilla groups, making the rebel forces much more formidable than before.[22] On the other hand, Havana has steadfastly denied that it has, or intends to play, a significant military/logistical role in the region's revolutionary armed struggles. And despite all its rhetoric about such Cuban interventionism, the Reagan administration has been unable to prove otherwise. Instead its efforts to do so have often backfired. First its White Paper on El Salvador was discredited not only by the liberal *Washington Post,* but also by the conservative *Wall Street Journal.*[23] Then there was the so-called "smoking Sandinista," a Nicaraguan arrested in El Salvador in early 1982 who was allegedly a rebel leader. He escaped into the Mexican embassy in San Salvador, which announced that he was an innocent student passing through the country and granted him asylum. Finally, in March 1982 the State Department produced a young Nicaraguan soldier who, it said, had admitted to being trained in Cuba (and Ethiopia) before being sent by his government to fight in El Salvador. But once before the U.S. press he repudiated his "confession," saying that it had been obtained under duress; he insisted that he was a volunteer who had joined the guerrillas on his own initiative. Such public relations fiascos have created widespread misgivings about the credibility of Washington's charges of substantial Cuban military intervention in Central America. *Newsweek's* comment regarding El Salvador is typical:

> The Cuban-Nicaraguan connection exists, but less decisively than Washington contends. Neither Havana nor Managua has sent troops to advise or fight beside the guerrillas in El Salvador, and what was always a minor flow of arms to the rebels has now ebbed to a trickle, according to sources in the area. Says one U.S. official in Central America: "I read statements coming out of Washington, and sometimes I wonder what the hell they're based on."[24]

In short, most informed observers have concluded that rather than being the creatures of Cuban meddling, as the White House argues, the Basin's revolutionary movements have basically developed on their own (including their military capabilities) in response to indigenous sociopolitical stimuli. It is, say Reagan's critics, his inability, induced by his Cold War ideology, to grasp this central point that has seriously distorted his understanding of the roots of Caribbean instability.

Keeping the above macrocritiques in mind, the major challenges to U.S. policy emanating from the Basin and the viability of the Reagan administration's specific responses can now be discussed.

Caribbean Challenges and the U.S. Response

The Developmental Challenge

Although Washington has emphasized external subversion as the main cause of political turmoil in the Basin, the destabilizing impact of the area's massive economic problems cannot be underestimated. By early 1982 even the White House had begun to recognize this fact:

> These countries [said President Reagan] are under economic siege. . . . Economic disaster is consuming our neighbors' money, reserves, and credits, forcing thousands of people to leave for other countries—for the United States, often illegally—and shaking even the most established democracies.[25]

How the United States responds to the challenge of promoting Caribbean development will be crucial in determining the nature of its future role in the region.

The first aspect of what is essentially a binary crisis involves the impact of external factors on Caribbean productivity and income. Over the past several years Basin countries have experienced a general economic deterioration due to increased petroleum costs, price drops on the world market for their commodity exports, burgeoning debts to cover trade deficits, and the transferal of U.S. stagflation through dependency relationships. Even Costa Rica, long considered the Switzerland of Latin America, was virtually bankrupt by late 1981 and unable to make the interest payments on its massive foreign debt.[26]

In both the island Caribbean and Central America, the devastating effect of worldwide recession on employment and national productivity, combined with often runaway inflation, has eaten away at individuals' real incomes.[27] And, as is frequently the case, the hardest hit have been the economic *marginales*—people barely making it at present. Only people who can adjust to the increased cost of living are not seriously hurt, and the overwhelming majority in the Caribbean do not fall into this category. Thus inflation wreaks havoc on a grand scale, driving many over the brink of desperation.

The second and much more insidious dimension of the Basin's developmental problems, aggravating the suffering associated with the productivity crisis, is the inequitable distribution of income (see Table

TABLE 1.1
Income Distribution (percentages)

Country	Year	Highest 5%	Highest 10%	20%	Highest 20%	20%	to Lowest 20%	20%
Bahamas	1970	21.0						3.0
Barbados	1970	20.0						7.0
Costa Rica	1960	35.0						6.0
	1970	23.0						5.0
	1971		39.5	54.8	19.9	13.3	8.7	3.3
Colombia	1960	36.0						3.0
	1970	33.0						4.0
Domin. Repub.	1970	26.0						5.0
El Salvador	1960	33.0						6.0
	1970	20.0						4.0
Guatemala[a]		----	----	----	----	----	---	---
Honduras	1967		50.0	67.8	16.9	8.0	5.0	2.3
	1970	29.0						3.0
Jamaica	1960	30.0						2.0
Mexico	1960	29.0						4.0
	1970	36.0						4.0
	1977		40.6	57.7	20.4	12.0	7.0	2.9
Nicaragua[b]		----	----	----	----	----	---	---
Panama	1960	35.0						5.0
	1970	33.0						3.0
Trinidad Tobago	1976		31.8	50.0	22.8	13.9	9.1	4.2
Venezuela	1960	27.0						3.0
	1970		35.5	54.0	22.8	12.9	7.3	3.0

Sources: World Bank, World Development Report 1981 (Washington: World Bank, 1981), pp. 182-183; World Bank, Poverty and Development (New York: Oxford University Press, 1980), pp. 84-85; and World Bank, World Tables 1976 (Baltimore: Johns Hopkins University Press, 1976), pp. 514-517.

[a] Data not available. See note 28.
[b] Data not available.

K. Baby Doc of Haiti

1.1)[28] and related benefits. While a simple rich-upper/impoverished-lower class analysis would project a grossly inaccurate picture of the complexity of social dynamics in the Caribbean, it is fair to say that there is sharp economic polarization between the "haves" and the "have-nots" in these countries. The haves are usually a class-heterogeneous collection, including not only the very rich, but also portions of the middle sector (particularly persons holding managerial positions, military officers, and government bureaucrats) and highly organized workers (the labor elite), who are usually found in modern, urban-based industries. Due to deeply entrenched patterns of systemic maldistribution, the burdens of recession fall most heavily on the have-nots while the fruits of prosperity tend to go disproportionately to the privileged few, thereby creating a potentially explosive situation fueled by feelings of serious relative deprivation (i.e., the perception on some people's part that the socioeconomic gap between them and a superordinate reference group is large and is widening rather than narrowing). Indeed there are theorists who contend that a sharp intensification of relative deprivation is the main cause of civil strife and revolutionary upheavals within societies.[29] In any case, the question of distributive justice is as much an element of the Caribbean developmental challenge as is increasing the region's overall productivity.

The U.S. Response. Washington has not totally ignored the need to attack the problem of maldistribution in the Caribbean. The Reagan administration, for example, supported President José Napoleón Duarte's efforts in El Salvador to enlarge peasant holdings by restructuring the country's land tenure system[30] and indicated after the March 1982 elections there, in which right-wing parties won a majority of the votes, that it would strongly oppose any attempt by a new government to roll back those reforms. Nevertheless, increasing productivity has been Washington's main thrust, as epitomized by Reagan's Caribbean Basin Initiative (CBI).

The CBI, which was formally announced in February 1982 and which excludes the leftist governments of Cuba, Nicaragua, and Grenada, is essentially a three-pronged policy.[31] First, it provided for $350 million of emergency U.S. aid in 1982 (with $750 million projected over three years), thus bringing the total fiscal year 1981/82 economic assistance package for the Basin to almost $824 million. Second, it asks Congress to allow most Caribbean exports to enter the United States duty-free for twelve years. Finally, and probably most important from the Reagan administration's standpoint, the CBI will strongly promote U.S. private investment in the Basin by providing tax incentives for U.S. companies to operate there and by negotiating treaties to protect their investments. Discussing this point, Assistant Secretary of State for Inter-American

Affairs Thomas O. Enders said that the emphasis on encouraging private investment

> would be achieved in part by "investment treaties covering the relationship between governments and private investors."
>
> Asked if these proposed treaties meant that countries would have to provide assurances against nationalization, Enders said "yes."[32]

Within this general scenario Jamaica has been targeted as the regional model for the free-enterprise development that Reagan would like to see applied throughout the Third World. Beyond the CBI the administration has tried, with mixed results, to use its influence in financial institutions such as the International Monetary Fund (IMF) and the Caribbean Development Bank to channel multilateral assistance to Basin regimes that it considers ideologically acceptable and away from radical "outcasts" such as Grenada.[33]

Evaluation of the U.S. Response. Basically Washington's reaction to the Caribbean's economic problems has been to prime the capitalist pump—to rely on, as President Reagan likes to call it, the magic of the marketplace to increase productivity, assuming that a trickle-down effect will then make available to the masses enough benefits of the new prosperity to keep them politically quiescent. This strategy, which in many respects resembles an internationalization of the Reagan administration's domestic economic program, has several fundamental weaknesses.

First, the CBI's developmental potential is questionable. Its free-trade provisions may be more show than substance:

> About 87 percent of all goods imported from the countries of the Caribbean basin already enter America duty-free under the Generalized System of Preferences, which is designed to help developing countries build overseas markets. Textiles (which will continue to be subject to tariffs) make up an additional 4 or 5 percent. As a result, Reagan's plan would affect only about 8 percent of products currently shipped to the United States.[34]

Moreover, the private investment upon which the CBI counts so heavily may not be sufficiently forthcoming because many American businessmen feel that the Basin, especially the island Caribbean, lacks the necessary infrastructure (e.g., airports, transportation networks, etc.) to support new industries. Developing such facilities quickly would require an infusion of U.S. government aid far greater than Washington is willing, and perhaps able, to provide. And even if the foregoing considerations prove not to be problems, the very real possibility exists that increased

U.S. investment plus the CBI's trade preferences will mean that the profits of much of the increased (export-oriented) productivity will go into the pockets of American entrepreneurs rather than into the local economies. As *Granma,* the Cuban Communist party's newspaper, noted in a blistering critique:

> Given the fact of overwhelming domination by the Yankee transnationals over the production and even more over the marketing of the export products of the underdeveloped countries, "duty-free entry" is shown to be a gimmick which in no way alters the control of the companies. On the contrary, they make even more profits, and the structural relations between imperialism and the underdeveloped countries which are the root cause of poverty and backwardness remain untouched.[35]

In other words, whose pump is really being primed—that of the U.S. business community or that of broadbased Caribbean development?

Second, given the existing patterns of systemic maldistribution, it is unlikely that whatever developmental benefits do filter down will be enough to make a significant dent in the Basin's endemic poverty and deprivation. Certainly the Alliance for Progress experience in the early 1960s demonstrated that seed money, whether public or private, injected into a context of structural malapportionment generates a minimal payoff for the dispossessed. Instead it is diverted, legally or illegally, to serve mainly the interests of the already privileged.

What is required to achieve Washington's goal of prosperity-induced stability is distributive reform. The Basin's record in this regard has not, however, been encouraging, primarily because a symbiotic linkage impeding change has often developed between the United States and conservative Caribbean governments (especially in Central America). A main impetus behind this relationship has been the oligarchic nature of many Caribbean political systems wherein participation has been limited to a few elite groups. These groups have not sought popular support because they have feared that any attempt to mobilize the masses politically might get out of hand and endanger the status quo within which their interests receive top priority. To compensate for their lack of a broad domestic constituency, such oligarchic regimes have looked for external allies to bolster their power; and traditionally Washington has responded with economic and military assistance, thereby enhancing its influence in the area and frequently receiving in return concessions that have facilitated the entry or expansion of U.S. business activities. Because the Washington connection has been seen as guaranteeing their survival, elitist Caribbean governments have had little incentive to respond positively to indigenous demands for distributive reform (which would require the oligarchy to sacrifice some of its power and privileges). Thus broadbased development has not occurred, and the chasm separating the haves from the have-nots has grown wider. Reagan's willingness to provide help, especially security assistance, to besieged conservative Basin regimes to prevent leftists from coming to power seems likely to perpetuate this legacy of oligarchic politics, thereby dimming the prospects for the distributive reforms that are so necessary to transform the trickle-down into a stability-producing deluge.

Finally, long-term Caribbean development probably demands—no matter whose strategy is chosen—structural alterations in the present international economic system dominated by the U.S.-led industrialized states. Third World representatives have repeatedly voiced such sentiments, calling for the formation of a New International Economic Order. But generally the United States has not been sympathetic to the NIEO concept, being inclined to see it as an illegitimate, leftist-inspired plot to redistribute existing wealth on a global scale. This has definitely been Reagan's attitude:

> The Reagan administration opposes shifting billions of dollars from rich to poor nations pressing for a global economic bargain.
> Myer Rashish, Under Secretary of State for Economic Affairs, said in an interview that growth in Asian, African and Latin American economies depended on creating more wealth, not on sharing existing resources.[36]

This productionist proclivity was reaffirmed in October 1982 at the North-South summit conference in Cancun, Mexico, much to the chagrin of the gathering's organizer, Mexican President José López Portillo, who had hoped that Washington would go beyond its symbolic conciliatory gestures and display a willingness to enter serious NIEO negotiations.[37]

Richard Fagen has aptly summarized the feeling that attempts to export the U.S. developmental model are doomed. He wrote in 1978:

> If the history of modern Latin America teaches no other lesson, it should by now be clear that the combination of formal democracy . . . and late-industrializing capitalist economies has not and probably cannot significantly reduce the appalling inequities in economic and social conditions. . . .
> In U.S. policy circles, this key fact of hemispheric life is not understood.[38]

The Insurgent Challenge: Guerrilla Politics

The economically rooted polarization noted above has in many instances spilled over into the political realm, effectively eliminating or preventing the emergence of a viable moderate center and thereby triggering a violent confrontation between intransigent defenders and radical opponents of the sociopolitical status quo. This phenomenon has been most common in Central America, where small oligarchies, backed by armies with a penchant for repression, have reigned supreme for generations. But even the Commonwealth Caribbean, with its heritage of Whitehall parliamentarianism, has begun to experience it, as noted in 1980 by a U.S. diplomat stationed there:

> The broad middle ground in the [English-speaking] Caribbean that is pro–Britain, pro–United States and [pro–]Canada is going to be eaten away as the economic situation continues to worsen. All the conditions that cause instability around here are going to worsen.[39]

Island officials have sounded similar warnings, declaring that "the Caribbean by and large is a region of existing democratic governments that are near the point of exhausting their options in dealing with economic problems."[40] Bishop's coup in Grenada and the violent, albeit still democratic, 1980 Jamaican elections illustrate the extent to which the area's political cauldron has begun to boil.

As such polarization has developed, those normally inclined toward peaceful innovation—the moderate center, in other words—have increasingly faded from the political picture. In some cases they have come to terms with the (oligarchic) authorities; in others they have been intimidated, if not physically eliminated, by extremist attacks (the most notorious examples being the operations of right-wing death squads in El Salvador and Guatemala). There have also been those still committed to bringing about change who, recognizing the futility of trying to do so by working within the existing system, have joined the radical left in armed struggle. These latter reformers have, in short, become violent revolutionaries.

Although leftist *guerrillaismo* has a long tradition in the Basin, its practitioners have suffered one defeat after another. In fact, before 1979, except in Cuba and possibly Mexico, every attempt guerrillas made to seize *and consolidate* power had failed. Recently, however, the tide has begun to shift in their favor in some countries. Where this occurred, the following two factors seem to have been conspicuously present and important:

1. Abandoning the divisive, discredited foco theory, the historically fragmented radical left has achieved an unusually high degree of internal cohesion and also has forged alliances with various groups—including elements of the Catholic church—that have never before been willing to embrace the strategy of armed struggle. Central commands have been created to coordinate the operations of previously autonomous paramilitary forces. Grassroots organizations designed to unite the opposition into mass fronts for concerted political action in support of the guerrillas have been established. Consequently governments have found that their most reliable control mechanism—divide and conquer— has, to a great extent, been neutralized.

2. The rebels have received considerable moral and/or material assistance not only from Communist states, but also from the world community. For example, the Sandinistas and, to a lesser extent, El Salvador's insurgents have been backed in various degrees by Mexico, France, the Socialist International (SI; an association of parties that includes England's Laborites and West Germany's Social Democrats, both of whom have stood behind the SI's Caribbean policies), the Movement of Nonaligned Nations, and the UN General Assembly.[41] Such multifaceted support has conferred international legitimacy on the guerrillas, making it extremely difficult for their opponents (including Washington) to drive them into an isolated, vulnerable corner by portraying them as nothing more than Soviet-controlled puppets engaged in a conspiracy of indirect aggression.

The U.S. Response. A fundamental Reagan principle has been to fight fire with fire. In a moment of perhaps unguarded candor, Secretary Haig reportedly explained this perspective on dealing with turmoil in the Basin by stating, with regard to El Salvador, that

> America's mistake in Vietnam was its preoccupation with winning hearts and minds; in El Salvador, Haig said, the United States would concentrate instead on helping the government win a military victory.[42]

Consequently U.S. counterinsurgency efforts and security assistance programs in the Caribbean have been expanded. For the most part Washington has concentrated on supplying arms, equipment, and money, although advisors have been dispatched to some countries (particularly El Salvador and Honduras) and training activities, both in the United States and at U.S. bases in the Canal Zone, have been stepped up.

Linked to this aid scenario has been the Reagan administration's emphasis on elections in the Basin. Recognizing that numerous considerations have motivated the United States to encourage electoral politics in the Caribbean, it is likewise clear that Washington's enthusiasm has had a military dimension: it is much easier to justify increases in security assistance to Congress and the American public if the recipient government can be said to enjoy a popular mandate. This strategy has had mixed results. It worked well in Jamaica, but failed miserably in Guatemala, where the March 1982 presidential elections were nullified when the armed forces carried out another in their long series of successful coups.[43] The outcome in El Salvador was more ambiguous. Although the massive turnout for the balloting there, also in March 1982, surprised even Washington, the absence of a liberal alternative, due to a leftist boycott of the elections plus the inability of the U.S.-backed Christian Democrats to win a clear majority, produced a coalition government dominated by extreme right-wing elements. These groups' reputation for violating human rights has aroused serious misgivings in the minds of many U.S. citizens about sending them any military aid at all.[44]

In addition to providing bilateral security assistance, the Reagan administration has tried to stimulate greater cooperation in military affairs among Basin states, hoping to minimize the need for direct Pentagon involvement and to allow the United States to maintain a low profile by funneling its aid through multilateral channels. Accordingly, in January 1982 Washington promoted formation of the Central American Democratic Community (CADC), whose members are Costa Rica, Honduras and El Salvador. The organization will, among other things, facilitate "certain undefined security measures, interpreted as the exchange of intelligence information."[45] Indeed, even before the CADC was established, Honduras had been allowing (with strong U.S. approval) Salvadoran troops to enter its territory in "hot pursuit" of guerrillas and to search its teeming refugee camps for rebel sympathizers.

Obviously confrontation has taken precedence over negotiations in Reagan's Basin strategy. Occasionally the administration has indicated a willingness to pursue discussions with the opposition, as it did in early 1982 when Mexico offered to act as a mediator between Washington and the Salvadoran insurgents. But then U.S. aversion to substantive talks reasserted itself. The basic rationale behind this position was that

a negotiated settlement . . . would give the guerrillas power that they had won neither on the battlefield nor at the ballot box. Negotiations would vindicate guerrilla warfare by abandoning the principle that an insurgency should not be allowed to force a government to the bargaining table by means of violence. . . .

What is more, a negotiated settlement would undercut the U.S. position in the East-West struggle with the Soviet Union; it would be proof that the leading power in the West could not find a way to protect a friendly government close at hand. The U.S. would appear to lack the strategy, the power and the will to influence events in the world at large.[46]

Reagan's willingness to discount the diplomatic option has been reinforced by his conviction that military power can eliminate the rebels or at least contain them long enough for his economic initiatives to generate stability.

Evaluation of the U.S. Response. Any conclusion regarding Reagan's security assistance projects depends heavily on what is perceived to be their goals. If the ultimate objective is a decisive military triumph over the guerrillas, one must question the aid's long-term viability. Admittedly some precedents suggest that such an approach will work. In the mid-1960s, for example, U.S. counterinsurgency programs contributed significantly to defeating rural insurrections in Venezuela, Colombia, Guatemala, Peru, and Bolivia.[47] Also, in the early 1970s Washington helped to eradicate the urban-based Tupamaros in Uruguay and the Monteneros in Argentina. Since then, however, conditions have markedly changed. Contemporary rebels now have much greater unity and external support than did their predecessors. Consequently the correlation of forces has become more balanced; so much so, in fact, that even within the Reagan administration doubts have begun to develop about its aid strategy. Such skepticism has been most pronounced concerning El Salvador, where "some [U.S.] officials were said to believe that a government victory would be virtually impossible without the introduction of combat troops from either the U.S. or some other foreign country."[48] Without clearcut victories—or, as Secretary Haig called them, quick fixes—the polarization process will probably continue, thereby intensifying political instability, strengthening the insurgents, and leading to protracted wars of attrition, which, strategists have concluded, the United States and its Caribbean allies are not likely to win.

If, on the other hand, the White House's primary goal is to buy enough time to put the Caribbean economies back on their feet, then its security assistance makes more sense. Indeed its efforts could even be labeled highly successful since the Basin has not been overwhelmed by a leftist tide. A closer inspection, however, reveals a potentially fatal internal contradiction—Washington's counterinsurgency initiatives are meaningful only if broadbased economic development occurs, but, as noted previously, they generally function to keep in power oligarchic governments that are highly unlikely to make the distributive reforms such development demands. Consequently U.S. military aid programs are forced, in effect, to revert back to the dubious "victory model."

Orchestrating cooperation between the Basin's armed forces has been quite attractive to the Reaganites because it provides a means to increase military pressure against insurgents without creating a serious domestic backlash from a Congress and a public wary of foreign entanglements.[49] Nevertheless it is still a very risky strategy because open involvement in the area's conflicts by U.S. allies might stimulate counterintervention by less friendly third parties. And in the Caribbean, the most powerful armed forces are controlled not by pro-U.S. governments, but rather by Washington's two main adversaries—Cuba and Nicaragua. Thus it would seem to make little sense for the White House to do anything that might serve to enlarge the region's sphere of hostilities.

The inadequacies in Reagan's military responses to the challenge of Caribbean insurgency, plus the fact that elections have seldom, if ever, proven effective in resolving violent political struggles in polarized systems, would seem to justify reexamining the negotiations option. Specifically Washington might consider brokering power-sharing agreements in countries torn by civil strife. Admittedly such arrangements would not in themselves remedy the socioeconomic problems underlying the Basin's turmoil, but they would (1) open up oligarchic governments to groups committed to the distributive reforms necessary for long-term stability and peace; (2) lay the groundwork for cordial, rather than confrontational, U.S. relations with revolutionary regimes that might eventually emerge from such settlements; and (3) remove a major irritant from U.S. ties with such crucial countries as Mexico, France, and West Germany, all of whom have supported the idea of negotiations.

The Nationalist Challenge

Nationalism has long been deeply ingrained in Latin America's political culture. Following World War II, however, its winds blew most strongly in Asia and Africa. But over the past decade, spurred by the tendency of many hemispheric states to identify more closely with the Third World, the area's nationalistic tradition has begun to reassert itself strongly. This renaissance has not been warmly welcomed in Washington, for Latin nationalism has always included a heavy dose of anti-Yankeeism; its adherents have usually insisted that in order to control their own destinies they must drastically reduce, if not totally eliminate, the immense political and economic influence that the United States has traditionally exercised over them.

In the Basin, anti-American nationalism has manifested itself in various ways. Countries such as Grenada, Guyana, Jamaica, Nicaragua, Panama, Suriname, and Trinidad/Tobago have followed Havana, a charter member, in joining the Movement of Nonaligned Nations. Support for the NIEO concept, which is seen by many dependency theorists as necessary to end U.S. economic hegemony, has grown. Indeed even some normally pro-American conservative governments have launched nationalistic tirades against Washington for allegedly meddling in their internal affairs, as did Guatemala's ruling generals in 1977 when they refused to accept further U.S. military aid because the Carter administration insisted that they had to improve their human rights record in order to receive it. But perhaps most dramatic has been the emergence of indigenous powers that seem willing and able to compete with the United States for influence and are dedicated to building a new regional political order within which the United States would be reduced from producer/director to just another actor on the Caribbean stage. Cuba, Nicaragua, and Grenada have promoted such nationalism from the radical left. Recently, however, heavy attention has focused on the challenge being mounted by a country in the political center—Mexico.

The first signs of Mexico's more assertive foreign policy occurred during the presidency of Luis Echeverría (1970–76), whose aspirations for Third World leadership were epitomized in his Charter of Economic Rights and Duties of States, which was overwhelmingly passed by the UN General Assembly in late 1974 as an important first step in the drive for an NIEO. But the person primarily responsible for thrusting Mexico into the Caribbean limelight was his successor, José López Portillo (1976–82).

His confidence bolstered by the announcement of Mexico's massive oil reserves, López Portillo launched a campaign to build Mexico into a major power in Basin affairs.[50] To consolidate his left flank (where the United States exercised practically no influence), he pointedly embraced Havana and extended strong support to the Sandinistas in their struggle against Somoza. In the latter case he played a pivotal role in frustrating Carter's plan to send an OAS peacekeeping force to Nicaragua to prevent a Sandinista takeover. These highly visible gestures to Caribbean radicals were supplemented by low-profile, but nevertheless effective, efforts to court more moderate, even conservative, Basin governments with programs of economic and energy assistance.

By seizing the middle ground and maintaining cordial ties with all but the extreme right, López Portillo clearly sought to establish Mexico as the Basin's premier diplomatic broker. In pursuing this strategy, he offered on several occasions to mediate U.S.-Cuban and U.S.-Nicaraguan reconciliations. In February 1982 he proposed a grand scheme for

regional peace involving Mexican facilitation of multidimensional negotiations between Washington, Havana, Managua, San Salvador, and
the Salvadoran insurgents.[51] Such attempts to midwife a new Caribbean
political order were but another indication of the desire on the part of
Basin nationalists to escape the U.S. shadow and to take charge of
charting their own futures.

The U.S. Response. The Reagan administration's tendency to perceive
and respond to Caribbean problems within a bipolar framework appears
to have hindered its ability to empathize with the Basin's nationalistic
sensitivities. Granted, President Reagan has developed very close, friendly,
personal relationships with some of his regional counterparts, especially
Mexico's López Portillo, and has made such goodwill gestures as
extending his first invitation for a U.S. state visit to a Caribbean leader,
Jamaica's Prime Minister Edward Seaga. But on a *programmatic* level
the picture has been somewhat more ambiguous.

In both the style and substance of Reagan's policies there have been
elements with considerable potential to arouse nationalistic trepidation
about U.S. hegemony. The CBI, for example, has several such aspects:
its pressure, explicit or implicit, on participants to adopt the U.S. free-
enterprise model of modernization could be construed as an attempt
to impose its social ideology on the area; its heavy emphasis on U.S.
private investment raises the specter of massive penetration or control
of Caribbean economies designed to lock recipients into a condition
of neocolonial dependency; and its insistence that aid go only to
governments with acceptable positions on international questions appears
to be a refusal to recognize the right of Basin countries to pursue
independent foreign policies. Moreover, the administration's occasional
allusions to its willingness to resort to unilateral force, such as imposing
a naval blockade on Cuba or sponsoring CIA-orchestrated destabilization
operations against Nicaragua, has resurrected deep-seated nationalistic
fears of Yankee military interventionism.

Certainly Washington has not shown any significant inclination to
accept a redistribution of regional influence by acquiescing to an expanded
role in the Basin's political affairs for its emerging middle powers.
Indicative of this stance has been a reluctance to react positively to
Mexico's efforts to function in a brokerage capacity. While appreciating
Mexico's value as a communication link, especially to Caribbean radicals,
and encouraging it to act as such, the United States has been quite
hesitant to include Mexico in substantive negotiations, preferring instead
a bilateral format. This general attitude was clearly demonstrated by
the reported U.S. response to Mexico's attempt to follow up on López
Portillo's peace proposal in February 1982:

Haig downplayed Mexico's role. Said he: "The U.S. will present and receive proposals on its own behalf." One of the main reasons for the Haig-Castañeda meetings, U.S. officials said, was simply to "massage the Mexican ego a little."[52]

Evaluation of the U.S. Response. There has been a definite inclination in Washington circles to link the idea of the United States as a global power to its ability to maintain its preeminence in the Basin, as illustrated by such comments as:

El Salvador is a mini-state in the backyard of the U.S. If this country cannot sustain the junta by a limited application of muscle, then it should quit the great power business.[53]

We simply cannot remain passive. If we cannot protect Central America, how can we defend the Persian Gulf and its oil? The international credibility of the United States is at stake.[54]

What would the Egyptians or the Saudi Arabians—or the Russians— think if they saw us back out of Central America. They would conclude that even that close to home, the Americans have no staying power.[55]

This psychology is abhorrent to many Latin Americans, evoking bitter memories of Manifest Destiny, gunboat diplomacy, and Yankee domination enforced by the Marines buccaneering through the Basin, or the CIA hatching its subterranean plots. And as long as it continues to prevail, the United States will not be able to react in a mutually satisfactory manner to the Caribbean nationalist challenge.

To deal with Basin nationalism, the United States must come to terms with its own flawed history. It must realize that much of the anti-Yankee sentiment there is a legacy of its own actions. By treating the area as its special sphere of influence for many years and functioning as a regional policeman, enforcing its own law and its own order, Washington has contributed significantly to the aura of suspicion that often permeates inter-American relations. Thus it would seem appropriate for the United States to make some major moves toward reconciliation. Carter attempted to do so with the Panama Canal treaties. But to think that Reagan, who opposed returning the Canal, would publicly disassociate himself from an imperialist tradition that he has never acknowledged is absurd. Probably the most that can be expected is a pragmatic response that would behaviorally (but not normatively) accept the legitimacy of demands by Caribbean nationalists—including those on the radical left (e.g., the Cubans, the Sandinistas, the Grenadians and the Salvadoran/Guatemalan guerrillas)—for an accommodation.

For such a rapprochement to occur, Mexican mediation would almost surely be required. But to be persuaded to play such a role,

> Mexico seeks something more than a crass quid pro quo; something quite intangible but in some respects even more important to the Mexicans: equality of treatment as a nation and utmost respect in future bilateral contacts.[56]

By so dealing with Mexico, Washington would implicitly be recognizing the emergence of new regional power centers and a new Caribbean political order. Once this crucial step is taken, the way would be open for serious negotiations to resolve the outstanding issues involved not only in the nationalist challenge to U.S. policy, but also in the developmental and insurgent challenges. If it is not taken and the United States continues along the same paths as before, Washington may soon find itself at a dead end. Avoiding this fate and instead becoming a constructive, egalitarian member of the Basin community is indeed the greatest contemporary challenge confronting U.S. Caribbean policy.

Notes

1. Ronald Steel, *Pax Americana* (New York: Viking Press, 1967), p. 292.

2. William G. Demas, "Foreword," in Richard Millet and W. Marvin Will (eds.), *The Restless Caribbean: Changing Patterns of International Relations* (New York: Praeger Publishers, 1979), pp. vii–x, explains that geopolitically the Caribbean can be seen in terms of three concentric circles. These are, from the inside outward: (1) the English-speaking, or Commonwealth, Caribbean islands; (2) the Caribbean archipelago, which includes all the islands plus the mainland "extensions" of Guyana, Suriname, and French Guinea in South America and Belize in Central America; and (3) the Caribbean Basin, consisting of the archipelago group as well as the littoral states of Central and South America. Here we are using the Basin conceptualization, including in the littoral category Venezuela, Colombia, Panama, all of Central America, and Mexico.

3. For a more detailed analysis of the Reagan administration's perceptions regarding U.S. interests in the Basin, see H. Michael Erisman, "Colossus Challenged: U.S. Caribbean Policy in the 1980s," in H. Michael Erisman and John D. Martz (eds.), *Colossus Challenged: The Struggle for Caribbean Influence* (Boulder, Colorado: Westview Press, 1982), pp. 12–18.

4. *Wagner Latin American Newsletter,* vol. IX, no. 11 (May 20, 1981), p. 2, notes that Guatemala is reported to have oil reserves as large as those of Alaska; and Judy Butler, "The Wider War," *NACLA Report on the Americas,* vol. 15, no. 3 (May-June 1981), p. 31, states that "new explorations [for oil in Guatemala] being conducted by Texaco and Amoco promise to supply 10 percent of U.S. needs."

5. Such a reorientation of sources may already be occurring: "The CIA's recent report of the world's oil reserves . . . points out that, in the near future, Latin America and other areas of the so-called Third World will be replacing the Middle East as world suppliers of hydrocarbons when deposits in the Middle East are exhausted.

"The accuracy of the report is made evident by the fact that the United States has been spending heavily on oil prospecting in more than 50 developing countries, many of them in Latin America, and chiefly in Central America and the Caribbean." ["The Danger Behind the Vile Campaign Against Cuba," *Granma Weekly Review* (April 20, 1980), p. 6.]

6. U.S. Department of State, Bureau of Public Affairs, "President Reagan: Caribbean Basin Initiative," Current Policy No. 370 (February 24, 1982), p. 5.

7. Richard E. Feinberg, "Central America: No Easy Answers," *Foreign Affairs,* vol. 59, no. 5 (Summer 1981), pp. 1123–1124.

8. X (George Kennan), "The Sources of Soviet Conduct," *Foreign Affairs,* vol. 25 (July 1947), pp. 566–582.

9. Only declassified and made public more than twenty years after it was written, "NSC-68, A Report to the National Security Council: United States Objectives and Programs for National Security" (Washington, D.C.: mimeographed, April 14, 1950) is one of the seminal documents of the Cold War. For an excellent brief discussion of it, see James A. Nathan and James K. Oliver, *United States Foreign Policy and World Order* (Boston: Little, Brown and Company, 1976), pp. 126–136.

10. Other Soviet goals that have been mentioned are: establishing a military presence in the eastern Caribbean (e.g., in Grenada) in order to be able to interdict strategic U.S. trade and logistical routes and divert Washington's attention from other vital areas, such as the Persian Gulf, by brewing trouble in the Basin.

11. Tad Szulc, "Confronting the Cuban Nemesis," *New York Times Magazine* (April 5, 1981), p. 39. See also "Reagan's Goal: Cutting Castro Down to Size," *U.S. News and World Report* (April 6, 1981), pp. 20–22, where it was revealed that a high-level State Department task force operating under Haig's overall direction had produced an ambitious plan to "bring the Cuban ruler into line." Options included, among others, a total air-sea blockade of the island, promoting internal subversion in hopes of toppling the Fidelista regime, and a U.S. military invasion.

12. A detailed official presentation of this analysis can be found in U.S. Department of State, Bureau of Public Affairs, "Cuba's Renewed Support for Violence in Latin America," Special Report No. 90 (December 14, 1981).

13. The concept of a penetrated political system is explained in James Rosenau, "Pre-Theories and Theories of Foreign Policy," in R. Barry Farrell (ed.), *Approaches To Comparative and International Politics* (Evanston, Illinois: Northwestern University Press, 1966), pp. 63–71; the essential aspects of Cuba's dependence on the USSR are described in Jiri Valenta, "The Soviet-Cuban Alliance in Africa and the Caribbean," *World Today* (February 1981), pp. 46–47.

14. U.S. Department of State, Bureau of Public Affairs, "Communist Interference in El Salvador," Special Report No. 80 (February 23, 1981), p. 1.

15. For details, see "Taking Aim at Nicaragua," *Newsweek* (March 22, 1982), pp. 20–29; and "A Lot of Show, But No Tell," *Time* (March 22, 1982), pp. 20–21. U.S. support for Great Britain in the 1982 war over the Falkland Islands destroyed, at least for the time being, the prospects for Argentinian participation in such covert operations.

16. Feinberg, "Central America" (note 7 above), p. 1130. For details regarding the stinginess of Soviet aid to Michael Manley's regime, see T. D. Allman, "Killing Jamaica with Kindness," *Harper's,* 258:30–36 (May 1979), p. 33.

17. An excellent, although somewhat more skeptical, analysis of the USSR's Caribbean policy can be found in Jiri Valenta, "Soviet Policy and the Crisis in the Caribbean," in Erisman and Martz, *Colossus Challenged* (note 3 above), pp. 47–82.

18. These Angolan developments are noted in William LeoGrande, "Cuban-Soviet Relations and Cuban Policy in Africa" (Paper presented at the 1979 International Studies Association convention in Toronto, Canada), p. 27; Gerald J. Bender, "Angola, The Cubans, and American Anxieties," *Foreign Policy,* no. 31 (Spring 1978), p. 26; and the *New York Times* (December 14, 1978), p. A14.

19. The other major incident occurred in Ethiopia when Havana rejected Russian entreaties to use its 16,000–17,000 troops in the country to help the radical Mengistu regime to defeat the secessionist Eritrean forces. For an excellent discussion of the extremely complex Eritrean issue, see Nelson Valdes, "The Evolution of Cuban Foreign Policy in Africa" (Paper presented at the 1979 International Studies Association convention in Toronto, Canada), pp. 122–145. Other less spectacular, but still noteworthy cases of the Cubans and the Soviets operating at cross purposes in Africa are chronicled in LeoGrande, "Cuban-Soviet Relations" (note 18 above), pp. 15–16 and 21–23.

20. Among the best of the recent works detailing the evolution of Cuba's foreign policy under Castro are Martin Weinstein (ed.), *Revolutionary Cuba in the World Arena* (Philadelphia: Institute for the Study of Human Issues, 1979); and Cole Blasier and Carmelo Mesa-Lago (eds.), *Cuba in the World* (Pittsburgh: University of Pittsburgh Press, 1979). The brief summary of Cuban foreign policy presented here is developed at much greater length in H. Michael Erisman, *Castro and Cuban Globalism: The Politics of Restrained Nationalism* (unpublished).

21. The foco theory was popularized by Regis Debray, *Revolution in the Revolution?* (New York: Grove Press, 1967). For an excellent collection of critiques of Debray's ideas, see Leo Huberman and Paul M. Sweezy (eds.), *Regis Debray and the Latin American Revolution* (New York: Monthly Review Press, 1968).

22. U.S. Department of State, Special Report No. 90 (note 12 above), pp. 6–8 and 10, reports that Castro mediated unity pacts among guerrilla groups in Nicaragua, El Salvador, and Guatemala while trying unsuccessfully to do so in Colombia in 1980.

23. Robert G. Kaiser, "White Paper on El Salvador Is Faulty," *Washington Post* (June 9, 1981), p. 1A; Jonathan Kwitny, "Tarnished Report?" *Wall*

Street Journal (June 8, 1981), p. 1. See also Jonathan E. Maslow and Ana Arana, "Operation El Salvador," *Colombia Journalism Review* (May/June 1981), pp. 53–58.

24. "How Havana Helps," *Newsweek* (March 1, 1982), p. 26.

25. U.S. Department of State, Current Policy No. 370 (note 6 above), p. 2.

26. Costa Rica's economic problems are summarized in "Raiding Grandma's Cabinet," *Time* (September 28, 1982), p. 42; and in "Costa Rica," *Mesoamerica,* vol. 1, no. 1 (January 1982), p. 8, which notes that Costa Rica is the first Latin American country to default on its international debts.

27. *Facts On File,* vol. 42, no. 2152 (February 12, 1982), p. 95, reports that in every Central American country except Panama, per capita income actually declined sharply in 1981.

28. No data is available for Guatemala, but since its demography is mainly rural, land tenure patterns can provide a good indication of income distribution. Alan Riding, "Guatemala: A State of Siege," *New York Times Magazine* (August 24, 1980), p. 20, notes that 70 percent of the land is owned by only 2 percent of the population. Thus the situation in Guatemala seems consistent with the income maldistribution appearing in Table 1.1.

29. The main proponent of the relative deprivation theory is Ted Robert Gurr, "Psychological Factors in Civil Strife," *World Politics,* vol. 22 (January 1968), pp. 245–278; and "A Causal Model of Civil Strife: A Comparative Analysis Using New Indices," *American Political Science Review* (December 1968), 62:1104–1124. James C. Davies, "Toward a Theory of Revolution," *American Sociological Review* (February 1962), 27:5–19, also relies heavily on the concept of relative deprivation in formulating his J-Curve theory.

30. Considerable controversy has emerged regarding Duarte's land reform. The radical right has viewed it as akin to Communism while the left has attacked it for being essentially symbolic and/or a cover for repressive rural pacification. The latter analysis is summarized in James C. Stephens, Jr., "Agrarian Reform: Hope Turns to Terror," *NACLA Report on the Americas,* vol. 15, no. 1 (January-February 1981), pp. 36–39. Other pessimistic appraisals can be found in "Land Reform Under Fire," *Newsweek* (January 19, 1981), p. 44; and "Salvadoran Military Begins Training with U.S. Weapons, Advisers," *Washington Post* (January 25, 1981), p. A15.

31. Details regarding the CBI can be found in U.S. Department of State, Current Policy No. 370 (note 6 above); and "Reagan's Blueprint," *U.S. News and World Report* (March 8, 1982), pp. 20–22. For a general overview of Reagan's 1982 bilateral aid proposals for the hemisphere, see U.S. Department of State, Bureau of Public Affairs, "Latin America and the Caribbean: Bilateral Assistance," Current Policy No. 269 (March 23, 1981).

32. *Facts On File,* vol. 41, No. 2133 (October 2, 1981), p. 728.

33. Washington's campaign against Grenada is covered in the following issues of *Caribbean Contact:* "Grenada Needs CARICOM Support Against Hostile USA" (June 1981), p. 1; "In Trouble, But Not for Sale" (July 1981) p. 3; and "Maurice Bishop's Revealing Letter to Ronald Reagan" (March 1982), pp. 7–8.

34. "The Fire Next door," *Newsweek* (March 1, 1982), p. 23.

35. "A 'Proposal' to Make the Rich Richer and the Poor Poorer," *Granma Weekly Review* (March 14, 1982), p. 2.

36. "Haig Aide Says U.S. Opposes Sharing the Wealth," *New York Times* (August 7, 1981), p. A6.

37. The Reagan administration's position on North-South economic issues is summarized in "Third World: Uncle Sam's Tough New Stand," *U.S. News and World Report* (October 26, 1981), pp. 20–24.

38. Richard R. Fagen, "The Carter Administration and Latin America: Business As Usual?" *Foreign Affairs,* vol. 57, no. 3 (1978), pp. 666–667.

39. Quoted in Karen DeYoung, "The Caribbean: A Developing Storm," *Washington Post* (September 28, 1980), p. A18.

40. Ibid.

41. Among the analyses emphasizing the importance of such diversified external support are Feinberg, "Central America" (note 7 above); and Roger Burback, "Central America: The End of U.S. Hegemony?" *Monthly Review* (January 1982), pp. 1–18.

42. "Storm Over El Salvador," *Newsweek* (March 16, 1981), p. 35.

43. These Guatemalan developments are summarized in "The Coup That Got Away," *Time* (April 5, 1982), pp. 28–30.

44. The most controversial figure in the rightist coalition is former national guard officer Roberto d'Aubuisson, leader of the National Republican Alliance party (ARENA), who apparently has close ties with right-wing death squads and who also, during his military intelligence career, was nicknamed Major Blowtorch for his reputed proficiency in using blowtorches to interrogate prisoners.

45. "Significance of Not One But Two U.S. 'Initiatives,'" *Caribbean Contact* (April 1982), p. 15.

46. "Terror, Right and Left," *Time* (March 22, 1982), p. 32.

47. The failures of these revolutionary movements are discussed and analyzed in Richard Gott, *Guerrilla Movements in Latin America* (New York: Doubleday and Company, 1971); and H. Michael Erisman, *Revolution and Revolutionary Elites in Latin America* (Ann Arbor, Michigan: University Microfilms, 1972).

48. *Facts On File,* vol. 42, no. 2153 (February 19, 1982), p. 104.

49. Opinion polls have shown that U.S. citizens are strongly opposed to *any* military involvement in such places as El Salvador. For example, a poll published in *Newsweek* (March 1, 1982), p. 19, showed that an absolute majority opposed sending U.S. military supplies, advisors, or troops to El Salvador and instead wanted Washington to stay completely out. Daniel Southerland, "U.S. Options in El Salvador," *Christian Science Monitor* (March 22, 1982) reports that a *New York Times*-CBS poll released March 21, 1982 confirmed these sentiments.

50. Excellent analyses of Mexico's foreign policy can be found in Edward Williams, "Mexico's Central American Policy: Revolutionary and Prudential Dimensions," in Erisman and Martz, *Colossus Challenged* (note 3 above), pp. 149–169; Bruce Bagley, "Mexico in the 1980s: A New Regional Power," *Current*

History, vol. 80, no. 469 (November 1981), pp. 353–356+; Daniel James, "Mexico: America's Newest Problem?" *Washington Quarterly* (Summer 1980), pp. 87–105; and John F. McShane, "Mexico's Foreign Policy: A Return to Restrained Nationalism" (Paper presented at the 1979 convention of the Southern Political Science Association in Gatlinburg, Tennessee).

51. For details, see "A Week of Mixed Signals," *Time* (March 19, 1982), p. 28; and see "Talking About Talking," *Time* (April 5, 1982), p. 16.

52. "A Week of Mixed Signals" (note 51 above).

53. Joseph Kraft, "Caribbean Gamble Seen," *Erie* (Penn.) *Daily Times* (February 26, 1981), p. 10A; syndicated column.

54. An unidentified Reagan administration official quoted in Tad Szulc, "Can Central America Be a New Vietnam?" *Parade Magazine* (January 24, 1982), p. 12.

55. An unidentified U.S. diplomat quoted in "Taking Aim at Nicaragua" (note 15 above), pp. 26, 29.

56. James, "Mexico" (note 50 above), p. 104.

Macroanalyses

2

The Ideological and Idiosyncratic Aspects of U.S.-Caribbean Relations

J. Edward Greene

Introduction

The complexities of international relations cannot be overstated. In the contemporary period interactions in the global arena must take into account a multiplicity of issues that are affected by an increasing number of nation-states, most of which can be described as developing-dependent countries. Central to this drama is the persistent hegemonic activity of the superpowers, the United States and the Soviet Union. Global competition is underscored by ideological considerations regardless of whether their manifestations are economic, military, or moral. This chapter identifies some of the ideological dimensions in the relationships between the United States and the Caribbean, focusing on the English-speaking CARICOM (Caribbean Community) nations to illustrate the analyses. Examined here are the features of world ideological dominance, the nature and scope of Washington's hegemonic power, and the contemporary formation of the Caribbean state system in response to the preeminence of the United States. The complicating factors involved—e.g., the role of middle powers in the hemisphere, bilateralism vs. regionalism, and subregional competition—are compared with the shifts in U.S. perceptions of its hegemonic authority.

Establishing a Hegemonic Ideology

When probing the impact of ideology in international relations, it is generally agreed that because ideological orientations are essentially

Barry University Library

Miami, FL 33161

33

influenced by domestic politics, diplomatic relations established on this basis are not necessarily stable; they are subject to alteration with changes in regimes.[1] This is more true for small states than for hegemonic powers. Hegemony is based not only on ideological but also on economic and cultural dominance. The three are deeply interrelated. Achieving global ideological hegemony involves creating the core of the world order, the underpinnings of which are aptly described as follows:

> The construction of a world hegemonic ideology is a continuing task. Theories are elaborated on trade and economic development, population and resources, the social relations of production, investment and technology, civil and political rights and the principles of political institutions. In all these and other fields, ideology gains the force of accepted rationality and comes to appear as an expression of an inherent order of nature rather than of a particular historical world power configuration.[2]

Although the hegemonic ideology is structurally institutionalized in the international order, its effective application depends on minimizing conflict between "core" and "peripheral" societies. It may, however, be modified by emerging demands within the system or by factionalism in the periphery and ultimately could be superseded by various idiosyncracies (including the demise of the core society).

In assessing the U.S. hegemonic ideology with special reference to the Caribbean, it is necessary to establish whether, as a core system, the United States has been able to sustain the regulatory mechanisms of the international economy, examining such variables as the effects of the conflicts and contradictions within its sphere of influence, the comparative strength of countervailing ideologies, and the emergence of alternative world views and alternative centers of ideological construction. The focus here is on determining whether Washington's hegemonic influences have dominated other networks of relations such as those established by the English-speaking states within the Lomé Convention's framework, within the Nonaligned Movement, or in the diplomatic sphere of the immediate Latin American geographical environment.

The Scope of U.S. Hegemony

Although there has been an upsurge in hemispheric relations in the immediate post–World War II period,[3] what can too easily be overlooked is the fact that U.S. policies toward Latin America generally, and the Caribbean more particularly, commenced as early as 1823 with the

Monroe Doctrine, whereby Washington gave a clear warning to European powers to stay out of the Western Hemisphere. Basically America's expansionist policies have focused on access to markets and natural resources, profitable overseas capital investment, and security-related issues. By 1850 the United States had expanded its Western frontier and steadily increased its interests in the Caribbean in the wake of interventions there by European powers.[4] Indeed the Clayton-Bulwer Treaty (1850) between Great Britain and the United States was an agreement to jointly monopolize the area. Between 1860 and 1890 the United States gradually increased its trade, and in spite of the prominence of European capital, U.S. entrepreneurs were able to penetrate the Basin and to consolidate their growing position, especially in Cuba and Mexico. By 1898, when Washington acquired Cuba and Puerto Rico from Spain by force, the U.S. position was greatly enhanced in the international capitalist economy. It was, therefore, a logical culmination of events when in 1904, under President Theodore Roosevelt, the United States created a sphere of influence in the Caribbean Basin as an addendum—the Roosevelt Corollary—to the Monroe Doctrine.[5]

As U.S. private investors were busily establishing themselves in the region, Washington expanded its military presence in Cuba, Mexico, Guatemala, Honduras, Nicaragua, Panama, Colombia, the Dominican Republic, and Haiti. Subsequently, having secured its hemispheric hegemony, the United States declared its Good Neighbor policy, thereby renouncing its right to military intervention. But as Michael Martin points out, the Good Neighbor policy was not intended to foster democratic political institutions. Instead, he notes, "the United States prepared Somoza to overthrow the elected Government and supported him to seize Nicaragua, [and] did [not] inhibit the dictators Trujillo and Duvalier from consolidating their control over the Dominican Republic and Haiti."[6]

The end of World War II ushered in a period of intense ideological confrontation, as manifested by the global Cold War and the Cuban revolution, which signified Moscow's growing influence in the Caribbean. President Kennedy's Alliance for Progress, launched in 1961, was designed to support U.S. capitalism against the countervailing growth of progressive and socialist movements in the Basin. But the Alliance succeeded only minimally in its attempt to prop up national elites by upgrading the military establishments erected to protect them and the largely U.S.-based multinational corporations.[7] In this context ideological motivations were indistinguishable from economic and military strategies for hegemonic superiority, with the external threat being identifed as Soviet totalitarianism.

All these events, among others, dramatize the long history of Washington's involvement in Latin America and many are illustrative of the ideological paradox so aptly described by Bradford Burns:

> In a ten-year span, military rule replaced thirteen constitutional Governments and the United States had supported lavishly the Latin American military. In truth, over two-thirds of Alliance for Progress funds went to military dictators or to military controlled civilian governments, despite the intention that the funds would be used to buttress democracy. Economically the area's condition was certainly more precarious in 1971 than it was in 1961.[8]

It was during the Alliance era that the countries of the English-speaking Caribbean were gradually acquiring their legal independence from Great Britain. First came Jamaica and Trinidad and Tobago in 1962, followed by Guyana (1966), Bahamas (1973), Grenada (1974), and the spate of the Leeward and Windward island territories and Belize from 1974 onward. By and large, the political culture of constitutionalism on which these newly independent states were formed created an image, which was to last well into the 1970s, of a generally safe zone within the U.S. sphere of influence. This was true in spite of the United States' role in repressing the growth of the Marxist-oriented regime in Guyana under Cheddi Jagan during the early 1960s and its direct intervention in the Dominican Republic (1965) to prevent a progressive movement from taking power. With the Cuban revolution already entrenched, the unrest in Guyana and the Dominican Republic had some implications for the stability of the region. Basically the U.S. strategy was to isolate Cuba and therefore preserve Washington's hegemonic authority. But problems in the global economic system and the political vagaries within the hemisphere made sustaining this policy difficult.

By the end of the 1960s the international financial and economic structures, which had been created at the 1944 Bretton Woods Conference by the United States on the assumption that its economy would flourish within a relatively open global environment, were precariously poised on the brink of disaster. From 1950 to 1970 the Gross National Product of the Western industrialized nations grew at unprecedented rates. However, between 1965 and 1979 the world order did not produce as rapid an improvement in per-capita Gross Domestic Products, especially in the poorest states, where over 50 percent of the human race lives. In addition, the mechanisms of currency stabilization and balance-of-payments adjustments were chaotic. International debt management appeared uncontrollable while private capital had practically usurped the functions of the World Bank group, a trend that has become even more prevalent in the early 1980s with the gargantuan loans, outstanding mostly to Third World countries, made by private banks, governments, and other financial institutions. This in turn has affected international production and trade. With the scientific and technological revolution giving a relative advantage to Japan and Western Europe over the United States, Washington's hegemonic power in the capitalist international order has been weakened.

The challenge to the United States was further dramatized when the Organization of Petroleum Exporting Countries (OPEC) quadrupled oil prices in 1973 and imposed an embargo against states that supported Israel in the Yom Kippur war. These actions undermined the possibility of indefinite economic growth, the basic assumption on which the U.S. concept of world order had been based.[9] Proposals for a New International Economic Order were not only a response to this global dilemma, but also highlighted the extent to which the postwar political and economic system had been weakened and politicized.

Increasing Caribbean radicalism in the 1970s—partly a reaction to the ramifications of international economic instability and more specifically to the private-enterprise philosophy that failed to promote growth and development—was perceived by Washington as endangering U.S. interests. Illustrating the U.S. stake in the Basin, Hilbourne Watson points out that the United States imports from the region over 50 percent of its bauxite and alumina; 7 percent of its nickel (provided by the Dominican Republic); 17 percent of its sugar; 15 percent of its cocoa, cigars, and tobacco; and a significant proportion of its bananas, coffee, spices, and tropical hardwood. Furthermore, several Caribbean entities—Trinidad and Tobago, the Netherlands Antilles, the Bahamas, St. Croix, and Venezuela—produce or refine most of the oil and petroleum products that come into the United States for use on the eastern seaboard. Finally, U.S. direct investments in the Caribbean are estimated at $10.52 billion; and of an estimated $14.76 billion combined capital flow into the area (including multilateral and bilateral aid), U.S. sources contribute $12.78 billion or 86 percent.[10] All these factors make the Caribbean a zone of relative importance to the United States. And, of course, its proximity to North America further increases its strategic significance.

Caribbean Responses

The newly independent states of the Caribbean are among those most directly affected by the vicissitudes of the global economic order. The international production crisis has resulted in high unemployment rates of 20 to 35 percent; chronic inflation ranging from 10 to 30 percent; and foreign-exchange and balance-of-payments problems that led to international debts in 1980 of $41 milion for the Bahamas, $60 million in Barbados, $430 million in Guyana, $417 million in Trinidad and Tobago, and slightly over $1 billion in Jamaica.[11]

Many of the political developments in the Basin between 1970 and 1980 were outgrowths of the downturn in the industrial cycle of international capital. In domestic terms increasing economic instability spurred interest in modernization models other than the free-enterprise system. In foreign affairs the appeal of Third World internationalism provided a basis for solidarity with various extrahemispheric national liberation movements. The conjunction of these internal and external reactions to the global recession has reinforced radical and left-wing tendencies within Caribbean societies, which in turn have contributed to the emergence of a new form of political struggle and the proliferation of mass movements promoting some type of socialism. What distinguishes the present popular organizations from those of the 1930s, 1940s, and 1950s is their basic shift from "laborism" as the basis of their demands for change. In the earlier period the prototype for political radicalism in the Commonwealth Caribbean was the British Labor Party. The emphasis on unionism and welfarism encompassed in the principles of Fabian socialism offered the Caribbean anticolonial movements a practical way of fusing nationalist aspirations with the only form of government, the Westminster system, in which they had tutelage. Once the two-party competitive model was rooted in a coalition with the union movement, party leaders found it relatively easy to manipulate the masses, and the British government found it even easier to manipulate both the leaders and the led. The mere granting of home rule acted as a palliative, satisfying the fundamental urge to substitute local for foreign office-holders.

The contemporary mass movements, however, have been operating at a time when anticolonial sentiments can no longed be used by local party leadership to divert attention from the issue of continuing economic underdevelopment. The Cold War, the growth of nonalignment, and the identification with Third Worldism have all generated alternatives to the Westminster model and liberal Fabianism. Especially after the 1968 Rodney crisis in Jamaica and the Trinidad and Tobago Black Power disturbances in 1970, social movements have forced the nationalistic dialogue to take place at an ideological level that poses the conflict between capitalism and socialism in sharper terms than before.

To a large extent government leadership rests with an entrenched old guard of West Indian nationalists or has been captured by a newer breed of reformists-nationalists who are likewise committed to curbing radical mass demands. This is most evident in Trinidad, where the ruling party was incapable of providing an acceptable successor to Dr. Eric Williams in 1974 even though widespread dissatisfaction both within and outside the People's National Movement was evident; a change in leadership took place only after his death in 1980. More important, however, is the failure of Caribbean mass movements to consolidate their positions either because of their inability to sustain support on the basis of a unified ideology or because of the growing tendency of governments to usurp their programs by *apparently* moving to the left.

Outside the dominant political parties many radical groups, such as the Worker's Liberation Party in Jamaica and the Working People's Alliance in Guyana, have, in various forms, contributed greatly to the ideological debate in the Caribbean and have placed on the agenda demands for social transformation that run counter to U.S. hegemonic interests. Such organizations have given expression to a new wave of activism calling for socialist change as well as fostering linkages with Cuba's Communist party and the Soviet bloc. While their popular support may not be as broadly based as Grenada's New Jewel Movement prior to its March 1979 revolution, their articulation of issues rooted in social discontent makes them at least viable political factions within the region.

Within the smaller, less developed territories of the Leeward and Windward islands, political instability was also manifesting itself in the increasing radicalization of those engaged in socioeconomic protest. For instance, the March 1979 coup in Grenada was greatly influenced by the repressive practices of the Eric Gairy regime as well as the economic crisis within the island. Subsequently Grenada's revolution stimulated leftist activism in neighboring St. Vincent, St. Lucia, and Dominica; but its main significance lies in the fact that it was the first successful armed uprising by a left-wing party in the Caribbean since the Cuban Revolution of 1959. The event immediately generated ideological polarization in the CARICOM as Jamaica and Guyana provided overt support to the new regime, Trinidad and Tobago remained noncommittal, and Barbados and various Windward and Leeward islands expressed serious concern over the unprecedented creation of an unconstitutional state controlled by the area's only nonelected government.

Cuba's role in this process of radicalization cannot be readily ascertained. However, its growing acceptability in the region can be inferred from the numerous technical and other missions dispatched by Caribbean states to Havana and vice versa, as well as by the growth of Marxist groups and political parties that have invited Cuban Communist officials to their rallies and conferences. The proliferation of

TABLE 2.1
Changes In Communist Country Relations And Representation
   in Selected Caribbean Countries, 1971-1980

	1971	1976	1977	1980
Number of Missions Established With Communist Countries	2	38	14	20
Number of Communist Countries Establishing Missions	2	11	12	12
Number of Communist Countries Without Missions	13	3	2	2
Number of Missions Held by USSR	1	5	7	8
Number of Missions Held by Cuba	1	6	6	10
Number of Missions Held by PRC	0	6	8	8
Total Number of Trade Missions Established	1	3	-	1

Source: Compiled by Hilbourne Watson from U.S. Department
of State, Bureau of Intelligence and Research, Communist
Diplomatic, Consular and Trade Representation in Latin
America and the Caribbean, Report No. 681 (January 11,
1977), Report No. 937 (March 14, 1978), and Report No. 1344
(March 18, 1980).

projects involving Cuban technical assistance in construction, health, and education was most evident in Jamaica from 1976 to 1980. Also, the Cuban state airline began operating regular flights between the English-speaking Caribbean and Havana. As a result, Cuban aircraft that were transporting troops in Angola in 1976 were, for a while, permitted to refuel in Barbados. Washington interpreted these developments as support on the part of Errol Barrow's government for Havana's military intervention in Africa, which was particularly reprehensible to the United States because it believed that Cuba was acting as a surrogate on behalf of the USSR. Most Caribbean nations, however, felt that Cuba had a right as an Afro/Latin state to assist legitimate black-African liberation struggles and therefore did not equate its involvement in the Angolan war with advancing the interests of the Soviet Union.[12]

The rapid growth of diplomatic, consular, and trade relations (see Table 2.1) with the Communist world is one indication that the Caribbean countries were trying to move out of the U.S. sphere of influence. One writer comments on this phenomenon:

> The expansion of Moscow's interests in the Caribbean is illustrated dramatically by the striking increase in the range of formal relations between Caribbean states and the USSR and its allies. . . . Yet these ties most Caribbean leaders will argue are motivated not by anti-American designs but by the desire to enlarge the range and number of possible foreign aid and trade options. Furthermore, Caribbean states have also increased their ties with Communist countries that are weakly linked or even antagonistic to the USSR. The People's Republic of China (PRC), for example, is one of the region's most important countries.[13]

The weakening of America's hegemonic power in the mid-1970s was related as much to the crisis in the world economy as it was to the Carter administration's moralistic tendencies, which are illustrated in the following comments by Secretary of State Cyrus Vance:

> The surest way to defeat terrorism is to promote legal, economic and social justice. Summary justice negatively affects the future that it tries to promote and only produces more violence, more victims and more terrorism. Respect for the legal regime promotes justice and eliminates the goals of subversion. When a government abandons that respect it lowers itself to the abyss of terrorism and loses its best weapon: its moral authority.[14]

But despite Carter's apparently moralistic approach to foreign affairs, his policies never intended to undermine or abandon Washington's world ideological hegemony. Indeed he sought to restore the legitimacy of U.S. paramountcy, but was thwarted partly by the magnitude of the domestic crisis preceding his presidency and, after his succession to power, by the crippling realities of the state of the world capitalist system. By the end of 1979 the principles of ideological pluralism and human rights that had previously guided his foreign policy were deemphasized and the Cold War rhetoric about external (Soviet) threats was rejuvenated.

Apparently Jamaican Prime Minister Michael Manley misjudged Washington's mood when, in his address to the Nonaligned Summit Conference in 1979, he made reference to the significance of the Russian Revolution of 1917 and, among other things, criticized the U.S. role in Puerto Rico:

We join our voices with those who assert the right of the Puerto Rican people to self-determination. While we would never seek to impose our will on any country we feel it to be the duty of the members of the Movement to support those who struggle for Puerto Rican independence regardless of whether they are in the minority at this time, because the principle is fundamental at this time.[15]

The tenor of his speech was clearly anti-American and came at a time when Jamaica's Minister of Finance, Eric Bell, was negotiating with commercial banks about refinancing the island's external debt of approximately $450 million. It also coincided with Carter's hard-won battle in Congress for the ratification of the Panama Canal Treaty and with the difficulties Washington was experiencing in trying to arrange a diplomatic resolution to the crisis in Nicaragua resulting from burgeoning anti-Somoza sentiments. These problems, among others, resurrected the external-threat syndrome in the United States. What was essentially opposition to Cuban and Soviet policies developed into hostility toward any nation identifying with their positions, notably on matters relating to Angola and Ethiopia. Accordingly Grenada was viewed by the United States as a strategic center for Moscow and Havana in the Eastern Caribbean because it supported the Russians on Afghanistan, and Cuba and Jamaica on the Puerto Rican issue. The subsequent U.S. effort in 1981 to prevent the European Development Fund from providing technical aid to Grenada was only one of the attempts to isolate a perceived external threat.

Washington's animosity towards Jamaica (1979–80) and Grenada (1980–81) highlights the continuity of the U.S. hegemonic trajectory across the Carter and Reagan regimes. Indeed from the time of the Monroe Doctrine and the Roosevelt Corollary, U.S. policymakers have customarily perceived hemispheric affairs primarily, though not exclusively, in terms of security.

Reagan, in announcing the Caribbean Basin Initiative, declared that "the United States will do whatever is prudent and necessary to ensure the peace and security of the Caribbean."[16] Specifically, his main objectives were: (1) to expand the U.S. military presence in order to contain the spread of popular social revolutions in the Basin; and (2) to implement an economic development program that would not only maintain the predominance of U.S. capital in the Caribbean, but in the overall capitalist world economy as well. The CBI's economic implications are discussed elsewhere in this volume, but it is important to point out here that it is neither a novel idea nor substantial enough to promote significant development in the region. Operation Bootstrap in Puerto Rico during the 1940s, the Alliance for Progress in the 1960s, and Nixon's Action Proposals in the 1970s were all similarly designed, and all produced deleterious consequences that perpetuated underdevelopment and dependence on U.S. money and markets. The CBI provides perhaps the clearest indication that foreign policy under Reagan is dominated by the perception of an East-West ideological struggle. The overriding concern is to limit Cuban/Soviet influence, specifically in the case of Grenada in the Caribbean and Nicaragua and El Salvador in Central America. The attempt to link the Caribbean and Central America within the so-called Caribbean Basin framework has clearly been influenced by ideological and strategic concerns. Unfortunately the Basin view imposes an arbitrary geopolitical definition that takes little account of the structures of subregional integration created by the governments of the Caribbean (CARICOM) and of Central America (CACM or the Central American Common Market).

The CBI further underscores the economic dimensions of Washington's aspirations for ideological dominance insofar as its proposals for increased capital flow to the Caribbean emphasize primarily foreign private investment and ultimately the development of capitalist societies modeled along U.S. lines. In other words, the Basin concept flows from a hegemonic strategic framework that incorporates U.S. social philosophy and is designed to facilitate U.S. economic/ideological penetration of the Caribbean and Central America. Recognizing the danger involved, CARICOM foreign ministers expressed their dissatisfaction with the potentially fragmentary impact on the area that could result from implementing the CBI as originally formulated.[17]

U.S. Hegemony and the Middle Powers

Continued U.S. hegemony in the Caribbean has been facilitated by various geopolitical factors. For instance, CARICOM has not contributed to regional economic viability in the manner anticipated. Hence the weakening economies of the small states have forced them to break ranks and to grasp at all forms of bilateral assistance. Another phenomenon that can affect (either positively or negatively) Washington's influence is the existence of action-spheres between subregions with the potential for eliciting both cooperative and competitive tendencies simultaneously. Venezuela represents an excellent example of this foreign policy dualism. Its claim to approximately two-thirds of Guyana's territory has led the Forbes Burnham government to internationalize the issue and to seek support and allies in the United Nations, the Western Hemisphere, and the Third World. The controversy has also intricately involved Brazil, whose decision to mute its own territorial claims in Guyana has been interpreted as a protective device and acts as a possible constraint on Venezuelan expansionism. Venezuela's claim to 3,000 kilometers of coastline along the Caribbean Sea creates another but lesser kind of boundary dispute with Trinidad and Tobago that includes issues related to fishing rights. On the other hand, Caracas has made available a variety of economic aid packages to the Windward/ Leeward islands and together with Mexico offers special oil concession facilities to the Caribbean states. It also participates in the Caribbean Development Bank. This increased economic activity in the CARICOM area has often been perceived as being supportive of Washington's efforts to contain the expansion of Havana's ideological and diplomatic influence.

The importance of the hemispheric middle powers (i.e., Mexico, Brazil, Venezuela, and Cuba) is their potential, both individually and multilaterally, to challenge Washington's traditional Caribbean hegemony. The relations among the middle powers are simultaneously *cooperative* and *competitive* with respect to Brazil, Venezuela, and Mexico and largely *competitive* between these three and Cuba because Havana's role in foreign affairs, especially its military activities and security assistance programs, is more expansive in both hemispheric and global terms. In the final analysis the relative diplomatic closeness among Brazil, Venezuela, and Mexico, compared with their distance from Cuba, is implicit in their relationship with the United States, which is normally hostile to Cuba.

If the gap between Havana and the other middle powers can be ascribed to ideological factors, the apparent gap between the CARICOM countries and Latin America is based on historical as well as cultural differences. The reservations held by those in the English-speaking Caribbean about the attitudes of the Hispanic nations are illustrated by Eric Williams's comment that "there has been a feeling in our direction of a certain resentment that our rights as members of the American family are not recognized and that we have to depend upon what ultimately appears to be something of grace instead of . . . a right."[18]

Williams was an advocate of sustaining the Caribbean archipelago and mainland Guyana against the rimland states, especially after 1973, when Venezuela's growing financial role in the region allowed it to compete with Trinidad and Tobago for greater influence. Caracas also instituted some low-profile military aid programs, one of which (a standby facility that was never used) was ironically in reponse to Williams's request for assistance during the 1970 Black Power riots in Trinidad. Venezuela's regional aspirations were bolstered in the mid-1970s by Jamaica, whose government was committed to a wider conception of the Caribbean in order to expand the system's resource base. Kingston's position conflicted with that of Trinidad and Tobago, which consistently resisted anything that they felt might weaken the integrity of the area.

The question of geopolitical relations between CARICOM and the wider Latin American framework remains unresolved in an institutionalized sense. Nevertheless, the functional ties already developed via the economic and security resources of the middle powers may yet lead to the development of a new system of trade and diplomatic arrangements between the subregions of the hemisphere. The creation of the Caribbean Development and Cooperative Committee, composed of CARICOM and Latin American states, is an attempt at such institutionalization. But simply establishing such organizations cannot by itself ensure the viability of regionalism. This is especially so when the hemisphere's hegemonic power—the United States—takes a firm stand on external threats and thereby discourages ideological pluralism, preferring instead, under Reagan, to identify the restoration of private enterprise in Jamaica as a top priority while seeking to isolate Cuba, undermine the People's Republic of Grenada, and reimpose control over a bankrupt Guyana.

Conclusion

Future relations between Washington and the Caribbean are far from predictable. Recently a wave of pro-U.S. sentiment has apparently emerged in the islands. The 1980 victory in Jamaica of Edward Seaga over Michael Manley was perhaps the single most important turn of events in the consolidation of U.S. ideological hegemony in the area. This was reinforced in 1981 by the return to power of Tom Adams in Barbados, the reinstatements of Vere Bird as prime minister in Antigua and John Compton in St. Lucia, and the installation of Eugenia Charles as prime minister of Dominica. In an electoral sense, then, there has been a movement from left to right. That this phenomenon has coincided with similar tendencies in Washington's foreign policy appears to be significant.

Regarding the prospects for U.S. intervention in the region, the role of the middle powers (except, perhaps, the increasingly isolated Cuba) will be crucial. For instance, Mexico's position vis-à-vis the CBI and Belize, Canada's rejection of U.S. attempts to block European Economic Community aid to Grenada, and Brazil's mediation in the Guyana-Venezuela border issue have all been positive counterbalancing forces in U.S.-Caribbean relations. Moreover, the Kremlin has not, except through Cuban surrogacy, made any overt attempts at penetrating the region using economic assistance. This is not to say that Moscow is not interested in undermining U.S. hegemony in the Caribbean. It is more a matter of geopolitical and geostrategic priorities, as Jamaica discovered in 1978–80, when it was unable to secure preferential agreements or "most-favored nation" trading terms with the Soviet bloc at a time when such concessionary arrangements would have reduced the impact of harsh conditionalities by the International Monetary Fund and growing U.S. hostility. Guyana, too, has had similar experiences with the Russians.

Given the economic instability currently sweeping the islands, it is likely that (Marshall-type) aid packages from Washington will be seized upon by some Caribbean regimes as a means of survival. Also two middle powers—Mexico and Brazil—are presently in the throes of financial crises occasioned by huge foreign debts and will almost certainly have to rely heavily on U.S. help to resolve them. This in turn will place some informal, but very real, constraints on their inclination to pursue foreign policies incompatible with Washington's interests. If these trends persist in the long run, the idiosyncracies within the Caribbean may yet be absorbed by the United States in its quest to reassert its strategic and ideological hegemony.

Notes

1. Vaughn Lewis, *The Commonwealth Caribbean Countries' Diplomatic Decolonization and Relocation: Relations with Hemispheric Middle Powers,* Working Paper Number 96 (Washington, D.C.: The Wilson Center, Latin American Program, 1981).

2. Robert W. Cox and Harold K. Jacobson, "The United States and World Order: On Structures of World Power and Structural Transformation" (Unpublished paper presented at the International Political Science Association Conference in Rio de Janeiro, Brazil, August 1981), p. 7.

3. Among the sources that deal extensively with notions of U.S. hegemony in the contemporary world are William P. Avery and David Rapkin, *America in a Changing Political Economy* (New York: Longman Inc., 1982); and James Petras, "U.S. Foreign Policy: Revival of Interventionism," *Monthly Review* (February 1980), pp. 15–27.

4. E. Bradford Burns, *Latin America: A Concise Interpretive History* (Englewood, N.J.: Prentice-Hall, 1982), p. 282.

5. Robert F. Smith (ed.), *The United States and Latin American Spheres of Influence* (Melbourne, Florida: Krieger, 1981).

6. Michael T. Martin, "From Cancun to the Caribbean Basin Initiative: The Political Economy of Regional Stabilization and Underdevelopment" (Unpublished paper presented at the Fourth Annual Conference of the Association of Caribbean Studies in Havana, Cuba, 1982), p. 6.

7. Ibid., p. 7

8. Burns, *Latin America* (note 4 above), p. 281.

9. A very good discussion of this issue is provided by Cox and Jacobson, "The United States" (note 2 above).

10. Hilbourne Watson, "The Internationalization of Capital and Economic Development: Accumulation and Unequal Development" (Paper presented at the Seminar on Democracy and Development in the Caribbean II, Inter-American Politics Seminar Series, May 6–9, 1979).

11. International Development Bank Annual Report (1979).

12. A full discussion of this is presented in Alfred Stepan, "The United States and Latin America: Vital Interests and the Instruments of Power," *Foreign Affairs*, vol. 58, no. 3 (1980), pp. 685–691.

13. W. Raymond Duncan, "Caribbean Leftism," *Problems of Communism* (May–June 1978), p. 21.

14. Unpublished speech by Secretary of State Cyrus Vance before the OAS General Assembly in Grenada (June 1977).

15. Address delivered at the Sixth Conference of Heads of States or Governments of Nonaligned Countries in Havana, Cuba, September 3–9, 1979 (Havana: Editorial de Ciencias Sociales, 1981), pp. 333–334.

16. "A Plan for the Caribbean," *New York Times* (February 25, 1982), p. 3.

17. Report of CARICOM Ministers of Foreign Affairs, Belize (Guyana: CARICOM Secretariat, 1981).

18. Quoted in Lewis, *The Commonwealth* (note 1 above), p. 15.

3

The Military and Security Dimensions of U.S. Caribbean Policy

Josefina Cintron Tiryakian

Introduction

At first sight, the heavy economic emphasis of President Reagan's Caribbean Basin Initiative[1] seemed to indicate a shift from the earlier focus on security and military concerns. However, Washington's behavior since the CBI (which included a military assistance component) was announced in February 1982 has left no doubt about the significance that the United States attaches to such matters in the Caribbean.

It is precisely the Reagan administration's security priorities that have distinguished most markedly its Caribbean policy from that of its predecessor. Both posited the need to support economic development in the Basin. Carter, however, minimized security considerations and followed a policy of demilitarization through arms denial and opposition to military regimes. For Reagan, on the other hand, security has constituted a primary justification for downgrading human rights, assisting dictatorial governments, and escalating weapons transfers.

The various U.S. security-related actions in the Caribbean during the 1980s indicate a clear pattern of militarization. Washington's conduct reveals that in the economic sphere its words have spoken louder than its actions while militarily its actions have undoubtedly spoken louder than words. Thus the United States seems to be offering baby carrots and wielding a big stick.

Often the U.S. approach to the Basin has been perceived as responding to regional conditons and its larger dimensions have been overlooked. This has been especially true with respect to the military component of Reagan's policy. And yet, in both the economic and military spheres, the general global principles behind U.S. foreign policy have been incorporated into Washington's Caribbean posture.

This chapter focuses on the geopolitical significance of the Caribbean Basin concept and analyzes key global and regional aspects of the Reagan administration's military policy there. It examines the pattern and some economic, political, and diplomatic functions (as well as possible consequences) of militarizing the area and assesses the potential impact of the Falkland Islands conflict on U.S. policy.

The Caribbean Basin Concept

One of the more significant and innovative aspects of the CBI has been the redefinition of the Caribbean Basin as a geopolitical unit that includes the islands, Mexico, Central America, Colombia, Venezuela, Guyana, and Suriname. This expanded perspective was, however, first used programmatically in November 1981 when the Defense Department reorganized its regional defense network under a single umbrella: the U.S. Forces Caribbean Command. The new command comprises the Caribbean Joint Task Force at Key West, the Antilles Defense Command in Puerto Rico, a naval force, and units from the Army, Air Force, and Marine Corps. The command's area of responsibility includes "waters and islands of the Caribbean, Gulf of Mexico, and parts of the Pacific bordering Central America."[2] This organizational consolidation is indicative of a new unified conceptualization of the region in U.S. strategic thinking and of the growing importance that Washington ascribes to military considerations in the resolution of Caribbean conflict.

Similarly, the Basin idea represents an important shift in U.S. political and economic perceptions. Traditionally the Caribbean, although never quite precisely defined, had a much more restricted sense—it referred to the sea and the islands. What is now called the Caribbean Basin was once treated by policymakers as a group of discrete zones toward which the United States had different policies.[3] But recently, operating through an ideological, political, economic, and military prism, Washington has been trying to develop interlocking mechanisms that will forge its geopolitical construct into a permanent reality. These have included traditional aid, trade, and investment as well as energy and military linkages. The United States has also sought to impose ideological purity in the Caribbean and has supported the adoption of a specific political and economic developmental model. Further, it has provided the military means to dislodge from the region "alien" influences; that is, competing models and ideologies.

The Basin concept, although novel in U.S. strategic thinking, did not originate with the Reagan administration. Rather it has emerged as a result of Caribbean events in the past decade. Fidel Castro began to grope toward this geopolitical vision in an effort to end Cuba's hemispheric isolation after Ché Guevara's failure to revolutionize South America. Michael Manley also took a wider view as he tried to assert Jamaican autonomy in the 1970s. More recently Nicaragua's Sandinista government has turned to the island Caribbean to forge ties outside its traditional Central American zone. Finally, both Venezuela and Mexico have been flirting with the idea of the Basin as their natural sphere of influence.

The Caribbean Basin paradigm has provided the basic framework within which the United States has responded to such developments. This approach poses similar policy prescriptions for the Spanish-speaking areas (traditionally U.S. clients or protectorates) and the recently de-colonized English-speaking countries that are in the process of defining their place in the global system. It also seeks to accommodate Venezuelan and Mexican aspirations by ascribing to them the role of minor partners, contributing energy and petrodollars for the stabilization of the region. But probably the most salient aspects of Reagan's strategy have been the proposed isolation of Cuba from the rest of the Caribbean and the rejection of the Nicaraguan socialist experiment as a prelude to Marxism. Insisting that instability in the area, regardless of its manifestations, has been inspired and supported by the Soviets and their Cuban clients and that consequently it constitutes a security threat to the United States, the CBI has operated on the premise that the whole Basin is of strategic importance and hence falls under the protective custody of the United States.

The Pattern of Militarization: Global Dimensions

Since Caribbean militarization reflects in great part a global trend, it is appropriate to set the stage for this analysis by referring to George F. Kennan's characterization of the East-West relationship as involving "anxious competition in the development of new armaments, blind dehumanization of the prospective adversary's motivation and inten-tions, [and] steady displacement of political considerations by military ones in the calculations of statesmanship. . . ."[4] If one substitutes "acquisition" for "development," Kennan's comments are equally ap-plicable to the Basin and are indicative of the reflective character of Caribbean militarization.

U.S. military policy in the Basin is an outgrowth of the Reaganites' efforts to develop what the former chairman of the Joint Chiefs of Staff, David C. Jones, described as a "comprehensive strategic vision that integrates regional issues within a larger global framework."[5] Washington's blueprint for the 1980s, however, shuns the worldwide commitments assumed during the Cold War and instead expects Europe and Japan to shoulder not only their own defense, but also that of the Third World. It calls for "a new division of labor [that] must also lead to a more equitable sharing of defense commitments in [Third World] regions of cultural importance to the West, and a more equitable acceptance of the risks inherent in such commitments."[6] Considering the developing areas the foremost challenge for the industrial world, Washington's new strategy assigns to each of the trilateral powers a key security role in their traditional spheres of influence: Japan in Southeast Asia, Europe in black Africa, and the United States in Latin America and especially the Caribbean.[7] U.S. programs to militarize the Basin reflect this basic division of labor in rearming the noncommunist world, which in turn is the centerpiece of Washington's global defense strategy for "fortress America."[8]

In contrast to Carter's relatively restrained posture, Reagan has given arms sales to developing nations high priority on his international agenda. Early in 1981 Under Secretary of State for Security Assistance James L. Buckley indicated that the administration considered such transactions an essential instrument of foreign policy[9] and a key component in responding to the Soviet global challenge.

In some Third World regions (e.g., the Middle East) such behavior does not represent a radical change. But in Latin America, and especially the Caribbean, it constitutes a significant departure since Carter's restrictive arms sales policies and human rights legislation were most strictly enforced in the Western Hemisphere.[10] Both the Carter and the Reagan administrations used arms sales as an instrument of foreign policy. Carter, however, sought to weaken through denial military regimes that lacked his administration's approval. Conversely, Reagan's policy of arms promotion has been intended to bolster governments supportive of U.S. global and regional interests. This shift from a theology to an ideology of arms sales resulted in renewed military aid to Guatemala for the first time since 1977[11] and significantly increased assistance to El Salvador, which included training at Fort Bragg and Fort Benning. Honduras, having received Pentagon aid to upgrade its forces and expand and improve airport facilities, has participated in Caribbean exercises with the U.S. Navy. Honduras has also allowed American military personnel to patrol its border with Nicaragua.[12] Table 3.1 shows the escalation of arms transfers from 1980 to 1983.[13]

The United States has also been training the armed forces of Suriname and Belize, and Reagan's UN Ambassador Jeane Kirkpatrick suggested that Costa Rica, the only country in Central America without a standing army, should organize one, offering Washington's help in doing so.[14]

TABLE 3.1
U.S. Military Assistance To Some Caribbean Basin
    States, 1980-1983 (millions of dollars)

Recipients	Military Sales and Assistance Deliveries, 1980	Budgeted and Emergency Allocations 1981	1982*	Budget Request 1983
Eastern Caribbean	None	.1	5.8	5.8
Dominican Republic	.6	3.4	5.5	10.3
Jamaica	None	1.7	2.1	6.7
El Salvador	1.6	35.5	81.0	61.3
Honduras	1.1	8.9	10.7	15.3
Panama	.6	.4	5.4	5.5

*Does not include $60 million in supplemental military aid

Sources: 1980 data from Department of Defense, Foreign
Military Sales and Military Assistance Facts (December
1980), pp. 12, 42, 56.   1981-1983 data from Fact Sheet,
Caribbean Basin Policy, p. 37.

Finally, the administration agreed to sell F-5 fighters to Mexico and twenty-four F-16s to Venezuela.[15] The F-16 deal, which represents the first time any major supplier has made its most advanced combat jets available to a developing nation in the Western Hemisphere, will seriously escalate the level of weapons sophistication in the Basin, thus giving greater impetus to the process of regional militarization.

More specific aspects of the U.S. global defense posture have been incorporated as well into the Caribbean military policy. The first concerns using security assistance to bolster the capability of indigenous forces to protect U.S. interests.[16] This strategy was adopted after the Vietnam war as a cost-efficient means of securing Washington's interests in the Third World and as a politically acceptable alternative to the commitment of its troops. Reagan, however, has not clearly excluded the possibility of direct military intervention in the Basin should local forces fail. On the contrary, one of the objectives of his buildup in conventional arms has been to allow the United States to move swiftly into any area. Accordingly the administration vetoed a UN Security Council resolution sponsored by Panama barring any intervention in Central America,[17] although both the secretary of state and the undersecretary for Latin

America have declared that Washington prefers collective security mechanisms to solve Caribbean crises.[18]

A second global principle of U.S. policy calls for arms sales instead of grants. The grant option is to be used only in exceptional cases to countries of strategic importance unable to afford defense expenditures. In 1982, for example, out of an allocation of $81 million to El Salvador, $63.5 million was in grants and $16.5 million in credit sales ($1 million was for military training, which is usually in grant form). The 1982 budget for the rest of the Caribbean was $4 million in outright aid and $25 million in credit sales.[19]

The above principles antedate the Reagan administration, yet they dovetail perfectly with the cardinal postulates in its Third World policy of self-help and "trade not aid." They also reflect the administration's insistence that its allies and clients contribute to global defense.

Washington's plans to establish military installations in Central America are another regional adaptation of its new strategy. During the last decade, when the United States was committed to reducing its bases on foreign soil, the Pentagon consolidated its Caribbean facilities into areas considered to be national territory: Guantanamo, the Panama Canal, and Puerto Rico. But secret discussions between the Reagan administration and Central and South American officials about setting up a network of bases in the hemisphere suggest a reversal of this trend.[20] Certainly stationing U.S. forces on the southern rim of the Basin, outside of Panama, would add a new dimension to Washington's presence in the region and would reaffirm the area's status as a U.S.-policed protectorate.

The F-16 deal indicated Washington's intention to extend to the Caribbean another global pattern: the establishment of surrogates in areas of strategic importance. In this respect Venezuela's position seemed akin to that of Saudi Arabia in the Persian Gulf, the sale of F-16s to the former and AWACS to the latter symbolizing preferential U.S. ties with these countries and their elevation to a position of junior partners with local police functions.[21] The similarities between the two nations extend beyond the fact that they are both OPEC suppliers to the United States. Both have political leaderships sharing Washington's anticommunist views and aspiring to regional leadership. Both have entered into U.S.-supported alliances with minor powers in their respective areas.[22] In each instance their local military supremacy complements their growing economic and political influence—in Caracas's case as a key capital and energy supplier and as the emerging Caribbean leader of elements oriented toward Western democratic social models.

From Venezuela's perspective the acquisition of F-16s represented the climax of the country's military trends since 1973. During this period its armed forces embarked on a modernization program that included major purchases and the creation of a national arms industry. By 1979 its defense expenditures were as high as those of Chile and Peru, two of the hemisphere's military big spenders.[23] Indeed, the F-16s will make Caracas's air force the most technologically advanced in Latin America.

Venezuela's position, under President Luis Herrera Campins, as a junior partner in the Basin represented a significant shift from the international objectives of the preceding Carlos Andrés Pérez regime, which focused on promoting Caracas's status as a Third World leader and a herald of the New International Economic Order. Caribbean policy under Pérez was framed within this North-South context. Its realignment reflected Herrera Campins's ideological and political preferences as well as the influence of the country's business and military elites, both of which have had close ties with their U.S. counterparts for many years. This new role may have also stemmed from Venezuela's shrinking foreign-policy options. Caracas had become increasingly isolated in both South America and the Basin; it was involved in border disputes with Colombia and Guyana; its relations with Brazil and Trinidad and Tobago were at a low ebb; and the Argentines were frankly hostile. Herrera responded with what he termed "Diplomacy of Projection," the overarching goal of which was to promote Caracas as the preeminent Latin American power in the Basin and as Washington's preferential ally.[24]

Venezuela has not been the only major hemispheric petropower that the United States has courted with military hardware. As mentioned before, the Reagan administration approved the sale of at least a dozen F-5 fighters to Mexico, reversing the Carter policy of denial. Furthermore, well-informed sources have reported that "American pressures . . . seek to strengthen the [Mexican] army and to have Mexico spend petrodollars to acquire modern weapons."[25] Whether in response to such prodding or for other reasons, in 1981 Mexico, until recently a leading proponent of Latin American disarmament, increased its defense budget by 54 percent.[26] Furthermore, the Mexican armed forces, noted for their subordinations to civilian authority, have recently expressed disagreement with the government's foreign policy and a desire for a stronger voice in policy decisions.[27]

A similar pattern seems to have developed regarding Guatemala, where the Reagan administration has agreed to sell equipment and technology for local arms production.[28] Until the spring of 1982 Guatemala's limited petroleum output did not generate enough foreign exchange for such an expensive venture. However, the fall of General Romero Lucas Garcia in March 1982 (partly for his refusal to heed demands by the country's economic elites and its multinationals to increase crude oil production) opened the door for a less nationalistic oil policy and a higher production level. Whether, as the left claimed, Washington was directly involved in the March military coup or, as the *New York Times* reported, U.S. officials only were aware of its preparations, the results will be the same: increased oil exports to the United States and the generation of foreign exchange to pay for Guatemala's military imports.[29] Following the overthrow, the Reagan administration again sought to convince Congress to put aside human rights considerations and approve expanded arms sales to the new regime.

The Pattern of Militarization: Regional Dimensions

One of the salient aspects of Reagan's Latin American policy in general and his Caribbean policy in particular has been the influential role played by U.S. military and intelligence officers. The ascendancy of the military extended to both high-level policymaking and actual diplomatic contacts between Washington and hemispheric governments. In the State Department the administration's personnel changes in the Latin American section moved to the forefront men with military backgrounds and quite conservative views.[30]

The most significant appointments were those of General Vernon Walters as ambassador without portfolio and retired Army General Gordon Sumner as a special aide to the assistant secretary of state for Latin American affairs. General Walters, former deputy director of the CIA and once employed by one of the oil multinationals operating in Guatemala, was entrusted with the delicate mission of winning hemispheric support for Reagan's Central American policy when it was first formulated and with conducting shuttle diplomacy throughout the region.[31] In the spring of 1982, when events in Central and South America threatened to undermine the administration's positions, Walters troubleshot in both areas, accompanying Secretary Haig to London and Buenos Aires as Washington attempted to mediate the Falkland Islands conflict and meeting with the leaders of the main political parties in El Salvador to impress upon them the conditions for continued American aid and to abort Roberto D'Aubuisson's bid for the presidency.[32] He also visted Havana where he had extensive talks with Fidel Castro, reportedly on the terms for a solution to the Central American situation and on the possible reintegration of Cuba into the Western camp.[33]

General Sumner, former chairman of the Inter-American Defense Board, retired from active duty partly in protest over Carter's human rights policy, which he blamed for the serious deterioration of the hemispheric collective security system. He subsequently joined the Washington-based Council for Inter-American Security, a lobbying and public information organization whose objectives include the promotion of U.S. security policies and cooperation among young non-Marxist political, academic, and business leaders in Latin America.

Sumner's views on Latin America typify the Reaganite Cold War ideology. For him the preeminent role of the United States "as leader of Western civilization and traditional values" is to mobilize hemispheric regimes in the fight against world Communism and in defense of "Western civilization, as we in the Americas know it."[34] An early exponent of the Kirkpatrick dichotomy between totalitarian and authoritarian governments, Sumner has been highly critical of the "grievous geo-strategic error" that in his view Carter and his "new left" policymakers committed in failing to make this distinction, and he blames them for the "the dramatic deterioration of the Inter-American Defense security system."[35] He has characterized the leaders of authoritarian military regimes in Latin America as "military technocrats trying to solve the socioeconomic and political problems that beset their respective countries," and, dismissing accusations of systematic human rights violations, he has argued that they have been carrying out "the traditional role of the soldier, which is to protect those who cannot protect themselves."[36]

Sumner's policy prescriptions focus on the resumption of friendly relations with Latin military governments. He supports unrestricted arms sales and training programs as instruments of foreign policy, stressing "the moderating and liberalizing impact [of military training programs]" and their effectiveness as a means of "giving young South and Central American leaders and their families an opportunity to experience the U.S. way of life" and of transferring at a modest cost "our concept of democracy and human rights."[37]

Pursuing a Walters/Sumner line, Washington sent various high-level Pentagon representatives to renew or improve relations with the military regimes in the region, welcomed Latin American officers to the United States, and conducted joint naval exercises with Honduras and Venezuela (together with Brazil and Argentina) as well as promoting other forms of military cooperation with countries in the region. In short, in the Reagan administration the military has become a primary instrument of Basin diplomacy, frequently bypassing professional diplomatic personnel.

A second significant regional dimension of Caribbean militarization has been the intervention of southern cone military regimes in Central American conflicts in support of U.S. policy. The most blatant examples have been Chile's training of Honduran cadets and its willingness to send advisors to El Salvador; Argentina's economic/military aid to El Salvador and its military assistance to Honduras and Guatemala; and the formation of an anti-Nicaraguan joint Venezuelan, Colombian, and Argentine paramilitary force financed by the United States.[38]

Before the Falklands war, Buenos Aires was Washington's primary partner in this scenario. However, Argentina's initiatives in Central America, like Cuba's in Angola, did not represent a simple case of superpower proxy participation, but were also motivated by economic, political, and ideological considerations stemming from its recent past. Besides symbolizing its allegiance to the United States in the hemispheric ideological struggle, the Argentines' support of Washington's Central American policy gave a certain legitimacy to their past counterinsurgency campaigns at home. Indeed, in some respects Argentina's involvement in El Salvador amounted to an extension into the Basin of its domestic struggle against the left. Also, its Central American military ventures opened what promised to be a strong market for its growing arms industry, which, like those of other Third World nations, depends heavily on foreign demand to remain viable. In short, Argentina's intrusion into the Caribbean reflected, like Venezuela's, both an ideological affinity for U.S. policy and political/economic self-interest.

Functions and Objectives of Caribbean Militarization

Reagan's immediate aim in the Basin was to defeat the area's leftist insurgents, but his ultimate objective, at least until the Falkland Islands conflict, was the creation of a high-powered anticommunist hemispheric alliance under U.S. leadership. As such, the administration seemed to be trying to resurrect the old Cold War environment wherein Washington was not only the recognized military leader of (as well as the hegemonic mediator between) Latin American countries, but also the region's major supplier of military equipment and training. Emphasizing the security threat posed by extrahemispheric ideologies, the United States entered the 1980s committed to revitalizing both its multilateral and bilateral defense pacts and to recapturing the Latin American weapons market.

Collaboration between Caribbean and southern cone regimes represented a first stage in the formation of a wider alliance to replace the defunct Inter-American Defense System. The U.S.-supported joint military activities of Venezuela, Colombia, and Argentina, as well as those of Guatemala, Honduras, and El Salvador, were intended to underline the community of interests of the countries involved and highlight the need to develop a new hemispheric security system. Colombia's call for the formation of an inter-American naval force to cope with leftist threats, an idea that was originally presented to the

Organization of American States (OAS) by President Reagan, indicated that Washington's efforts were succeeding.[39] Similarly, declarations by the Honduran chief of staff that Tegucigalpa would call for Pentagon intervention to halt armed aggression "from the Soviet Union by way of Cuba" were in effect recognition by the Honduran military of the country's status as a U.S. client and demonstrated their acquiescence to Washington's domination of the Basin.[40]

But of all the various aspects of Caribbean militarization, arms sales perhaps perform the most significant functions. First, they provide an effective mechanism for military integration. During the late 1960s and throughout the 1970s the United States maintained unilateral restrictions on credits and sales to the region. President Carter's policy of denial to human rights violators climaxed this trend. Consequently, as the Basin countries found such alternative suppliers as Great Britain, France, West Germany, Italy, Israel, and Australia, Western Europe displaced the United States as the hemisphere's major source of arms. Reagan, of course, has sought to reestablish American primacy. Should he succeed, a certain degree of compatibility in the area's weaponry would facilitate joint military actions and perhaps eventually the integration of regional forces.[41]

Second, arms transfers have significant symbolic meanings. They generally denote friendly ties between seller and buyer and often are the hallmark of a particularly special relationship. They may also be an expression of nonalignment, which in Latin America necessarily implies independence from the United States. Peru's purchase of Russian hardware in the 1970s signaled autonomy from Washington; similarly the Sandinistas' deal with France in 1982 indicated their commitment to a nonaligned posture and their determination to become neither a Soviet nor a U.S. client.

Third, weapons can function as a wedge to open a country for further political penetration. Establishing a supply relationship constitutes a major decision that entails not only the actual transfer of equipment but, more importantly, extensive personnel exchanges. Advisory and training programs have traditionally helped to secure U.S. access to Latin American decisionmakers. It is this aspect that can have the most significant impact in influencing Caribbean governments and especially their military establishments.

Yet the degree of influence resulting from such penetration is highly debatable. For example, the Kremlin's efforts in the Third World have not been particularly successful. However, U.S. transfers to the Basin are but one of several integrative mechanisms including trade, aid, and investment as well as support for ideologically compatible political and economic elites. Arms deals alone may not be a viable means to gain leverage, but as part of a package including political and economic ties, they can help to create dependency relationships that weaken the recipient's ability to pursue an autonomous course.

The Dominican Republic after Washington's 1965 intervention exemplifies the effectiveness of such a multifaceted approach. In the following decade Santo Domingo was the largest recipient of U.S. economic and military aid in the Caribbean (excluding Puerto Rico), and from 1966 to 1979 U.S. investment in the country quintupled.[42] Concurrently the Dominican Republic became one of Washington's most loyal clients, considered by U.S. congressional and business leaders to be a model for the region.[43] A key indicator of superpower influence— voting behavior at international forums—confirms the extent of U.S. influence: Dominican representatives have consistently voted with Washington on key issues at the United Nations.

The fourth important effect of weapons transfers is to maintain the status quo and to eliminate dissent, as was done in the 1960s after the State Department warned President Johnson that the pace of Latin American social upheaval was likely to increase and recommended continued emphasis on internal security programs.[44] More recently the Caribbean Basin has been targeted. For example, a 1982 IMF confidential report on El Salvador suggested that the threat of repression can be quite effective in keeping labor disciplined and wages low.[45] And in the early 1980s Washington escalated military assistance to Jamaica, the eastern Caribbean, and the Dominican Republic—areas with minimal Cuban influence, but with growing labor and political unrest.

Finally, arms sales can be quite profitable, although some observers have argued that Latin American expenditures are too low to be of much financial significance to the United States and that Washington's hemispheric aid policies have been guided by politics and security rather than economic considerations. This probably was the case during the Cold War when U.S. transfers involved mostly grants of obsolete surplus equipment. Since then, however, Washington's emphasis has been on sales. This shift, along with the decision of many regional governments to embark on modernization programs, substantially increased the economic ramifications of arms sales to Latin America. From 1970 to 1979, for instance, there was a 650 percent rise in hemispheric arms imports.[46] Although, compared to other Third World areas, Latin America has had the lowest level of arms expenditures relative to GNP, the trend is definitely upward.[47]

The lucrativeness of the hemispheric arms market has generated persistent (and successful) efforts by Western European and Israeli manufacturers to penetrate it. From 1968 to 1972, while Washington maintained its policy of restrictive sales, the Western Europeans sold

$1.3 billion to Latin America.[48] The State Department has calculated that the human rights policy in Argentina cost over $813.5 million in sales that were not approved by the U.S. government.[49] This sum does not include potential orders that Buenos Aires did not even consider placing because of the expectation that they would be rejected. Obviously arms transfers to the Caribbean islands, and even to Central America, are not going to reach such magnitudes. Nevertheless, purchases by the larger countries in the Basin could be significant, the Venezuelan F-15 agreement being one example.

Another factor to consider when evaluating the economic importance of the Caribbean is the growing dependence of the defense industry on overseas markets. Many U.S. defense contractors openly admit that their survival is contingent on foreign sales, and this situation is expected to intensify in the next decade.[50] Furthermore, looking toward the end of the century, the Reagan administration's commitment to technological innovation will release a whole new generation of surplus weapons for disposal in the Third World.

The Falkland Islands Crisis and Caribbean Military Policy

For the majority of Latin governments, U.S. support for what they condemned as England's atavistic colonial claims to the Falkland Islands belied President Reagan's February 1982 statements before the OAS about the brotherhood of American nations and their shared "traditions and common values." In retrospect the president's indignation at the "new kind of colonialism [that] is not of our hemisphere, but . . . threatens our hemisphere," sounded hollow.[51] More important, the sense of betrayal expressed by the Argentine junta sent waves of doubt among Washington's friends about its trustworthiness as an ally. The eventual impact of this psychological blow to U.S.–Latin American relations is hard to assess, but it should not be lightly dismissed.

Certainly the Falklands conflict undermined the viability of the Caribbean Basin concept, as was demonstrated by the split at the United Nations between the English-speaking Caribbean nations (who supported the British) and the majority of Spanish-speaking states (who favored Argentina).[52] This fissure reflected fundamental differences that are bound to reappear on other issues. On the other hand, the crisis probably helped to align the English-speaking Caribbean more closely with the United States.

The Falkland crisis also aborted the process of East-West polarization in the hemisphere, which Washington had been carefully and successfully nurturing as an ideological justification for its collective defense strategy.

The Soviet Union, Cuba, and Nicaragua showed considerable finesse in their handling of the situation. Moscow's sympathetic but temperate response, Havana's expressions of Third World and Latin solidarity regardless of ideological differences, and the fact that neither overtly tried to profit by promoting tension elsewhere considerably enhanced their image. Whether these short-term benefits will translate into extended political and economic advantages remains to be seen. But henceforth the White House will have a hard time convincing its OAS colleagues that there is a Red menace at their door or that it is in their interest to rally behind the United States.

It is almost inconceivable, however, that in the post-Falkland period a critical mass of hemispheric countries will unite against Washington because such a move could seriously disrupt economic relations with the United States that are crucial to the continued financial health of most Latin American nations. But it is probable that many Latin leaders will perceive the Soviet Union as a useful counterfoil to Washington's hegemonic power and consequently will either adopt a policy of non-alignment or at least begin to think more in (Third World–oriented) North-South rather than (Reaganite) East-West terms.

These propensities were strengthened by Washington's inability to mediate the dispute successfully. The shift in negotiating momentum from the United States to the United Nations, the institutional center of North-South confrontation, represented a serious loss of prestige for the Reagan administration. Even more revealing of the sad state of U.S.–Latin American relations was the call by Venezuela and Costa Rica for the removal of the OAS from Washington and for the formation of another inter-American political organization that would exclude the United States.[53]

Compounding Washington's problems was Buenos Aires' postwar enthusiasm for Latin American integration, a cause that it had never before embraced. This "conversion" injected new life into the Latin American Economic System (SELA), which proposed a new strategy to assert "the right of Third World countries to an independent development" and vowed to make it impossible for the developed nations to exert upon any of them the type of economic pressures imposed on Argentina during the Falkland conflict.[54] The most vocal SELA members threatened a hemispheric revival of the NIEO demands to restructure the global economy. Should this revival materialize, economic nationalism is likely to resurface as a divisive domestic political issue within the Caribbean and as a source of conflict with the United States.

The South Atlantic war also hurt Washington's arms sales policy. It is now improbable that the United States will become Argentina's or the hemisphere's major supplier. Buenos Aires has already expressed interest in resuming purchases of European weapons, and others are also likely to emphasize diversification of sources (along with the further development of their own defense industries) to minimize arms-dependence vulnerability. The Soviet Union may even be able to strike some deals. But whoever the suppliers may be, there is widespread agreement that the next decade will witness a major effort among Latin Americans to acquire sophisticated hardware.[55]

Undoubtedly the conflict seriously damaged the hemispheric support network that the Reagan administration had been building for its Central American policies. In particular it dealt a death blow to Washington's projected collective security alliance, considering that Buenos Aires recalled its military advisors in Guatemala, Honduras, and El Salvador as well as its paramilitary force aimed at Nicaragua[56] and that a major middle power, Venezuela, resolutely sided with (and was reported to be sending aid to) Argentina.[57] Thus two key supporters of Reagan's Central American and Caribbean policies distanced themselves from the United States. Also, it is widely believed that U.S. opposition to Buenos Aires' call at the OAS for measures against Great Britain jeopardized the future of the Rio Treaty. Peru, for example, reacted by proposing a new pact that would give the Latins more autonomy in regional security decisions.[58]

The collapse of these collective security plans should have prompted Washington to reassess its position on Caribbean militarization. Before the Falkland crisis the Reagan administration promised to seek multilateral solutions to any serious threats emerging in the Basin. But immediately after the war, there did not appear to be much of a chance for a truly hemispheric defense agreement. Thus Washington shifted to a subhemispheric approach, concentrating on building a Central American consensus behind its increasingly hardline policies there. Honduras was drawn into the spreading regional conflict as a U.S. proxy, and Panama, heretofore a critic of Washington's Caribbean policy, joined Reagan's anticommunist crusade after a palace revolt led by the head of the national guard.

Before the South Atlantic war, the United States viewed Honduras as a buffer state protecting El Salvador and Guatemala from the Sandinista "virus," and as a base for the destabilization of Nicaragua. Although Honduras did not have any serious guerrilla problems, the Pentagon tripled its military assistance from 1980 to 1982 and built its in-country advisory mission to the largest in the region. Thus Tegucigalpa's armed forces (especially its air force) became the best equipped in Central America. Washington justified such aid to what was then a peaceful country by arguing that it would enable Honduras "to defend itself and avoid the possibility of any direct American intervention. . . ."[59] But the real rationale revolved around strategic considerations—Honduras borders on Nicaragua, El Salvador, and Guatemala—and the fact that Tegucigalpa's relatively clean human rights record made it easy to obtain Congressional approval.

In the post-Falkland period Honduras' role became much more clearly that of a U.S. surrogate. With the departure of Argentine forces, Tegucigalpa openly stepped into the Central American fray by sending 2,000 troops to help the Salvadoran army and by intensifying its involvement in U.S.-sponsored covert anti-Nicaraguan forces.[60] Such proxy activities outside its borders were accompanied by the flaring up of guerrilla activity within the country, the intensification of domestic repression and human rights violations, and the appearance of death squads and conscription.[61]

Panama's ideological shift and its strong support for U.S. policy represented a significant change. Under Omar Torrijos the government was vocal in its support of the Third World (which backed its Canal renegotiation demands) and maintained close relations with Cuba and Nicaragua. After Torrijos's accidental death his protégé and successor, Arístides Royo, followed similar lines. For instance, during the Falkland crisis he accused Washington of betraying Latin America, offered to send Panamanian national guard forces to Buenos Aires, visited Havana to discuss the conflict with Castro, and proposed the formation of a hemispheric conference that would exclude the United States.[62]

Royo's anti-Americanism was deeply disturbing to the Reagan administration because Panama is one of the major banking and U.S.-military training centers in the Basin. Moreover, a pipeline to carry Alaskan oil across the isthmus was finished in 1982, and a multinational commission was about to be formed to study the construction of a new sea-level canal—an enterprise of great strategic and commercial importance to Washington.[63] Royo's forced resignation by Panama's new strongman, General Rubén Darío Paredes, and his replacement with a U.S.-trained banker as figurehead president, eased Washington's fears.[64] Paredes, a candidate for the 1984 presidential elections and a rigid law-and-order man, announced after taking charge that there would be no place in Panama for Communism, closed all newspapers for a week, and asked for the resignations of most civil authorities, declaring, "We are going to innoculate our democracy against disorder."[65] He fully shares Reagan's Cold War perspective and supports U.S. participation in all inter-American meetings; and, in an interview with the commander-in-chief of the Pentagon's Southern Command, he suggested increased military collaboration between Washington and Panama because of "what is occurring . . . in Central America and the Caribbean."[66] Given the existing Honduran cooperation with El Salvador and reports that Guatemalan troops had also joined the Salvadorans, Paredes's position brought closer to realization the creation of a U.S.-trained and sponsored Central American force to fight the left in the region.[67]

Washington also stepped up its efforts to destabilize the Sandinista regime. Besides holding provocative border maneuvers with Honduras in July 1982, it intensified its naval surveillance off the Nicaraguan coast, increased its support for right-wing Somozan national guardsmen and Cuban exiles operating in Honduras, and distanced itself from more recent Nicaraguan exiles from both Managua's business community and the Sandinista leadership.[68] In August 1982 the U.S. Senate approved the Symms sense-of-Congress resolution supporting the use of "whatever means necessary to block Cuban aggression in the hemisphere." The resolution was widely interpreted in the Basin as a possible prelude to another U.S. intervention in Nicaragua.[69]

Washington's policy toward Havana was equally severe. It stepped up economic pressures, continued to push for the establishment of Radio Marti to be beamed toward the island, and was tepid toward a Cuban offer to withdraw its troops from Angola and cut completely any arms flow to Central America in exchange for lifting the U.S. trade embargo.[70] Washington's failure to respond to this proposal, which meets its two key conditions for negotiations, gave credence to Havana's claims that in previous secret meetings U.S. officials had demanded a break with Moscow as their price for normalization.[71]

Caribbean Policy: The Negative and the Positive

The loss of support among key hemispheric nations for U.S. Caribbean policy, the fact that its strategy in El Salvador has rendered a military victory improbable, and the growing number of critics among analysts with long experience in Basin affairs all indicate that what Washington needs is not a hard line aimed at turning the clock back to pre-1959 days, but rather initiatives that take into account the vast changes that have occurred in the region in the past two decades.[72] Such a shift hinges on the resolution of three issues: the war in El Salvador, U.S.-Cuban tensions, and relations with Nicaragua.

Furnishing arms and military training to Salvadoran forces is not likely to give them the ten-to-one advantage over the insurgents that they need to succeed.[73] The alternatives are direct U.S. intervention or a political settlement. The first would be too costly to even consider; it would provoke almost universal hostility in Latin America and widespread protest in Western Europe. A UN peacekeeping force to maintain order while negotiations (which would include the guerrillas) take place seems to be an honorable and pragmatic solution.[74] Moreover, including Caracas in this process would be a significant step in healing the U.S.-Venezuelan rift.

Washington also needs to come to terms with Cuba and Nicaragua (which would entail accepting ideological pluralism and nonalignment in the Basin), especially since both have made promising gains on the hemispheric diplomatic front. In 1982, for instance, Brazilian corporate leaders visted Havana to renew trade links, and in the wake of the Falkland crisis the Argentine foreign office described its relations with Cuba as "extremely good."[75] The same can be said for Nicaragua. Its Brazilian economic connection dates from the early days of the Sandinista regime, and its ties with Argentina are also "extremely good." These developments portend the emergence of some kind of regional realignment in which Havana and Managua will not be isolated anymore. Hence the United States should move to reconcile with them. Otherwise it risks alienating itself further from the more important countries in Latin America. Moreover, Castro and the Sandinistas are facing critical economic problems and thus have shown a serious interest in establishing cordial contacts with Washington. Each recognizes the economic advantages that normalization would bring and is willing to pay a reasonable political price for it. Also, the Soviet Union, burdened with a $3-billion annual subsidy to Havana, supports a U.S.-Cuban rapprochement and is equally receptive to better relations between Washington and Managua.

Détente with Cuba and Nicaragua and a political solution in El Salvador may also be the most effective means to contain leftist insurgency in Guatemala and Honduras and to promote stability in the Basin. Rapprochement would open the door to reintegrating Havana and Managua into the Basin. And given the serious financial problems facing both countries, development is bound to take precedence over the promotion of Caribbean conflict in their calculations once U.S. relations are normalized. Certainly establishing close economic ties would give Washington more leverage over the two countries than it has at present. On the other hand, destabilizing them would lead to civil wars, which would probably send shock waves throughout the Basin.

Since the Falkland crisis, U.S. relations with Latin America have sharply deteriorated. A multifaceted political initiative in the Caribbean would contribute considerably to turning the tide toward hemispheric cooperation and would be well received by Washington's European allies. In 1981 Secretary Haig proclaimed that a military victory in El Salvador would be a test case of U.S. global leadership. A shift toward a political solution in all crisis areas in the Basin would be a much more effective gauge of Washington's ability to lead the West.

Notes

1. U.S. Department of State, *Fact Sheet, Caribbean Basin Policy* (Washington, D.C.: 1982).

2. *Latin American Index,* vol. 20, no. 20 (December 1, 1981), p. 81.

3. On the various zones and their economic ties with the United States, see Josefina Cintron Tiryakian, "Puerto Rico's Status and Changing Caribbean Relations: Implications for the United States" (Paper presented at the 1980 meeting of the Latin American Studies Association held at the University of Indiana in Bloomington).

4. George F. Kennan, "Cease This Madness," *Atlantic Monthly,* vol. 247, no. 2 (January 1981), pp. 25–28.

5. U.S. Department of Defense, *United States Military Posture for Fiscal Year 1982. An Overview* (Washington, D.C.: 1981), p. i.

6. Richard Burt, "In Defense of Western Values," U.S. Department of State, Current Policy No. 368 (February 5, 1982), p.1.

7. James L. Buckley, "Security Assistance for FY 1983," U.S. Department of State, Current Policy No. 378 (March 11, 1982), p. 7.

8. For an excellent analysis, see Michael T. Klare, "Une strategie de défense globale pour l'Amérique Forte," *Le Monde Diplomatique* (September 1981), p. 1.

9. James L. Buckley, "Arms Transfers and the National Interest," U.S. Department of State, Current Policy No. 279 (May 21, 1981), p. 2. See also Andrew J. Pierre, "Arms Sales: The New Diplomacy," *Foreign Affairs,* vol. 60, no. 2 (Winter 1981/82), pp. 277–282.

10. On the Carter policy, see Richard R. Grimmett and Robert G. Bell, "The Conventional Arms Trade in Latin America: Implications for U.S. Policy," *Arms Trade in the Western Hemisphere* (Hearings, Subcomittee on Inter-American Affairs, House Committee on International Relations, 95th Congress, 2nd session, June-August 1978), pp. 205–243 (hereinafter cited as "Hearings"). U.S. hemispheric military sales had been declining since the mid-1960s. In the early 1960s the United States accounted for 40 percent of the total arms transferred to Latin America, but by 1975–76 it was providing only 15 percent according to statements at the hearings by Cesar Sereseres and David F. Ronfeldt, p. 113.

11. In June 1981 the Reagan administration approved a $3.2-million sale of military trucks to Guatemala. See *Wall Street Journal* (June 19, 1981), p. 1.

12. *Washington Report on the Hemisphere,* vol. 2, no. 1 (October 6, 1981), p. 3; *U.S. News and World Report* (May 31, 1982), p. 47; and Loren Jenkins, "Honduras on the Edge," *Atlantic Monthly,* vol. 250, no. 2 (August 1982), pp. 16–20.

13. The upward trend in arms transfers to the region began under the Carter administration. See William G. Bowdler, "Foreign Assistance Proposals, Latin America and the Caribbean," U.S. Department of State, Current Policy No. 166 (April 16, 1980), pp. 4–5.

14. *Le Monde,* international edition (December 4–10, 1980), p. 6; *Latin American Index,* vol. 10, no. 2 (February 1, 1982), p. 8; and *Le Monde,* international edition (September 3–9, 1981), p. 5.

15. *Latin American Index,* vol. X, no. 14 (August 1, 1982), p. 56.

16. U.S. Department of Defense, *Annual Report FY 1982,* p. 30.

17. Panama introduced the resolution on behalf of Nicaragua. See *Latin American Index,* vol. 10, no. 8 (May 1, 1982), p. 30.

18. Alexander Haig, "An Agenda for Cooperation in the Western Hemisphere," U.S. Department of State, Current Policy No. 351 (December 4, 1981), p. 1; and Thomas O. Enders, "Strategic Situation in Central America and the Caribbean," *Department of State Bulletin,* vol. 82, no. 2059 (Feburary 1982), p. 81.

19. *Fact Sheet* (note 1 above), p. 37.

20. *Latin American Index,* vol. X, no. 6 (April 1, 1982), p. 24; and *Le Monde,* international edition (March 4–10, 1982), p. 8. Washington has denied reports that base negotiations in the Caribbean have focused on the islands of Amapala and San Andres off the coasts of Honduras and Colombia, respectively.

21. U.S. Department of State, Current Policy No. 369 (February 5, 1982), strongly supported the sale as a means to promote the national interest: "It strengthens our ties with an important nation, enhances its capabilities, lessens the burdens on the United States, and contributes to the stability of our 'third border,' the Caribbean."

22. The Gulf Cooperation Council, consisting of six Persian Gulf nations, and the Central American Democratic Community of Costa Rica, Honduras, El Salvador, Colombia, and Venezuela were established in early 1982. See U.S. Department of State, Current Policy No. 364 (February 1982), p. 3. Because of its human rights violations, Guatemala was not invited to join until after the Rios Montt military coup, when it became a member. See *Le Monde,* international edition (August 5–11, 1982), p. 3.

23. Augusto Varas Fernandez, "La reinserción de América Latina en el marco estratégico mundial" (Paper presented at a conference on la internacionalizacion de la politica y el proceso de democratizacion en America Latina in Rio de Janeiro, August 1981), p. 14.

24. Carlos A. Romero, "The Venezuelan Foreign Policy in the Caribbean Since 1979" (Paper presented at the 1982 Caribbean Studies Association meeting in Kingston, Jamaica), pp. 24–26.

25. Alain Joxe, "L'Amérique et ses modeles," *Le Monde Diplomatique* (January 1982), p. 17.

26. Andrew J. Pierre, *The Global Politics of Arms Sales* (Princeton, N.J.: Princeton University Press, 1982), p. 248. Mexico was also shopping in Argentina, Europe, and Israel for military equipment.

27. *U.S. News and World Report* (December 14, 1981), p. 37.

28. *Washington Report on the Hemisphere,* vol. 2, no. 1 (October 6, 1981), p. 3. The deal was possible in spite of the ban on arms sales to Guatemala because it was classified under commercial transactions excluded from the restrictions.

29. Yvon Le Bot and Louis Morin, "Le role du patronat et des militaires dans le coup d'Etat au Guatemala," *Le Monde Diplomatique* (May 1982), p. 9; and *New York Times* (March 28, 1982), Sec. 4, p. 1.

30. *Latin American Index,* vol. 9, no. 20 (December 1, 1981), p. 82.

31. *Washington Report on the Hemisphere,* vol. 1, no. 20 (July 14, 1981), p. 6.

32. *Economist* (April 17, 1982), p. 19; and *Time* (May 3, 1982), p. 36.

33. *Le Monde,* international edition (April 22–28, 1982), p. 4

34. "Hearings" (note 10 above), p. 75. The convergence of views is traceable to the fact that members of the Council for Inter-American Security comprised the "Committee of Santa Fe," a group of very conservative scholars and retired military officers that reportedly was highly influential in the formulation of Reagan's hardline Caribbean policy. The committee recommended a war of national liberation against Cuba, according to the *Washington Report on the Hemisphere,* vol. 2, no. 5 (December 1, 1981), p. 3.

35. "Hearings" (note 10 above), pp. 71, 76. On the security crisis, see John Child, "The Inter-American Military System: Historical Development, Current Status, and Implications for U.S. Policy," in Tom J. Farer (ed.), *The Future of the Inter-American System* (London and New York: Praeger Publishers, 1979), pp. 155–203.

36. "Hearings" (note 10 above), pp. 68, 69.

37. Ibid., p. 74.

38. *Washington Report on the Hemisphere,* vol. 2, no. 16 (May 4, 1982), p. 2; *La Nación Internacional,* Costa Rica (April 2–8, 1982), p. 2; *Economist* (March 13, 1982), pp. 20, 56.

39. *Latin American Index,* vol. 10, no. 6 (April 1, 1982), p. 24.

40. *Latin American Index,* vol. 10, no. 7 (April 15, 1982), p. 28.

41. As General David C. Jones observed: "U.S. security interests are not advanced when U.S. military training, education and equipment are replaced by European or non-Western sources. To revitalize hemispheric collective defense, the U.S. must take the lead to fashion a credible coalition strategy which can elicit the cooperation of its Rio Pact allies" (Quoted in *United States Military Posture for FY 1982,* p. 20).

42. U.S. Department of Commerce, *U.S. Direct Investment Position Abroad* (December 31, 1979), unpublished; *U.S. Statistical Abstract 1979,* p. 369; and *U.S. News and World Report* (March 31, 1980), p. 61. On the political role of the Dominican military, see G. Pope Atkins, *Arms and Politics in the Dominican Republic* (Boulder, Colo.: Westview Press, 1981).

43. U.S. Congress, House Committee on Foreign Affairs, *Caribbean Nations: Assessment of Conditions and U.S. Influence* (Report of a Special Study Mission to Jamaica, Cuba, the Dominican Republic, and Guantanamo Naval Base, Committee Print, January 3–12, 1979), pp. 27–31.

44. Walter LaFeber, "Inevitable Revolutions," *Atlantic Monthly,* vol. 249, no. 6 (June 1982), pp. 76–77. This is an incisive comparison of the Reagan and Kennedy Central American policies.

45. Walden Bello and John Kelly, "Au Salvador: Le Fonds monétaire à la rescousse d'une économie en ruine," *Le Monde Diplomatique* (July 1982), p. 11.

46. U.S. Arms Control and Disarmament Agency, *World Military Expenditures and Arms Transfers 1970–1979* (Washington, D.C., March 1982), p. 9.

47. Arms Control and Disarmament Agency, *World Military Expenditures and Arms Transfers 1969–1978* (Washington, D.C., December 1980), p. 7. Until 1978 all Basin countries (except Nicaragua) spent less than 2 percent of GNP on arms.

48. Grimmett and Bell, "Hearings" (note 10 above), p. 227.

49. Joseph E. Karth, "Hearings" (note 10 above), pp. 270–271.

50. Jacques Gansler, *The Defense Industry* (Cambridge, Mass.: MIT Press, 1980), p. 213.

51. White House Press Release (February 24, 1982), pp. 5, 6.

52. *Le Monde,* international edition (May 27–June 2, 1982), p. 2; and *The Economist* (June 5, 1982), p. 22.

53. *Le Monde,* international edition (May 6–12, 1982), p. 3. In August 1982 the Latin American Parliament, at its tenth meeting, called for the reorganization of the OAS to make it more protective of hemispheric interests and to bring about "a real balance between industrial and Third World countries" [*Excelsior* (August 23, 1982), p. 3A].

54. *Excelsior* (August 20, 1982), p. 28; and Charles Vanhecke, "L'Argentine dans la guerre-là découverte du tiers monde . . . et de M. Fidel Castro," *Le Monde,* international edition (June 10–16, 1982), p. 4. Shortly before the conflict Argentina's foreign minister declared his government's priority to be loyalty to the United States, stating in Brasilia that he did not consider his country to be part of the Third World, but rather "part of the new world, the world of the Americas" [*Economist* (March 13, 1982), p. 56].

55. *Economist* (May 8, 1982), p. 3.

56. *Le Monde,* international edition (May 6–12, 1982), p. 3.

57. *New York Times* (May 23, 1982), p. 9; and *Le Monde,* international edition (May 27–June 2, 1982), p. 2.

58. Neiva Moreira, "Las viudas de Monroe," *Tercer Mundo,* vol. 5, no. 53 (June–July 1982), p. 33. Peru, Brazil, Ecuador, and Venezuela decided not to participate in UNITAS, long-established joint U.S.–Latin American naval maneuvers [*La Nacion,* Costa Rica (June 7, 1982), p. 4].

59. *U.S. News and World Report* (May 31, 1982), p. 47.

60. *The Economist* (July 1, 1982), p. 34; and *Latin American Index,* vol. 10, no. 14 (August 1, 1982), p. 53. The escalation of U.S. military assistance to Honduras since 1981 indicates that Washington was preparing Tegucigalpa for a proxy role in Central America. The Reagan administration sent Honduras the largest number of personnel in the region (from 60 to 110 military advisers and 147 diplomats) and asked Congress to approve funds to improve three Honduran airfields near the Nicaraguan border, which would enable Washington to land troops and fighter planes. See *U.S. News and World Report* (May 31, 1982), p. 47; and *Latin American Index,* vol. 10, no. 7 (April 15, 1982), p. 28.

In November 1981 CIA Director William Casey presented to the National Security Council a proposal to launch a major covert attack against Nicaragua from Honduras, reportedly later approved by the president [Jenkins, "Honduras" (note 12 above), p. 20]. In mid-September 1982 the Honduran Council for Peace reported a CIA-organized meeting in Tegucigalpa of U.S. military and intelligence personnel and Honduran chiefs of staff and cabinet members in preparation for the invasion of Nicaragua and the further regionalization of the Salvadoran conflict [*Excelsior* (September 20, 1982), p. 2A].

61. *Economist* (September 4, 1982), p. 33. The Honduran armed forces doubled from May 1982 (13,500) to August 1982 (27,500) [*U.S. News and World Report* (May 31, 1982), p. 47; and *Latin American Index,* vol. 10, no. 16 (September 1, 1982), p. 63].

62. *Le Monde,* international edition (December 3–9, 1981), p. 4; *Economist* (August 7, 1982), p. 33; *Tercer Mundo,* vol. 5, no. 53 (June–July 1982), p. 31; and *Time* (June 7, 1982), p. 38.

63. *La Nación Internacional* (June 11–17, 1982), p. 6.

64. *Le Monde,* international edition (August 26–September 1, 1982), p. 2.

65. *La Presse,* Montreal (July 31, 1982), p. B12; and *Latin American Index,* vol. 10, no. 15 (August 15, 1982), p. 59.

66. *La Nación Internacional* (June 4–10, 1982), p. 7.

67. Argentina had reportedly been helping to train a 1,000-man Latin American commando force to deal with Central American revolutions [*Latin American Index,* vol. 10, no. 5 (March 15, 1982), p. 20].

68. *Washington Post* (August 8, 1982), p. A12.

69. *Central America Report* (Guatemala), vol. 9, no. 32 (August 20, 1982), pp. 249–250.

70. *Economist* (August 28, 1982), pp. 12–13. On Cuba's previous efforts to negotiate, see Wayne S. Smith, "Myopic Diplomacy," *Foreign Policy* 48 (Fall 1982), pp. 161–166.

71. President Reagan had previously mentioned Cuba's break with Moscow as a condition for U.S. talks, but the two points that he and the secretary of state repeatedly stressed were withdrawal of Cuban troops from Africa and cessation of intervention in Central America. On the confusion over Reagan's Cuban policy objectives, see Smith, "Myopic Diplomacy" (note 70 above), pp. 159–160.

72. Besides works already mentioned, see James Chace, "Getting Out of the Central American Maze," *New York Review of Books* (June 24, 1982), pp. 20–26; H. Michael Erisman, "Colossus Challenged: U.S. Caribbean Policy in the 1980s," in H. Michael Erisman and John D. Martz (eds.), *Colossus Challenged: The Struggle for Caribbean Influence* (Boulder, Colo.: Westview Press, 1982), pp. 12–18; Richard E. Feinberg and Richard S. Newfarmer, "A Bilateralist Gamble," *Foreign Policy* 47 (Summer 1982), pp. 133–138; William LeoGrande, "Cuban Policy Recycled," *Foreign Policy* 46 (Spring 1982), pp. 105–119; Abraham F. Lowenthal, "Misplaced Emphasis," *Foreign Policy* 47 (Summer 1982), pp. 114–118; Robert A. Pastor, "Our Real Interests in Central America," *Atlantic Monthly,* vol. 250, no. 1 (July 1982), pp. 27–39; and Robert

E. White, "Central America—The Problem That Won't Go Away," *New York Times Magazine* (July 10, 1982), pp. 21–43.

73. *Economist* (February 27, 1982), p. 53. In March 1982 El Salvador was reported to have 5,000 guerrillas and 23,000 armed forces [*Economist* (March 27, 1982), p. 18].

74. Seweryn Bialer and Alfred Stepan, "Cuba, the U.S., and the Central American Mess," *New York Review of Books* (May 1982), p. 17. In the fall of 1982 the presidents of Mexico and Venezuela joined in an effort to bring about negotiations between the United States, Nicaragua, and Honduras [*Latin American Index,* vol. 10, no. 17 (September 21, 1982), p. 68].

75. *U.S. News and World Report* (May 24, 1982), p. 24. Argentina signed a $100-million trade agreement with Cuba and sent 7,000 tons of wheat to Nicaragua [*U.S. News and World Report* (June 21, 1982), p. 25].

4
The Economic Dimension of U.S. Caribbean Policy

Kenneth I. Boodhoo

Introduction

The United States' economic interests in, and relationships with, the Caribbean predate U.S. independence, having begun when the colonies became the region's primary supplier of basic foodstuffs. The economic relationship soon generated partisan involvement in the Basin's internal political affairs. For example, partially to protect a growing trade with Haiti, the United States helped the island's elite to suppress a slave revolt in the 1790s. The United States' hegemonic aspirations were formalized in 1823 by the Monroe Doctrine, which provided the rationale for occupying Cuba, Puerto Rico, Haiti, and the Dominican Republic early in the present century. Prior to these interventions, the United States played a significant role in facilitating Panama's secession from Colombia, acquiring in the process control of the ten-mile-wide corridor that would become the Canal Zone.

U.S. diplomacy in the 1930s was highlighted by President Roosevelt's Good Neighbor Policy, which, while promoting the withdrawal of U.S. troops from many Basin countries, has also been termed "a change of form rather than content."[1] From the 1940s onward the United States has emphasized the "Bootstrap" approach to development, which functioned to strengthen economic and consequently security linkages between the United States and Basin countries and in particular provided the foundation for the emergence of dependent capitalism in the Caribbean.

This chapter will survey and analyze U.S. economic linkages with, and U.S. domination over, the Basin with emphasis on the post–World

War II period, during which Washington's interests have intensified considerably both for economic and security reasons. Obviously instability in the Basin could threaten a large proportion of U.S. commerce. Currently almost one-half of U.S. trade, two-thirds of its imported oil, and more than half of its imported strategic minerals enter the country by way of the Panama Canal or through Caribbean waters. Moreover, while some of the United States' strategic mineral imports merely pass through the Caribbean, a significant amount actually originates there. For example, in recent years Jamaica has supplied over 50 percent of U.S. bauxite and alumina imports, while in 1976, 69 percent of total U.S. oil imports and 83 percent of residual fuel imports came from Caribbean refineries.

Early Development of U.S. Economic Interests

The American colonies were an important part in the triangular trade among Britain, the colonies themselves, and the Caribbean. In 1770 the colonies supplied the bulk of the islands' basic foodstuffs and other needs: half of the flour, all of the butter and cheese, one-third of imported dried fish, one-quarter of the rice, all of the lumber, and all of the pasture animals.[2] Indeed the prosperity of New England was due largely to its trade with the West Indies.

It was not that the Caribbean countries were physically unable to provide much of their own sustenance. Rather, two factors militated against any prospect for agricultural self-sufficiency. First, the islands were colonies, and a colony is never intended to be self-sufficient. Second, just as dependency was inherent in colonization, so also was division and specialization of production. Hence the Caribbean's designated function was to grow sugar while New England furnished food and Britain was the center for manufactured products. In summary, "the North American colonies [came] to have a recognized place in [England's] imperial economy, as purveyors of the supplies needed by the sugar planters and their slaves."[3]

The linkages between the colonies and Caribbean countries became so profitable after the United States gained independence that when Haiti's slaves revolted in the late eighteenth century, Washington displayed few qualms about sacrificing democratic idealism to crass economic self-interest by siding with the planters in putting down the rebellion. By the last quarter of the eighteenth century, Haiti had become the richest colony in the world, as illustrated by the fact that while *total* British colonial trade in 1789 was valued at five million pounds, Haiti *alone* accounted for 11 million of France's overall 17 million pounds. The island's affluence was based on a highly developed plantation system that produced sugar, coffee, cotton, and tobacco by ruthlessly exploiting the labor of tens of thousands of black slaves.

The United States maintained extensive commercial relationships with the Haitian planters. Some Americans even resided there to further their business activities. Two cities in particular, Philadelphia and Charleston, were the seats of extensive trading activity. Approximately 500 Yankee ships plied the Haitian route. U.S. exports, primarily food to feed the large slave population, amounted to about 20 percent of the island's imports. In exchange Americans bought sugar for themselves and their European customers, which meant that the Haitian uprising not only threatened U.S. trade with the Caribbean, but with Europe as well. Furthermore, the federal government was aware that U.S. merchants who had accepted drafts in payment for cargoes shipped to Haiti would suffer heavy losses if the United States did not extend financial support against the slave revolt.[4] Thus the new country provided approximately $750,000 in 1791. Additional money, arms and ammunition, food, and even fighting men were supplied by some U.S. states and plantations.

Economic considerations were obviously very influential in shaping U.S. policy toward the rebellion, but there were also other factors involved. Southern planters were extremely concerned about the possible demonstration effect that a successful uprising in Haiti might have upon their slaves. U.S. officials, meanwhile, were worried about a British takeover in Haiti, which would not only upset the balance of power in the region, but would also allow London to control the island's lucrative commerce. Nevertheless, U.S. assistance was too little and too late. Thus Haiti became the second nation (and the first black republic) in the hemisphere to gain independence. This setback for the United States was only temporary, however, with attention quickly shifting to Cuba and the Spanish Caribbean:

> The United States was the only power interested in the Caribbean in the nineteenth century. In 1811 Jefferson dreamed of an independent federation of all the Caribbean islands. When that prospect faded, Jefferson turned his eyes to Cuba.[5]

In 1823 President Monroe laid the broad outline for Washington's future relationship with the Basin and Latin America in what subsequently became known as the Monroe Doctrine, which sought to guarantee the independence of hemispheric countries from foreign influence while pledging the United States not to interfere in their affairs. It further declared that they "from henceforth [were] not to be considered as subjects for future colonization by any European powers." The Doctrine was followed within a few years by the idea of Manifest

Destiny, the belief that U.S. economic and political superiority would inevitably lead to regional domination.

It was within this context that Washington sought to purchase Cuba from Spain. This attempt failed, but dollar diplomacy continued with the United States unsuccessfully trying to purchase the Danish Caribbean in 1867 and then looking toward the Dominican Republic. But despite these efforts, Washington did not achieve a firm foothold in the Basin until the end of the century. The United States became a significant colonial power in the Caribbean after the Spanish-American War. Its hegemony ranged from the outright annexation of Puerto Rico to the appropriation of the canal corridor in Panama. Temporary occupations occurred in Nicaragua, Honduras, Haiti, and the Dominican Republic. But Cuba probably represents the best example of the interface between economic considerations and Washington's policy of Caribbean domination at this time.

In the decade preceding the Spanish-American War, U.S. investment in Cuba had steadily increased as the U.S. demand for sugar expanded. The influx of U.S. money into the production and processing of sugar led to a restructuring of the industry as the small independent farmers were bought out and their land consolidated into large plantations. These former growers were then relegated to the role of rural workers. Concurrently capital from the Sugar Trust in the United States led to the establishment of large sugar-milling centers. At this point the entire industry was not yet under U.S. domination,[6] but the foundation for eventual hegemony had been laid.

Following Spain's defeat, massive amounts of foreign capital flowed into Cuba during the first quarter of the twentieth century. U.S. investments, which totaled approximately $50 million in 1895, grew to $200 million by 1906 and then increased more than sixfold to $1,240 million in 1924. By that time U.S. companies controlled over 50 percent of cane production and had also bought heavily into the electrical, telephone, and transportation sectors.[7]

Due largely to the influx of U.S. money, technology, and plantation-scale mode of operation and to assured access to the mainland market, the Cuban economy assumed a clearly monocultural configuration during the first quarter of the twentieth century. Sugar's share of the island's exports went from less than 50 percent to approximately 90 percent by 1930. Meanwhile the tobacco industry, where small farms predominated, experienced a corresponding decline, going from 40 percent of the export market in 1902 to about 10 percent thirty years later.

U.S. economic penetration of Cuba was facilitated initially by military occupation of the island. As the Spanish troops departed, U.S. forces numbering 45,000 entered, and a U.S. military government under General John R. Brooke was proclaimed. Each province had a Cuban governor and a U.S. general at its head. Washington took over the customs, postal, sanitation, and health services. But perpetual occupation, no matter how politically or economically profitable, was not customary U.S. policy. Cuban independence, however, could possibly jeopardize the United States' broad interests.

The Platt Amendment of 1901 became the compromise solution to this dilemma. The Cubans were not permitted a choice in this matter; they were told to accept the Platt Amendment as an appendix to their constitution or the U.S. occupation would be continued. Basically the Platt Amendment prohibited Havana from entering into treaties that infringed upon its sovereignty and from contracting debts that would place undue financial burdens upon the state; granted Washington the right to intervene for the preservation of Cuban independence; declared that all laws enacted by U.S. occupation authorities would continue to be legally binding; and allowed the United States to purchase or lease lands necessary for coaling or naval stations. Almost a year after ratification of the amendment, General Leonard Wood formally proclaimed the end of the U.S. military occupation on May 20, 1902.

Against the backdrop provided by the Platt Amendment, President Theodore Roosevelt in 1904 declared his corollary to the Monroe Doctrine. It was essentially a claim by the United States that it, as the dominant power in the region, had a responsibility to maintain peace in the Western Hemisphere and to assure that Latin American governments did not behave in a manner that in any way could be construed as endangering the interests of their neighbors or the United States. This reaffirmed commitment to unilateral action to maintain stability served to promote U.S. economic interests in, as well as its hegemony over, the hemisphere. Operating under the Roosevelt Corollary, Washington militarily intervened in Latin America over thirty times, including three occasions in Cuba.

In 1906 the United States landed first 2,000 marines and then 6,000 other troops when the Cuban government collapsed under revolutionary pressure. Secretary of War William Taft was sent to Havana and acted as governor for a brief period before turning over the office to Charles Magoon, a Nebraskan lawyer formerly stationed in the Panama Canal Zone. The United States occupied the island until January 1909. With Taft as president, Washington again intervened in 1912, when, during a period of civil unrest, U.S. holdings were threatened. The third major incursion occurred during World War I. Once again, Cuba was in a state of turmoil. The United States, worried about its property and also fearful of the rise of pro-German sentiment, was determined that the island would remain peaceful. Consequently marines landed in

Oriente and Camaguez provinces in April 1917, ostensibly for training purposes. They remained until 1922. During the last year of this occupation General Enoch Crowder, who became the first American to hold the rank of ambassador to Cuba, controlled decisionmaking within the country to the point where he handpicked President Alfredo Zayas's cabinet.

The domination of the U.S. embassy in Havana over the Cuban bureaucracy continued in the early 1930s under Sumner Welles. In 1934, however, Franklin Roosevelt's Good Neighbor Policy led Washington to conclude a treaty with Havana that in effect abrogated the Platt Amendment.

The Cuban pattern was repeated all over the Caribbean Basin; U.S. economic penetration followed military intervention. U.S. capital entered Puerto Rico on a large scale after its occupation by U.S. forces in 1898;[8] and, like Cuba, sugar replaced the traditional crop (coffee), with the bulk of the financing, organization, and marketing controlled by mainlanders. Also following the Cuban model, Puerto Rico's sugar industry was gradually transformed from one characterized by small local farmers to one dominated by foreign-owned plantations. Four large U.S. companies held 25 percent of all cane land and produced over 60 percent of all plantation sugar.

The formal constitutional relationship between the United States and Puerto Rico was (and still is) quite different from that which Washington has had with every other Basin territory. Whereas the island was originally a U.S. colony, today it maintains free associate status, which has led some observers to conclude that "none of the [other] political experiments of the United States have proved more successful."[9] In any case, certainly "Puerto Rico and the United States have indeed come to be part of an economic unit as well as a political unit."[10]

The United States was not only keenly involved in the affairs of the island Caribbean, but also the bordering mainland states. Nicaragua is a good example of Washington's attitudes and policy toward Central America. Initially U.S. interest in the country was primarily motivated by the search for a cheap overland route from the Atlantic to the Pacific. Lake Nicaragua made this possible. In 1850 Washington concluded the Clayton-Bulwer Treaty with Britain, which ended the latter's hegemony over Nicaragua and provided for joint control over any future canal. Within seventeen years the White House violated that agreement by signing a pact directly with Managua granting the United States the exclusive rights of transit.

Liberal president José Zelaya, though opening Nicaragua to U.S. private investment from 1895 to 1909, attempted to negotiate a canal treaty with the Japanese, thereby leading the United States (which was determined after its 1903 agreement with Panama to monopolize all canal routes) to support his overthrow. Due to the unrest that followed, the marines landed in 1912 and maintained a presence until 1925.

The U.S. withdrawal in 1925 signalled a renewed civil war between Nicaraguan Liberals and Conservatives. Again the United States intervened "to protect American lives and property" and stayed from 1927 to 1933. While Washington began training a military police force (the Guardia Nacional) to take over after it left, all the Liberal leaders agreed to lay down their arms, with the sole exception of the nationalist Augusto Sandino. Thus from 1927 until 1933 the United States was mired in its "first Vietnam." By late 1933 Washington had withdrawn its forces, leaving behind U.S.-trained Anastasio Somoza to lead the National Guard. In 1934 Sandino was killed after attending a meeting with titular President Juan Sacasa to negotiate for peace, and Somoza quickly established control over the country.

The 1930s saw much turbulence in Basin territories due to the Great Depression and, equally important, due to the restructuring of their economies that was facilitated by U.S. economic penetration. The results were twofold. First, Caribbean indebtedness to the United States—and thus the latter's leverage over the former—increased dramatically. Second, rising unemployment and increasing poverty culminated in large-scale rioting, the areas hardest hit being Puerto Rico, Cuba, Trinidad, and Jamaica. These developments were, however, soon overshadowed by World War II.

Post–World War II Economic Policy:
The U.S. Connection

The war dramatically deepened the Basin's economic ties with the United States, as illustrated by the increasingly U.S. orientation of the region's trade (with U.S.-owned companies in the Caribbean contributing heavily to the process). Between 1937 and 1947 the share of total exports going to the United States rose from 45.1 to 77.2 percent in Costa Rica; from 60.1 to 77.5 percent in El Salvador; from 63.9 to 86.4 percent in Guatemala; from 27.9 to 59.6 percent in Haiti; and from 55.4 to 77.4 percent in Nicaragua.[11] In the postwar period these dependency patterns were further intensified by the particular approaches to modernization introduced into the area.

Four basic paradigms have been employed to generate economic development in Basin countries. The earliest and most pervasive was the Puerto Rican "Bootstrap" formula, of which modified versions continue today. The second is the import-substitution strategy (also known as the "ECLA Model," promoted by Raul Prebisch and the

Economic Commission for Latin America). The third (which led to the formation of the Central American Common Market and also became popular in the English Caribbean in the early 1960s following the demise of the politically oriented West Indies Federation) uses the concept of economic integration, which stresses that development can be achieved through complementarity, specialization, coordinated location of industry, and preferential assistance to less-developed member states. The final and most recently attempted approach can be described as the participation/partnership mode. While the first bootstrap model encouraged the influx of foreign capital by placing few restrictions on it, this fourth alternative requires co-ownership of developmental enterprises by the host state, or its nationals and by foreign investors, thus leading to expanded governmental involvement and/or majority shareholding (though not necessarily control) in what was formerly the private business sector.

Certain countries, including Trinidad, Jamaica, Barbados, and more recently Nicaragua, have tried all four models in their original or modified forms. The Dominican Republic, Haiti, Panama, and Belize have eschewed only integration. Haiti is the last in the area to use any of these strategies, having in the early 1970s put into practice the pure Bootstrap approach that continues there today. Guyana, as well as Nicaragua, has gone from partnership to state control, as did Jamaica for a brief period. Trinidad has also moved somewhat in this direction, although its pivotal petroleum industry remains essentially foreign-owned and controlled. Cuban-style Marxism represents, of course, a fifth option, which so far has not been seriously embraced by any other Basin nation.

The Bootstrap concept was introduced into Puerto Rico in the mid-1940s and has remained the primary formula for economic development in the region. In the English-speaking Caribbean it was modified and became popularly known as "industrialization by invitation." Insisting that significant industrial growth demands access to foreign capital, technology, management skills, and market connections, bootstrappers supported such generous incentives to foreign investors as rebates of tariffs, tax holidays, allowances for accelerated depreciation, and subsidized local services (e.g., factory sites, utilities, etc.).

The program experienced an impressive start in Puerto Rico. By 1953 over 300 manufacturing plants, providing more than 25,000 new jobs, were added to the local economy. The per-capita GNP increased from $122 in 1940 to $426 by 1953, and to $677 in 1960. By this time also, approximately 46,000 jobs had been added.[12] Almost all the capital was from the United States.

The early achievements of the Bootstrap model in Puerto Rico encouraged the English-speaking Caribbean countries, which were experiencing very high unemployment rates, to adopt it, obviously believing that entry into the U.S. industrial system by means of the branch plant would provide the solution to their woes. They made, however, a fundamental error by assuming that because the island's general economic situation was similar to theirs, they could successfully transplant its developmental model. This scenario ignored Puerto Rico's distinctive U.S. connection. It is precisely the uniqueness of that relationship that makes it unlikely that Bootstrap can be effectively replicated elsewhere in the Basin.

Of primary importance in understanding this linkage is the fact that the island's economy has been incorporated into the mainland's and thus does not operate as a separate entity. Consequently Puerto Rico does not have to confront the foreign exchange or monetary problems that independent states would normally experience in their international transactions. Also, the island's U.S. trade is tariff free. Because a major stumbling block to successful industrialization in underdeveloped countries is access to the markets of the first world, Puerto Rico's privileged access to the United States, subject only to the forces of competition, gives it a unique advantage. Finally, Puerto Rico receives considerable assistance from Washington in the form of grants, credits, loans, guarantees, and welfare and benefits immensely from open immigration to the mainland, which provides a release valve for economic and social pressures on the island.

Trinidad's passage of the Aid to Pioneer Industries Ordinance (1950) and its later approval of related legislation represented that country's attempt to copy Bootstrap. At that time sugar and petroleum, the main pillars of its economy, were stagnating. With workers being retrenched, Trinidad hoped that the Puerto Rican approach would not only curb rising unemployment, but also promote much needed economic diversification. As a result of this law, approximately 250 branch plants (mostly U.S. subsidiaries) were established in Trinidad between 1950 and 1965. But since these industries created only 7,000 new jobs while the labor force was growing by 100,000, unemployment continued to rise, increasing from 6 to 15 percent during this period.

Haiti's experience followed the Trinidad pattern. In a country where the economy has always revolved around farming (e.g., in 1978 agriculture accounted for 41 percent of the island's Gross Domestic Product and 61 percent of its export earnings), Bootstrap-type incentives managed to attract seven plants in 1967 and by 1978 had drawn approximately 200 producing such varied goods as sporting equipment, toys, textiles, and some electronics. Consequently industry's share of the GDP rose from 9.7 percent in 1968 to 16.5 percent ten years later. But these new factories, even though generating 20,000 to 40,000 jobs, employed only 1 percent of the Haitian work force and unemployment remained (almost unbelievably) in the 70–80 percent range.

Despite Bootstrap's early success in Puerto Rico (e.g., the island's per-capita income doubled during the program's first decade), an analysis of longitudinal data covering the broad period from 1950–1980 shows that its overall impact was much less positive than its initial short-term results. Currently Puerto Rico is the home to over 300 subsidiaries of major U.S.-owned corporations, with total profits exceeding $3 billion each year. Yet its average per-capita income of approximately $3,500 is only one-half that of the poorest mainland state (Mississippi). With unemployment at 25 to 30 percent, the island absorbs about 10 percent (or $850 million) of the U.S. food stamp program. Indeed more than one-half of the Puerto Rican population is dependent on such food benefits.

In contrast to Puerto Rico, El Salvador illustrates the impact of U.S.-controlled investment where (as was generally the case in Central America) industrialization has been encouraged more by ECLA policies of import substitution and economic integration. But in reality the actual programs implemented often were not in accordance with ECLA's plans for balanced economic growth and the establishment of "integration" industries on a regional location basis. In addition, pressure from Washington for open markets and the free flow of foreign investment seriously dimmed the prospects for achieving self-sustaining economic development, thus perpetuating Central America's system of dependent capitalism.

Superficially it would appear that El Salvador benefited enormously from the ECLA approach to industrialization. From 1960 to 1970 its manufacturing sector experienced annual growth rates of 8.1 percent, its share of exports rose from 5.6 to 28.7 percent, and its employment figures increased from 85,000 manufacturing jobs to approximately 250,000. A closer analysis, however, indicates much more limited gains than the overall picture suggests. While the total labor force expanded by 1.8 percent annually, its proportion of industrial workers actually declined from 13.1 percent in 1960 to 11.1 in 1970. Moreover, locating most new businesses in the capital further widened the income distribution gap between the city and the country as a whole.[13]

Generally experiments in Caribbean industrialization, as illustrated by the experiences of Trinidad, Haiti, Puerto Rico, and El Salvador, have involved extreme reliance upon foreign investment, technology, raw materials, and export markets. And in every case the primary beneficiary has been the United States. This Americanization of the

Basin's economies leads to further distortion. Because most new industries locate there, the urban sector has adopted the psychology of conspicuous consumption from the United States. Production processes are geared to satisfy the demands of this elite urban group, and consequently the basic needs of the majority of the society remain largely unmet.

Central America epitomizes this pattern. Ever since the sixteenth century it has been a focal point for investment and domination by foreign capitalists. In the post–World War II period, industrialization through import substitution was viewed as the way to escape external hegemony and fluctuating world prices for primary products. Because of the relatively small size of the individual countries, the creation of a regional market through integration was advocated as the best means to provide conditions conducive to economies of scale and thereby to open the avenue to self-sustaining development.

The Economic Commission for Latin America, the primary promoter of this philosophy, stressed that integration should be undertaken gradually and that trade liberalization should be instituted at a rate that would not threaten participants with unfair competition or a drastic loss of customs revenues. Consequently ECLA supported the idea of reciprocal industrialization, which would permit all members to modernize at a roughly similar pace and therefore minimize the stress on local economies. Ideally ECLA's strategy, which demanded regional planning, would result in the gains from integration being distributed equitably. These principles were embodied in treaties signed in 1958.

Even though the ECLA initiatives were grounded within a capitalist framework and would not unduly orient Basin economies away from the United States, Washington was not enthused about them because it feared that they would weaken the private sector, which the United States felt should be strengthened as much as possible to serve as a bulwark against any potential Communist threat to Central America. But primarily Washington wanted to assure that the region remained wide open to U.S. corporations. Thus it opposed any policies that would, by encouraging economic nationalism and central planning in any form, restrict free trade or foreign private investment and ultimately moved against the 1958 treaties.

Through diplomatic pressure and the promises of massive "aid" (read, "bribes"), Washington pushed for a common market to be quickly established and to allow free movement of goods, capital, and labor. In other words, it wanted "market forces" rather than planning policy to determine not only the pace of integration, but also the location of industry. These efforts were pursued independently of ECLA and led to the signing of the U.S.-inspired General Treaty of Economic Integration between El Salvador, Honduras, Guatemala, and Nicaragua in 1960. Costa Rica joined in 1963.

Using the 1960 agreement and a $100 million aid package, Washington began to institutionalize its penetration of the two foremost agencies of the common market: The Permanent Secretariat and the Central American Bank for Economic Integration. It established its regional office of the Agency for International Development—through which assistance to the common market countries was funneled—near the Secretariat and after a brief period of tension the relationship between the two "took on certain characteristics of an illicit love affair."[14]

"The Central American Bank," said one analyst, "owes its creation and continued existence to the U.S."[15] In its formation the Bank relied on United States expertise; in the implementation of its programs it has been subjected to constraints placed upon U.S. loans; and even in its interaction with other international donor agencies, pressure from Washington has prevented developments not in keeping with the interests of the United States. Indeed such domination has reached the point that it "allows the U.S. to use the Bank as an instrument of its foreign policy."[16]

The Economic Dimension of Contemporary U.S. Policy

Following the Alliance for Progress of the early 1960s, which was directed primarily toward Latin America, the United States had no coherent economic policy toward the Caribbean until the formal pronouncement of the Caribbean Basin Initiative in February 1982. Nevertheless its original economic objectives have remained basically unchanged. These include the maintenance of a stable climate for its foreign investment and its exports and the perpetuation of its influence and control over the region's raw materials, thus assuring itself reliable and continuous supplies. To achieve these goals, Washington has tried to minimize leftist (i.e., Soviet and Fidelista) influence in the Basin. Thus it has been quite willing to provide substantial economic and especially security assistance to anticommunist, pro-U.S. governments even if they have had unsavory reputations for repressing their own people. Pursuing such policies led the United States to support Rafael Trujillo, the Duvalier family, and the Somozas, to name but a few of the area's twentieth-century right-wing dictators.

It was the rise of Castro in Cuba, his exporting of revolution, and his rapid movement into the Soviet camp that prompted the United States to reexamine its hemispheric policies. Consequently Washington launched large aid programs to support friendly regimes and to encourage limited socioeconomic reform. With Latin America's economic situation steadily deteriorating, the United States provided $450 million to establish the Inter-American Development Bank and, shortly thereafter at the Bogota OAS meeting, granted another half billion dollars to establish a Social Progress Fund. In late 1960, nearing the end of his campaign for president, John Kennedy announced his Alliance for Progress.

The Alliance was formally initiated with the adoption of the Charter of Puenta del Este (Uruguay) in August 1961. Its scope was as broad as its objectives were ambitious, striving for annual Latin American economic growth rates of 2.5 percent. It sought a more equitable distribution of national income, economic diversification, accelerated industrialization and agricultural production, agrarian reform, and economic integration. Socially its primary aims were to end illiteracy and to increase life expectancy. The United States pledged to provide a major part of the funds needed.

In practice the Alliance had little impact upon economic development in Latin America and the Caribbean. Between 1961 and 1970 Washington furnished $11.5 billion of which $2.8 billion were for Export-Import Bank loans to buy U.S. goods. Another $1.4 billion were Public Law 480 loans to finance purchases of surplus U.S. food.[17] Thus according to the Economic and Social Secretariat of the OAS:

> During the period covered by the Alliance . . . Latin America seems to have been contributing to an appreciable degree to strengthening the balance of payments position of the United States without foreign aid provided . . . being sufficient to compensate fully for the deficit accumulated by Latin America in other transactions with the United States.[18]

The U.S. House Subcommittee on Inter-American Affairs concluded in 1969 that the Alliance's performance in promoting both reform and development had been disappointing. While GNPs expanded at an average of approximately 5 percent per year, the hemisphere's population explosion eroded *real* economic growth to about 1.5 percent per year.[19] Even so, the subcommittee never investigated whether these increases generated improvement in the standard of living for the millions of poor. In any case the Alliance, as it was originally conceived, died during the Johnson presidency and what remained was turned "into another foreign aid program."[20]

During the second half of the 1960s and through the 1970s, Washington devoted little attention to the Caribbean. This neglect was due to U.S. preoccupation with Vietnam and to the oil crisis that catapulted Mideast affairs to the forefront of its international agenda. Furthermore, the withdrawal from Southeast Asia and the mood of isolationism thereby

TABLE 4.1
U.S. Direct Investment 1966-1976
   (millions of dollars)

Year	Barbados	Guyana	Trinidad	Jamaica	Total
1966	3	N.A.	207	163	373
1968	6	40	215	295	566
1970	9	40	198	507	754
1972	18	36	280	624	958
1974	20	20	549	609	1,198
1976	20	21	713	577	1,331

Source: Adapted from Ransford Palmer, Caribbean
Dependency on the U.S. Economy (New York: Praeger
Publishers, 1979), p. 14.   Original source of data is the
U.S. Department of Commerce, Bureau of Economic Analysis.

created, together with the ethical climate arising from the Watergate experience, placed further constraints on U.S. foreign-policy activity, especially in terms of interventions.

However, U.S. private sector activity was not curbed at all by the restraints on public policy. To the contrary, U.S. business in the region flourished, as illustrated by Table 4.1. Analysis on a country-by-country basis reveals interesting variations. For instance, while U.S. direct investment in Barbados remained small, Trinidad experienced a 350 percent gain over the ten-year period. Although some of this increase was undoubtedly due to rapidly escalating petroleum prices in the post-1973 period, it was also a reflection of the development options that Trinidad chose. After a brief flirtation with nationalization/participation following the 1970 Black Power uprising, Trinidad had reverted by the mid-1970s to the basic bootstrap, dependent-capitalism path. This approach continued to attract U.S. investment capital, especially in the oil and oil-related sectors. In fact, at least 90 percent of direct U.S. investment in Trinidad is in the petroleum industry.[21]

The data for Guyana and Jamaica reveal a pattern very different from that of Trinidad. The relatively small U.S. investments in Guyana declined by 50 percent during the period 1966–1976. In Jamaica, 1976 investments were $50 million less than in 1972, yet still represented a 350 percent increase over 1966. Guyana's rapid decline was a direct result of the Burnham regime's decision to transform the country into a "cooperative republic," which opened the door to large-scale nationalization of foreign-owned property. The Jamaican government had espoused the philosophy of democratic socialism, which also permitted nationalization on a somewhat reduced scale.

Following the creation of the Central American Common Market, U.S. multinational corporations, spurred on by Washington's willingness to pressure local regimes to allow free and unfettered investment and by an array of Bootstrap-type incentives, entered Central America on a large scale. U.S. direct investment in the common market countries increased from $389 million in 1959 to $501 million in 1967, and to $677 million in 1977. The estimate for 1980 was over $1 billion.[22]

On the surface it would appear that the tripling of U.S. investments in Central America has introduced that region to the industrial age, thereby removing it from the dependency on U.S.-owned agriculture. But as one commentator wrote, "the postwar experiment with industrialization ended in failure. Industrialization came to mean the growth of U.S. industry in Central America, not the development of Central American industry."[23] And, the writer continued, "two decades of industrialization deepened the region's dependency on international capitalism and worsened its trade balance."[24]

The original intention of dependent capitalism (as practiced in Basin countries) was that industrialization would promote diversification of individual economies and that the import-substitution approach would reduce the region's dependence on the United States. In reality, however, the opposite occurred. Among the many problems that became apparent with the strategy, two are most obvious.

First, in response to integration agreements designed to reduce the ability of foreigners to export directly to Basin markets, U.S. corporations have simply moved their plants into the region, thereby avoiding high protective tariffs while also benefiting from the cheap labor and the investment incentives provided by host governments. Thus what is accepted as industrialization throughout the entire region consists largely of assembling semifinished products from the United States or bottling foods similarly imported. One study conducted in El Salvador found that the majority of industries there processed imported goods: ALCOA's plant produced aluminum sheets from imported materials; Pillsbury milled imported wheat grain; Crown Zellerback produced corrugated cardboard boxes from imported paper.[25] The same pattern has emerged in Trinidad, Puerto Rico, Haiti, and other countries.

The second problem concerns the level of employment generated by such industries. One of the major objectives of the Bootstrap model was to provide jobs for the rapidly expanding population in the region.

But as already demonstrated, although this approach did substantially increase the GNP, it did little to help the unemployment situation. The fact that U.S. branch plant industrialization has not alleviated Caribbean unemployment is clearly a consequence of the type of technology introduced. The U.S. economy is based on high-technology, capital-intensive industry. The developmental option chosen by Basin territories has permitted and even welcomed the transferal of U.S. high technology, which has contributed to substantial overall growth rates, particularly during the pre-1970 period. Thus their economies have grown, but they have not necessarily developed.

To ascertain whether a country is developing, Dudley Seers suggests examining what has been happening to unemployment, poverty, and inequality. If during a given period of time, he says, they have declined, then that economy and society is on the road to development.[26] Mahbub Haq has argued that for too long planners have been overly preoccupied with achieving high GNPs without recognizing that such growth may be accompanied by rising disparities within a society and that "very often economic growth has meant very little social justice." He therefore warns a state to be more concerned with the content of its GNP than with the rate of its increase. "Let us," he concludes, "take care of poverty and this will take care of the GNP."[27]

This, then, was the general situation in which the Caribbean Basin territories found themselves at the start of the 1970s. Rapid movement of U.S. investment into the region had stimulated economic growth in the manufacturing sector while agricultural exports were steadily declining. Very rapid population increases, among the highest in the world, were being experienced. Increasing birth rates together with more sophisticated health and welfare programs resulted in a large excess of labor, which the capital-intensive manufacturing sector was unable to absorb. Thus the revolution of rising expectations gave way to the revolution of rising frustrations. It is within this context that Jamaica under Michael Manley, who was elected in 1972 on the basis of a populist appeal, began gingerly to institute a program of democratic socialism.

Washington's response to these developments was rather cautious. While U.S. private industry in the Basin continued to expand, official policy toward the region was muted, at least in comparison to past activities. Nevertheless during Carter's tenure Somoza was overthrown in Nicaragua, a left-leaning movement staged a successful coup in Grenada, and the civil war in El Salvador dramatically intensified. At this tumultuous point Ronald Reagan took over the reins of the American government.

In February 1982, one year after his inauguration, Reagan formally announced his new Caribbean policy. And just as President Kennedy had promoted the Alliance for Progress based on the success of the Marshall Plan, the Reagan administration has attempted to "sell" the CBI by resurrecting the basic theme of the Alliance—"to demonstrate . . . that man's unsatisfied aspiration for economic progress and social justice can best be achieved by free men working within a framework of democratic institutions." But President Reagan's analogy was not entirely appropriate. The Alliance was presented as the heir to the successful Marshall Plan; the CBI is the progeny of a failure—the Alliance for Progress.

Three broad aspects of the CBI are significant. First, the White House proposed duty-free treatment for twelve years for most Basin products (with some important exceptions). Second, emergency economic and military support funds of $350 million were requested, bringing the total fiscal 1982 assistance package to $825 million. The fiscal 1981 figure was $420 million. Finally, the program called for increased tax incentives for U.S. investors and other measures to strengthen the capitalist sector in Basin economies. One Caribbean economist described the CBI as "a combination of economic self-interest and political fire-fighting,"[28] and a U.S. senator said, "Many in Congress consider the plan little more than a cover for increased assistance to El Salvador"[29] (more than one-third of the emergency aid was designated for that country).

The CBI's centerpiece is the one-way free trade (excluding sugar, textiles, and apparel) for Basin countries over a twelve-year period. It was this aspect of the program that came under the severest criticism; it eventually was amended by various Congressional committees even though 87 percent of Caribbean exports already enter U.S. markets duty-free.

The supplementary emergency assistance of $350 million is un-doubtedly a relatively small amount to be spread among well over a dozen countries. Also, because El Salvador, Costa Rica, and Jamaica combined would receive $248 million, or close to 75 percent, the majority of the recipients would get miniscule allocations. Indeed the $350 million was less than the $368 million that the state of Florida spent since early 1980 to care for Caribbean refugees.[30]

The CBI's tax incentives are based on the assumption that if Washington is more helpful to U.S. multinationals, they will be more willing to invest in the Basin. The question to be asked, therefore, must be: Is the tax incentive program designed to assist Caribbean development or to increase the profitability of American corporations? This in turn leads to the core issue—what is the true purpose of the CBI?

Many Caribbean skeptics argue that the main rationale for the CBI can be found in the numerous problems that have confronted the U.S. economy over the past decade, especially its trade deficits and the shrinking profit margins in some industries. Indeed a Commerce Department official pointed out that as Basin nations develop through the CBI, "their demand for imports for consumption and as inputs to their production processes will grow, opening new markets for U.S. products. . . . U.S. businesses are certain to fill a large part of the region's growing demand for imports." And, she continued, "the guaranteed duty-free access to the U.S. market . . . will make U.S. direct investment in the Basin countries more profitable."[31]

On a more general level one might argue that the CBI flows from a U.S. desire to preserve the old international economic order in the face of increasingly strident demands for a new one. Certainly Reagan's domestic policies, which stress the primacy of the private sector, free trade, and the "trickle-down" approach are rooted in this old order. Hence it could be said that the CBI, which is essentially an internationalization of his internal programs, is heavily geared toward reinforcing the prevailing pattern of global economics. Whether such an Americanization of the Basin will work, however, is highly dubious, for as Richard Fagen noted in 1978, the history of Latin America has demonstrated that the employment of a capitalist developmental model (as exemplified by the United States) "has not and probably cannot significantly reduce the appalling [hemispheric] inequities in economic and social conditions."[32]

If the CBI and overall U.S. policies toward the Basin are to succeed, it is insufficient to offer a pittance in aid or to increase investment incentives for U.S. business. Instead serious attempts must be made to deal with the fundamental issues facing the region. These include: rejuvenating agriculture; permitting, not inhibiting, exports of sugar to the United States; developing forms of industrialization relevant to the region and involving technologies that are labor, as opposed to capital intensive; integrating industry into the national economies; terminating quotas on textiles and apparel to the United States; establishing joint partnerships that complement rather than take over the local private sector; and launching programs to combat rapid population increases, health problems, and malnutrition. It is then, and only then, that the United States will contribute to developing rather than exploiting the Caribbean Basin.

Notes

1. Robert Smith, "Republican Policy and Pax Americana, 1921–1932," in W. Williams (ed.), *From Colony to Empire* (New York: John Wiley, 1972), p. 270.

2. Eric Williams, *Capitalism and Slavery* (London: André Deutsch, 1964), p. 108.

3. Ibid., p. 110.

4. Thomas Matthewson, "George Washington's Policy Toward the Haitian Revolt," *Diplomatic History,* vol. 3, no. 3 (Summer 1979), pp. 327, 334.

5. Eric Williams, *From Columbus to Castro* (New York: Harper and Row, 1970), p. 409.

6. John E. Fagg, *Cuba, Haiti, and the Dominican Republic* (Englewood Cliffs, N.J.: Prentice-Hall, 1965), p. 42.

7. Ibid., pp. 56, 72.

8. Gordon K. Lewis, *Puerto Rico: Freedom and Power in the Caribbean* (New York: Harper and Row, 1963), p. 3.

9. Chester Lloyd Lewis, *Caribbean Interests of the United States* (1916), Reprint Edition (New York: Arno Press, 1970), p. 98.

10. Ibid., p. 100.

11. As reported in Richard Bernal, "The Struggle for the Old International Order: The Caribbean Basin Plan and Jamaica" (Paper presented at the 1982 conference of the Caribbean Studies Association in Kingston, Jamaica), p. 13.

12. Lewis, *Puerto Rico* (note 8 above), p. 116.

13. Lisa North, *Bitter Grounds: Roots of the Revolt in El Salvador* (Toronto: Between The Lines, 1982), pp. 52–53.

14. *N.A.C.L.A. Latin American Report,* vol. 7, no. 5 (New York: North American Congress for Latin America, May 1973), p. 6.

15. Ibid., p. 7.

16. Ibid., p. 8.

17. Bernal, "The Struggle" (note 11 above), p. 17.

18. Jerome Levinson and Juan de Onís, *The Alliance That Lost Its Way* (Chicago: Quadrangle Books, 1970), pp. 12–13.

19. John Martin, *U.S. Policy in the Caribbean* (Boulder, Colo.: Westview Press, 1978), p. 103.

20. Ibid., p. 99.

21. Ransford Palmer, *Caribbean Dependency upon the U.S. Economy* (New York: Praeger Publishers, 1979), p. 15.

22. Tom Barry, Beth Wood, and Deb Preusch, *Dollars and Dictators* (Albuquerque, N.M.: The Resource Center, 1982), pp. 34, 40.

23. Ibid., p. 37.

24. Ibid.

25. Ibid., p. 35.

26. As quoted in Ken Boodhoo, "Eric Williams: Economic Ideas and Economic Policy," *Journal of Caribbean Studies,* vol. 3, nos. 1, 2 (Spring/Autumn 1982), p. 32.

27. Mahbub Haq, *The Poverty Curtain: Choices for the Third World* (New York: Columbia University Press, 1976), pp. 27, 29.

28. Bernal, "The Struggle" (note 11 above), p. 25.

29. Len S. Zorinsky, reported in the *Miami Herald* (March 26, 1982), p. A18. See also "Caribbean Vision, and Nightmare," *New York Times* (February 25, 1982), p. A30.

30. Heliodoro Gonzalez, "The Caribbean Basin Initiative: Toward a Permanent Dole," *Journal of Interamerican and World Affairs,* vol. 36 (Summer 1982), p. 33.

31. Al Hughes, "The Caribbean Basin Economic Renewal: New Opportunities for American Business," in U.S. Department of Commerce, *Business America,* vol. 5, no. 5 (March 8, 1982), p. 20.

32. Richard Fagen, "The Carter Administration and Latin America: Business As Usual?" *Foreign Affairs,* vol. 57, no. 3 (1978), p. 666.

Case Studies

5

The Politics of Confrontation: U.S. Policy Toward Cuba

Juan del Aguila

Introduction

Revolutionary Cuba continues to present Washington with a variety of regional and extrahemispheric challenges that neither moderate or liberal Democratic administrations, nor the present U.S. approach, have coped with effectively. As the record shows, actions against Havana have included an invasion, a secret war, diplomatic isolation and expulsion from the OAS, an economic embargo for over twenty years, failed attempts to assassinate Castro, and recurring campaigns questioning the regime's legitimacy. Current unresolved bilateral difficulties stem partly from what some take to be irreconcilable ideological conflicts, Havana's alleged role as a Russian "hired gun," Cuban activities in Africa on behalf of radical and pro-Soviet governments or liberation movements, the island's growing military capabilities in defensive and offensive weapons, and demonstrated Cuban involvement with, and assistance to, leftist and subversive groups in the Caribbean Basin, all of which have generated or could generate confrontations with Washington.[1] Indeed a 1980 report advised the new Reagan administration that:

the United States can no longer accept the status of Cuba as a Soviet vassal state. Cuban subversion must be clearly labeled as such and resisted. The price Havana must pay for such activities cannot be a small one. The United States can only restore its credibility by taking immediate action. The first steps must be frankly punitive.[2]

This chapter (1) analyzes the reasons, motivations, and conduct that explain the persistent tension-laden deadlock in U.S.-Cuban relations; (2) examines views and assumptions purported to clarify Havana's foreign-policy behavior; (3) discusses why antagonism between Havana and Washington has turned into a natural state of affairs; and (4) probes the limits of either accommodation or confrontation.

Definitions As Sources of Conflict

It has long been recognized that the language through which one characterizes a relationship either contributes or detracts from the ability to frame proper responses to either antagonists or friendly rivals. In the case of the United States and Cuba, periodic outbursts from various administrations singling out Havana as a major regional and global troublemaker, continued characterizations of Cuba as a Russian proxy (though admittedly an increasingly capable and audacious one), and the framing of explicit or implicit threats have all tended to induce noncompliance rather than fundamental alterations in behavior. For instance, public suggestions from the Reagan administration that Havana must cut its military ties to the Soviet Union if it wishes to reenter the inter-American system are perceived by the Cubans not as a minimal condition put forth by Washington in order to frame a political agenda, but as deliberate efforts to reduce their freedom of action on behalf of their own legitimate foreign policy interests. Similarly, what is considered adventurism by the United States (namely diverse Cuban activities on a far-flung scale away from its natural hemispheric habitat) is taken by Havana as genuine internationalist obligations to be pursued with vigor, without rendering an account to Washington. Obviously this bilateral context is also affected by the policies that each nation pursues vis-à-vis other actors. As such, if Cuba's conduct is taken to be a series of moves designed to alter local or regional balances in order to overextend U.S. capabilities or to gradually weaken its will to resist involvement in various places, then the response is likely to be framed along global or strategic lines. On the other hand, if Havana's moves are presumed to stem from either domestic or ideological factors, though they might have a strategic dimension, U.S. reactions have to be devised along quite different planes, involving political and value matters and not simply realist balance-of-power considerations. In sum, as serious-minded analysts have recognized,[3] complex motivations as well as actual behavior have to be understood and assessed in order to frame an effective policy derived from accurate conceptualizations.

Over the past three decades an ever-expanding sphere of conflict characterized by coercive measures, diplomatic warfare, and economic

TABLE 5.1
The United States and Cuba: Selected Punitive
    Measures Across Issue Areas, 1959-1982

Issue Area	Actors	
	United States	Cuba
Military/Stra-tegic	military exercises in Caribbean; Key West Task Force; explicit threats; exile raids	massive militariza-tion; collaboration with USSR
Economic Development	embargo since 1962; denial of CBI funds; pressure on lending institutions	debt refinancing; Third World and La-tin American trade; integration into CMEA
Diplomatic Status	isolation; expulsion from OAS; no normal-ization; viewed as proxy	calls for Latin American unity; le-gitimacy through nonalignment and the Soviet bloc
Political/Ideological	system depicted as "alien"; domestic order product of "bankrupt" ideology; described as totali-tarian	characterization as imperialist power; system depicted as "decadent"; descri-bed as monopolistic

Adapted from Elizabeth G. Ferris, "Toward A Theory For The Comparative Analysis Of Latin American Foreign Policy" in <u>Latin American Foreign Policies</u>, eds. Elizabeth G. Ferris and Jennie K. Lincoln (Boulder: Westview Press, 1981), p. 246.

boycotts have been the stuff of U.S.-Cuban relations. As summarized in Table 5.1, in typical action-response terms, initiatives pertaining to critical issue areas elicit various replies, often leading to high degrees of stress. A state of unremitting hostility, pierced by flashes of tension like the 1979 pseudocrisis over the Soviet brigade, has prevailed since the second half of the Carter administration, exacerbated by mutual intervention in the Caribbean and Central America. After initial gestures such as the establishment of interests sections in Havana and Washington, movement to restore normal diplomatic relations abruptly ended due largely to costly and provocative Soviet-sponsored Cuban campaigns in Africa.[4] Moscow's invasion of Afghanistan further compromised Havana, but by then the Carter administration had chosen to treat the island as a Russian proxy, a decision that had direct implications because from that standpoint

> the absence of any U.S. leverage within Cuba does not seem harmful. One does not create an independent policy towards a puppet. One attempts to influence the puppeteer. Cuba has been absorbed into the global functional category of the Cold War.[5]

Havana's strong and overt support for the Sandinista regime and the Salvadoran guerrillas added to Washington's discomfort. Believing that Castro and the Kremlin had taken advantage of Carter's naive moralism and vacillation and that the president's willingness to sacrifice friendly autocrats on the altar of human rights opened the gates for leftist forces, the Reagan administration set out to restore U.S. credibility by challenging Castro and moving to strengthen Washington's Basin clients. Cuba, as expected, took up the clarion, reviving cherished revolutionary doctrines, vastly improving its defenses, and continuing to cooperate with its Soviet protector.

Marxist-Leninist Morality and the Challenge of Internationalism

Havana's complex international conduct is generally viewed from three perspectives—one stressing its Russian connection; the second its commitment to world revolution; and the third, its developmental priorities.[6] In the first instance Cuba's activities, principally but not exclusively those outside of its immediate area, are presumed to be Soviet-sponsored or directed, thus reducing the island's ability to pursue less than strategic objectives and subordinating its priorities to those of its superpower patron. In short, Cuba is viewed as just another satellite. For example, President Carter remarked to members of the Board of Trustees of the Caribbean and Central America Action Group in April 1980 that Havana's failure to criticize the Soviet invasion of Afghanistan "shows a total absence of independence on the part of Cuba." One year later, former Secretary of State Haig expressed similar views, referring to Moscow's "exploitation of the Cuban proxy." Finally, in a statement to Congress in March 1982, Assistant Secretary of State for Inter-American Affairs Thomas Enders reviewed Havana's support for radical forces in Latin America and concluded that "we must be clear about Cuba. It is a Soviet surrogate." (Though he also alluded to its tradition of self-motivated ideological and political support for fellow revolutionaries.) Certainly, then, the evidence overwhelmingly indicates that leading officials in both the Carter and Reagan circles (as well as in prior administrations and probably subsequent ones) came to accept the notion that Havana's foreign policy serves primarily the Kremlin's interests, that the Fidelistas repay the Russians with overseas military and terrorist-spawning commitments, and that Cuba cannot, even if its leadership wished to, deviate from Moscow's dictates. Thus the island is seen as the Soviet empire's westernmost strategic outpost, sitting next to critical supply lines which it could presumably interdict in the event of a major conventional conflagration.

The second perspective stresses that Cuba's behavior stems from its leader's ideological convictions, personal ambitions (e.g., Castro's desire to be *the* undisputed leader of the Third World), and heroic Latin American machismo.[7] This view finds in such sentiments as "a revolutionary's duty is to make the revolution" a global call to arms against Western imperialism. Though tempered by calculated prudence, the call has been consistent over time. In addition, because Castro continues to lecture revolutionaries (in governments, in the universities, in the underground) regarding their solemn obligations on behalf of higher goals such as freedom for all mankind from the servitude imposed by imperialism, he is considered an uncompromising radical. Indeed, according to Fidel, the old idea of socialism in one country is already buried in history's dustbin. As Marxist-Leninists convinced of the inexorable march of human events, but reminded of the fact that "one must give history a push," revolutionaries the world over must, he says, transcend parochial attachments, consider their movements part of a worldwide struggle, and listen to those mature and experienced elder statesmen who have successfully defied imperialism. Logically, then, internationalism is but the highest manifestation of Marxism-Leninism, as Castro stated rapturously in 1978:

Internationalism and its ideals of solidarity and fraternity among peoples form the beautiful essence of Marxism-Leninism. Without internationalism, the Cuban revolution wouldn't exist. Being internationalists is one way of paying our debt to humanity.[8]

Assuming internationalist commitments means that Cuban personnel overseas engage in a variety of activities such as building roads and hospitals in Ethiopia, training freedom fighters in Yemeni camps, or providing assistance to Nicaragua's internal security apparatus. Earlier, influenced by Guevaraist doctrines, Havana's leaders sought to replicate their guerrilla experience by promoting armed struggle and insurrectionary urban violence in several Latin American countries.[9]

Through the 1970s and into the 1980s, ideological considerations continued to shape Cuban behavior. Indeed Carlos Rafael Rodriguez, vice president of the Council of State, contended that "in developing our foreign policy we subordinate the interests of Cuba to the general interests of the struggle for socialism and communism," adding that "the fundamental strategic premise of our foreign policy . . . presupposes a frontal and permanent struggle against imperialism and the various forms in which it manifests itself." Alluding to misconceptions about détente appearing in the U.S. press, Rodriguez categorically reasserted Havana's right to assist national liberation movements anywhere. Finally, pointing to one of the core issues preventing a U.S.-Cuban reconciliation, he noted:

> The U.S. imperialists claim that we should accept their idea of peaceful coexistence between themselves and the Soviet Union. This is totally unacceptable. They view peaceful coexistence as an agreement leading to a division of "spheres of influence" or a commitment obliging the peoples fighting for national independence and for socialism to water down and even end their struggles. Such struggles—in which imperialism is the main enemy—will not only continue, but must continually become more intense.[10]

There can be little doubt that Castro's own sense of grandeur along with neo-Guevaraist ideas are important components of the regime's foreign policy. As such, these factors continue to have a bearing on the present and future state of relations with the United States.

The third approach focuses on the idea that Cuba's foreign policy stems from its economic and developmental needs. For example, it is often argued that in order to obtain the trade, credits, technology, and even investment benefits offered by the industrialized nonsocialist countries, Havana must balance its unabashedly pro-Soviet positions and its more threatening overseas activities with respect for Western concerns.[11] Interestingly enough, Rodriguez, the militant theoretician of 1982, has apparently been the driving force behind this pragmatic tendency as part of a technocratic faction emphasizing "the need to promote Cuba's rapid and sustained economic development through rational methods of socialist planning, cost accounting and financing at home, and by greater trade and technological ties with the advanced countries of the socialist and nonsocialist worlds."[12]

But ultimately the point to emphasize here is that either as a Soviet proxy, as a nation led by a tropical megalomaniac championing a secular ideology, or as a developing socialist society, Havana's posture vis-à-vis the United States leads toward a confrontational rather than an accommodationist *modus operandi*. In other words, Cuba has been pushed by these influences (either singly or in combination) to align itself with pro–Third World, anti–Western, anti–U.S. interests and causes.

The Politics of Confrontation

Clearly swings between confrontation and hostility on the one hand and wary acquiescence on the other characterize U.S.-Cuban relations. Although the period of direct action by Washington gave way to efforts to start a dialogue, the rejuvenation under Reagan of a U.S. commitment to containment politics has resurrected the possibility of assertive responses to what is viewed as regional mischief by Havana. Likewise, as was the case in the 1960s, Cuba has reacted to perceived threats from the United States with a campaign calling for armed struggle and revolutionary violence as the only way to change stagnant and unjust socioeconomic orders. In this battle, Central America has become the focal point.

Understandably Havana assigns primary responsibility for the area's convulsions to past and present U.S. policies, simplistic and inaccurate as that may be.[13] As *Granma* put it:

> the roots of that rebellion [in Central America] are found in the systems of exploitation and oppression, and in the brutality of regimes imposed on those countries by American imperialism, in total disregard of fundamental rights.[14]

Conversely, arguing that external agents propounding a foreign ideology were involved in efforts to destabilize countries that were moving toward greater socioeconomic equity and had in fact elected governments democratically, President Reagan contended before the OAS in 1982 that:

> Since 1978, Havana has trained, armed and directed extremists in guerilla warfare and economic sabotage as part of a campaign to exploit troubles in Central America and the Caribbean. Their goal is to establish Cuban-style Marxist-Leninist dictatorships.[15]

Determined not to repeat the alleged mistakes of the Carter administration (e.g., his efforts to ease out authoritarian, but evolving, regimes without paying sufficient attention to the political and strategic consequences resulting from the victory of radical movements such as the

Sandinistas), Reagan has cast Havana as a regional villain, openly meddling in its neighbors' internal affairs using such time-tested means as subversion, terrorism, and guerrilla warfare. In short, Washington charges that logistical and political support from Cuba for armed insurgents is part of a well orchestrated destabilization campaign. Meanwhile Havana, aware that the United States has little effective leverage through which to induce a change in Cuban policies, has been able to capitalize on local struggles and find opportunities for extending its own influence, thereby refurbishing its revolutionary credentials at no more than marginal cost.

Simply put, each nation's views and actions in Central America move an already strained relationship even closer to confrontation. But Washington's policy arsenal deployable against Fidelista encroachments—including measures that may elicit Cuban compliance with U.S. objectives—is demonstrably short of effective means. Whether as a result of past blunders, the fact that Castro thrives on confrontations, or a radically changed political environment in the Basin, Havana's involvement may ultimately be reduced not by swaggering on Washington's part, but through concerted regional action by Cuba's *other* adversaries (including Mexico, Venezuela, Costa Rica, and, apparently, Panama).

Armed Struggle: The Ever-Present Option

U.S. concerns with real and perceived Cuban gains in the Caribbean Basin revolve around the presumed security threat that would materialize should hostile, Cuban-supported regimes replace weak U.S. clients there. Havana's role in the struggle against Somoza, correctly based on the conviction that Washington would not intervene on the dictator's behalf, brought it immense political and ideological payoffs in the form of an openly Marxist-Leninist, pro-Soviet, anti-U.S. government in Nicaragua, which domestically pursues quasipopulist and redistributive policies.[16] On the other hand, if an increasingly unpopular Sandinista administration, besieged internally as well as externally due in large measure to its own mismanagement, excesses, and provocations, survives and consolidates itself as a political puppet of Cuba with strong links to the Soviet bloc, then the idea that struggles for national liberation often lead to radical dictatorships will once again be proven. In other words, the evolution of the Nicaraguan revolution has a direct bearing on U.S.-Cuban relations insofar as it vindicates an old Castroite axiom that political change can only come about through violent means. As Fidel himself reiterated in July 1980:

The Guatemalan experience, the Salvadoran experience, the Chilean experience, the Bolivian experience, what have they taught us? That there is only one path: revolution. That there is only one way: revolutionary armed struggle! . . . And the peoples learned their lesson and saw that there was only one road to liberation: that of Cuba, that of Grenada, that of Nicaragua. There is no other formula.[17]

Some have argued that at times reviving the strategy of armed struggle is Castro's first line of defense when U.S. policies either threaten Cuba directly or lead to its regional isolation. According to this theory, Castro activates leftist networks in Latin America in order to shield the island from possible intervention since the U.S. appears to prefer putting out local fires rather than moving directly against Cuba itself. Without security-related incentives, Havana is seen as much less prone to promote violence. For example, one observer noted, during a period of détente and low tension in U.S.-Cuban relations, that due to "preoccupation with the task of institution-building and economic development, the Cuban regime, without repudiating its solemn commitment to continental social revolution, is no longer active in militarily exporting its own revolution."[18]

If, as the accumulated evidence strongly suggests, the idea of armed struggle is an integral part of the Cuban leadership's conceptual baggage, serving as a practical means through which Havana protects itself against the risks of a major confrontation with Washington, then why has it been revived during the last few years? To put it differently, do objective conditions in the region, as well as the correlation of forces globally, increase the likelihood that Cuban support for armed insurgency and subversion will grow and place conventional regimes in peril? To resolve these questions moves one away from the basic parameters of this analysis, but attempting to answer them points to the perennial dilemma in U.S.-Cuban relations around which secondary issues revolve; namely that these two nations view the world in diametrically opposed terms, that the values that each seeks to vindicate through its foreign policy make them natural antagonists, and that a permanent rivalry is built into their behavior. Obviously overt conflict does not have to be the outcome since confrontation can take many forms. It is also more than a question of management because some differences are subject to mutually satisfactory settlements, such as the antihijacking agreement. It is, in short, a struggle that revolves around ideas, beliefs, and values as much as will and capabilities, with the latter being constantly pressed to serve and advance the former.

Explanations and Consequences: Must Something Be Done?

Persistent calls for doing something about Cuba and Castro are often heard in Congress, in the media, and, one can be reasonably sure, in the inner councils of U.S. strategists, planners, and policymakers. Conversely, the view that Havana is a thorn in the flesh but not a dagger in the heart has gained legitimacy and acceptance in liberal sectors as well as among a good number of U.S. experts and researchers on Cuba. Extreme voices, coming from political descendants of Senators Orville Platt and William Borah, speak in openly chauvinistic terms; the sophisticated set, by comparison, often adopts a posture of flabby idealism supported by unabashed gullibility when disdainfully referring to the alleged Cuban threat. Interestingly enough, in the fringes one detects the feeling that, for different reasons, more than a few in each camp attribute Havana's conduct to U.S. policy failures from the Eisenhower to the Reagan administrations, though scholars like William A. Williams have argued that the tragedy of U.S. diplomacy in Cuba goes back to the Spanish-American War. In any case, Havana's behavior is seen as being *reactive;* that is, Cuba is inert until some external force pressures it to move in one direction or another. That was the way it was during the "pseudo-Republic," through the democratic period and the Batista dictatorship, and most importantly during the early years of the Revolution, which determined its subsequent pro-Soviet path. In short, Havana is not attributed a will of its own; it is what Washington does or fails to do that matters.

Contemporary analyses are not as crudely deterministic, but nonetheless still hold that if only the United States were to take the initiative, Cuba would then respond in a meaningful way and eventually most differences could be settled. This perspective stresses that coercive economic measures, military threats, the lure of normalization, and episodic political and diplomatic isolation have neither broken Havana's will to resist, weakened its ties to the Soviets, nor fundamentally altered its willingness to pursue its goals in the face of superior power, challenging U.S. hegemony in the process. In short, the policy of graduated hostility pursued by successive U.S. administrations, which "aims to force Cuba to cease activities objectionable to the [United States] by punishing Cuba for undertaking them,"[19] has not resolved bilateral conflicts in a manner that preserves legitimate U.S. interests.

A second view, running along similar but not entirely analogous lines, argues that Castro can be induced "both to cease his military activities abroad and to expel foreign troops from Cuba"[20] if Washington puts into effect a strategy combining sanctions with incentives. The argument goes that Fidel, as a pragmatist and a rational man, would find it in his interest to retreat from overseas commitments in order to rule out a potential U.S. move against the island, gain access to American technology, and get the embargo lifted. Indeed it is contended that regardless of whether such logic appeals to Castro or not, Cuba's economic difficulties, its heavy dependence on Moscow, its tarnished image in the Third World due to the Soviet albatross, and its unnatural isolation from the largest and most affluent market in the world will ultimately combine to make gradual accommodations with the United States an utmost necessity.

A third opinion, taking into account the fact that Havana has learned to live without access to the U.S. market and has in fact made a national virtue of its anti-Yankeeism, logically recognizes that the Cubans do not necessarily attach top priority to normalization and are unwilling, as a quid pro quo, to moderate their behavior just to gain the good graces of the United States. Still it is contended that "difficult as the dealings with Cuba may be, there is no plausible alternative to an effort to moderate Cuban foreign policy through positive incentives."[21] Presumably there is nothing to be gained by permanent hostility; the costs of confrontation are simply too high. Therefore U.S. interests are best served by rationally attempting to iron out differences. In sum, it is felt that insofar as Washington's policies offer the Cubans rewards rather than sanctions or threats, they will suppress their urge to promote subversion and Marxist revolution, quietly reassess their ties to the Soviet Union, and put themselves in a position in which some form of U.S. leverage is reestablished. This is a tall order indeed, but feasible if the United States takes the initiative and if Castro is persuaded that his chances for survival are enhanced by going along rather than by continued obstreperousness.

Each of these analyses concedes in one form or another the fact that Fidel may be convinced of his world historical role as a significant contributor to the victory of socialism over capitalism and imperialism. Each also assumes, however, that he is sufficiently pragmatic to consider opportunities that may lower tensions with the United States, bring about more than marginal economic benefits to Cuba, reduce Soviet leverage over Havana's foreign policy, and still maintain personal rule over a quintessentially totalitarian order. In a nutshell it is suggested that if Castro is made an offer that he cannot refuse, he will make substantive political concessions in order to enhance his own and his regime's security. Never mind that his position is presently secure and that threats to Cuba are not credible. Fidel will still gain more than he gives up, because, after all, hostility and confrontations serve no one, no matter how Machiavellian.

A second assumption is that it has for some time been in the security and other interests of the United States to move toward a reconciliation with Havana. In doing so, Washington would demonstrate real statesmanship, begin to outgrow its inability to deal pragmatically with revolutionary regimes, and show all men of good faith that as the

prodigal son once did, so can Castro come back into the fold. If only—
so the reasoning goes—the United States would recognize that the
Cubans appear to threaten U.S. security interests only because Washington confuses political change with threats to its security, then it
could gain more from Havana through a constructive dialogue than
from empty boasts or political intimidation.

A derivative point is that it may be in the economic interests of the
Kremlin, given the enormous, often wasteful spending needed to keep
Cuba afloat, to prod Castro closer to the United States. Part of the
reasoning here is that mounting domestic difficulties such as low
economic growth, unenviable productivity rates, agricultural shortfalls,
and noticeable consumer discontent, combined with escalating military
spending and tighter credits from Western sources, have produced major
financial hardship in the Soviet Union. If that is the case, the drain
on resources required by the open-ended occupation of Afghanistan
and the systemic crisis in Poland may dictate that priorities must be
met in Moscow's immediate security zone and that economic commitments to Havana must be reassessed in light of the latter's future
political and strategic value. Consequently, if Fidel can be persuaded
into a dialogue with Washington, he may come away with such gains
as new economic opportunities, reduced pressure from the White House
on Western banks if Cuba moves to the brink of default, only minor
and tactical political concessions on matters affecting U.S. interests in
Latin America, no retreat from Africa, and, most of all, ironclad
guarantees that Washington would not move against the island. Such
arrangements would, of course, suit the Kremlin well.

Obviously, no U.S. president could survive if such a deal is con-
summated: and as matters have stood for a number of years, the Cubans
refuse to even consider talking about what they define as matters of
principle, including their sovereign right to assist, in accordance with
their own capabilities, fellow revolutionaries the world over. Presumably
Cuba is not the only nation that has steadfast principles. In a dialogue,
it seems eminently reasonable to assume that the United States could
also designate some issues off limits. For instance, Washington could
insist that if the Fidelistas feel obligated to support radical leftists, then
it will back their opponents, adding that it too is unwilling to put the
question up for further discussion.

Assuming that principles become less than central behind closed
doors, even if an understanding with the United States on political
concerns could be achieved as part of a wider package involving security
guarantees and economic incentives, Havana would have to weigh the
consequences very carefully. Is Castro willing to make peace knowing
full well what that would do to his cherished radical credentials? Would

not the essence of Cuban foreign policy—permanent defiance of imperialism—vanish in a whiff of economic opportunism (a move for which Fidel has repeatedly denounced the Chinese)? Since the revolution's survival is not at stake, can Washington obtain lasting political concessions in exchange for allowing Havana to do business with U.S. firms once again? To put it differently, can Castro make a credible commitment to refrain from exacerbating local conflicts or exporting revolution so that the United States would not reimpose an embargo? These are not merely rhetorical questions, but rather concrete problems that have to be faced and ultimately resolved if anything approaching normalization can ever come about. At this point the prospects for commercial relations and bilateral trade, coupled with the advantages for Cuba of acquiring modern technology, are unlikely to deter Havana from pursuing objectives invariably at odds with those of the United States. In short, containing Cuban influence can be achieved through a variety of admittedly difficult and unsavory means, but to suppose that opening up the U.S. market to Cuban sugar, permitting U.S. firms to sell Cuba sophisticated hardware, or otherwise engaging the island economically will make Havana behave is inconsistent with practical realities.

Today Cuba's economic survival is not threatened by withholding U.S. goods, capital, or technology. Although improved economic performance and a higher standard of living is likely to result if the embargo is lifted, "the major impact occurred in the early 1960s. Since that time the marginal importance of the U.S. economic embargo has declined considerably."[22] Having adjusted to economic strangulation, though at a high cost, there is no reason to assume that Cuba would jump at the chance of opening itself up to capitalists and make major political concessions in the process as well. For example, despite the fact that Western banks and financial institutions underwrote Havana's trade deficit in the late 1970s, one study found that "there is no evidence that this lending made Cuba more friendly to Europe and Latin America." It concludes that while "it would be unwise to absolutely refuse to engage in negotiations, . . . it would be shortsighted for the United States to ease the financial burden of Castro's overseas military activities, as the Western banks seem to have been doing in the past few years."[23] Bankers, after all, are not in a position to assess political threats among states, nor are their judgments necessarily transferable to matters of statecraft. The fact that financial institutions choose to expose themselves by lending hundreds of millions of dollars to a dependent, low-growth economy speaks of avarice and shortsightedness, practices that ought not to be emulated.

To sum up, then, the view that Havana can be brought around by economic inducements ignores the fact that its long-term commitments with the socialist bloc are not easily reversed even if Cuba had the will to do so, which is questionable. Although states can carry on political rivalries and even challenge each other despite the fact that they maintain valued economic relationships, when one adds to the bitter political competition that has emerged between the United States and Cuba the ideological acrimony and a legacy of historical grievances (particularly on Havana's part), it is hard to imagine that a meeting of the minds could result from purely economic incentives.

The Question of Risks: Contamination and Expectations

For a controlled society like Cuba, where cultural pressures stress conformity, economic sacrifice, and political obedience, significant risks are involved if Havana decides to court U.S. capitalists in earnest. It is not simply a matter of attracting money or promoting trade. Given the psychological weight that U.S. culture still exerts on the island, even a gradual improvement in bilateral economic matters would lead to diffusion into other areas, including life experiences and person-to-person contacts. There is already abundant evidence that visits by returning exiles in 1979–80 had major social consequences due to the demonstration effect of sharp contrasts between the general vitality and economic achievement of the Cuban community in exile and the unending austerity and cultural isolation experienced by those remaining on the island.[24] Moreover, interviews with refugees from Mariel strongly suggest that revolutionary socialization has not been as successful as once thought and that a good many Cubans question—if not repudiate—the prevalent ethos. As Dominguez has noted, breaking Cuba's cultural isolation risks weakening "the norms of austerity and self-sacrifice that the leadership has cultivated for so long. The importation of conspicuous consumption from the U.S. may accelerate the process of demand-making from below."[25] Consequently, though Cuba's economic situation requires access to foreign capital and technology and setting up flexible guidelines for their operations on the island,[26] the leadership is not unmindful of the risks. As a matter of fact, in their most recent speeches Castro and other top officials have warned of the dangers of penetration and have stressed revolutionary militancy, voluntarism, and social commitment, which are values through which the Revolution's present and future Communist generations dedicate themselves to improving and perfecting the existing order.[27]

Hostility as a Natural Condition

The presumed tradeoff among economic inducements, mutual security guarantees, and foreign-policy moderation on Havana's part rests on questionable assumptions, takes little account of the fact that the Soviets still attach political and strategic value to Cuba, and pays insufficient attention to Castro's deep-seated revolutionary convictions. Moreover, if broadening contacts with the United States entail more than minimal risks for Cuba in terms of internal order, "ideological contamination," growing popular expectations, and even de-socialization, is the bilateral relationship frozen in permanent hostility? Part of the answer obviously lies with the ebb and flow of U.S. domestic politics as well as with whatever chances there may be for an acceptable regional settlement, Havana's own self-restraint (not necessarily induced), or a dramatic gesture on the part of a future U.S. president analogous to the China announcement in 1971. On the other hand, as time goes by and Cuba's linkages to the socialist bloc grow stronger, as budgetary problems affect the conduct of Washington's foreign affairs, and as international lending for struggling Third World nations is reduced for a variety of reasons, structural constraints will pressure policymakers on both sides to maintain the status quo.

Clearly Havana's situation in the Soviet empire has a bearing on its future prospects for normalization with the United States. Economic isolation, a host of internal factors, the vagaries of the world sugar market, and recurring problems in trade, deliveries, and quality of goods with fraternal countries reinforce rather than alleviate Cuba's dependent status. According to a congressional study, agreements signed with the Kremlin for the 1981–85 period and economic policies outlined at the Second Party Congress in 1980 commit Havana to "seek solutions through further integration in CMEA [Council for Mutual Economic Assistance] and dependence on the U.S.S.R." Assessing the island's economic future through the mid-1980s in critical areas such as investment, foreign trade, energy needs, sugar production, and tourism, and stressing the fact that servicing Cuba's staggering external debt of $2.6 billion takes away needed resources and foreign exchange, the report concludes that

in the 1980's the era of extensive growth based on ever-expanding resource transfers from CMEA—and especially the U.S.S.R.—is drawing to a close. In this environment, Havana's avowed pursuit of closer integration with CMEA is unlikely to achieve a level of economic advance necessary to

maintain (much less improve) the living standards of the Cuban population.[28]

Even if the Soviets have been encouraging Castro to seek détente
with the United States, that does not mean that they wish to divest
themselves entirely of their Cuban client, as is often assumed. In other
words, "if such accommodation led to the removal of a potential source
of renewed Cuban-American friction," the Kremlin would find the risks
of normalization tolerable and in its own interests because that "would
ensure the Soviet presence in the Caribbean without the risk of another
confrontation with the United States."[29] But the idea that Moscow can
pressure Castro to come to terms with Washington (short of threatening
to cut Havana's economic lifeline if Fidel is not forthcoming) is simply
not creditable. A politically militant and militarily powerful Cuba is a
major asset for the Russians, and they can live with the status quo in
spite of foreseeable economic losses.

Among the major reasons for the persisting hostility between Havana
and Washington is Cuba's policy of conscious and willful defiance of
the United States, its persistent attempts to exploit anti-U.S. sentiment
in Latin America and elsewhere (as was the case during the Falklands
war), its continuing efforts to fuel the fires in Central America, its
ideological alignments, and, in the final analysis, its categorical definitions
of principled self-righteousness. One should not confuse an occasional
willingness to receive congressional delegations or to use academic
contacts for the purpose of sending signals to the White House as
evidence that Havana has come to the realization that permanent
hostility has run its useful course and must gradually abate. As Horowitz
has observed regarding the impact that visits by various individuals,
business organizations, or congressional personnel have had in modifying
Cuban attitudes:

> Fidel's position, and hence that of his subordinates, has been unchanged:
> not a single concession on matters of principle, while at the same time
> every aggression is converted into principle. Cuba claims the right to
> participate or aid in the fomenting of guerilla insurgency throughout the
> world, and the shipment of military cadres and arms to all allies.[30]

The fact that Washington perceives Havana as a Soviet proxy and
economic satellite does not mean that communications have broken
off entirely; contacts have taken place to discuss conventional matters
such as migration, family reunification, entry visas to the United States
for former political prisoners, and the release of Americans held in

Cuban jails for a variety of crimes. These questions are hardly earth-shaking, however, and there is little likelihood at this time for wider political talks despite the well-publicized meetings in 1981 and 1982 between former U.S. Secretary of State Haig and Vice-President Carlos Rafael Rodriguez in Mexico City. Subsequently roving ambassador Vernon Walters conferred in Havana with Castro himself. Reportedly the principal subject in these conferences has been the ongoing crisis in Central America. But as of early 1983, no breakthrough had occurred and no improvement in the climate of U.S.-Cuban relations was evident.

On the other hand, the record also shows that during the first two years of the Reagan administration, on a number of occasions Havana attempted to broaden the scope of its contacts with Washington, presumably in order to move to an acceptable resolution of conflicts in the Caribbean Basin. For a variety of reasons, including the belief that if the costs of meddling in its neighbors' affairs were sufficiently high, Cuba would restrain itself, the White House chose not to pursue negotiations, feeling instead that "it could intimidate Castro."[31] Efforts such as these, even if Havana's motivation is earnest, do not contradict the earlier points here regarding the continuing value to it of a conflictual relationship with the United States. For instance, preserving gains in Central America is in Cuba's interest, as is the neutralization of potential moves to destabilize Nicaragua. The status quo, in short, favors Havana and its allies. If it can be secured through negotiations with Washington, then it is logical for the Cubans to move in that direction, seeking in effect U.S. ratification once Havana's interventionism has produced favorable political results and a *new* status quo has been created.

Now, as in the past, when U.S.-Cuban contacts have neither produced a meaningful change in Havana's policies nor led to a wider political dialogue, each blames the other. Washington, for example, takes the position that Cuba's intractability and its desire to have its cake and eat it too is responsible for continuing animosities. Conversely Havana, adopting a posture of injured innocence, argues that U.S. unwillingness to treat it as an equal deserving respect as a sovereign nation poisons the atmosphere and precludes entering into substantive talks. Additional difficulties arise because both sides have repeatedly set conditions prior to entering negotiations, such as the U.S. requirement that Cuba repudiate its ties to the Soviet Union, as a sign that it is ready to correct a historical mistake, and Havana's insistence that the U.S. embargo must be lifted as a goodwill gesture. Core issues that could presumably be handled through an admittedly long bargaining process are consistently placed up front not as matters for each nation to reconsider, but as absolute demands requiring a prompt and favorable a priori response.

Overall, then, the prospects for lowering tensions are inextricably linked to the resolution of the Caribbean Basin's conflicts and to the way in which Cuba manages its political and military relationship with the Soviet Union. Certainly if the past is any guide to the course of each nation's future policies, Washington will seek to restore its position and injured image through a mixture of bluster and vacillation, while Cuba, feeling ever more potent, will fuel regional fires and exploit local struggles, sending signals that it wants peace and tranquility while its interventionism continues unabated.[32]

Conclusion

U.S. policy toward Havana oscillates between uncompromising hostility and more moderate approaches stemming from the realization that Cuban behavior is subject to various limitations that its leaders consistently seek to minimize or circumvent. To a large extent, the overall climate of superpower relations affects Washington's perceptions of Cuba's intentions, shaping U.S. responses in mostly East-West terms. Consequently the island has been treated as a Soviet satellite even in periods of relative stability between the superpowers. Close military collaboration between Havana and Moscow in Africa, as well as the Cubans' loyal political support for Soviet foreign-policy objectives, strengthen the belief that in both form and substance Havana's policies are congruent with the Kremlin's designs. Thus international rivalries involving Havana in a variety of roles are bound to affect American assessments as to how best to cope with Castro's adventurism, with a variety of sanctions being continually tested.

Cuba, believing itself to be a chosen instrument for world revolution, does not accept the notion that only great powers can influence global trends, injecting itself into numerous struggles on behalf of either Soviet interests, Third World allies, or its own goals, all the time challenging the assumed hegemony of the United States. One of a few Third World states with a global foreign policy, Havana's activism belies its prostrate economic condition. Indeed its pursuit of political objectives has not been significantly deterred by economic sanctions, least of all those from the United States (whose bluster Cuba welcomes).

Carefully exploiting episodic confrontations with Washington to strengthen Soviet commitments to Cuba, to advance revolutionary causes among like-minded or neutralist Third World states, or for domestic consumption, Havana points to its proven ability to frustrate U.S. efforts designed to undermine its system as something that can still be replicated in the 1980s. Moreover, asserting that something like an international civil war pitting the forces of order against those of the underprivileged is necessary to enhance the status of the dispossessed in the international hierarchy, Cuba rejects U.S. and Western notions that social progress can be achieved through reformist or gradual means. Thus it demands in highly moralistic terms that Washington refrain from intervening in the Basin's internal affairs, always claiming to be defending the principle of self-determination while simultaneously assisting "progressive" forces in order to press local advantages and produce favorable outcomes.

Seeking to preserve influence in areas beset by political conflict and operating under self-imposed inhibitions regarding the limits of its capabilities, the United States grudgingly recognizes that democratic procedures frequently are not observed in marginal societies facing national breakdowns. Still it must cope with Havana's ideological challenge in a manner for which its domestic structures are ill-prepared and in an environment where the fragmentation of power has neutralized options once available to it when it exercised regional hegemony. Thus despite minimal economic assets and an often unappealing ideology, the Cubans continue to exploit the contradictions in Washington's behavior (especially its necessary support of unsavory clients in Latin America and elsewhere) in order to sustain their political leverage over their more powerful antagonist. Finally, the demands of U.S. domestic politics conspire against a consistent foreign policy. Neoisolationist pressure both within and outside the foreign-policy establishment adversely affects U.S. credibility, thereby increasing the possibility that Washington may be confronted with challenges from its adversaries that were once unimaginable. Certainly Castro, who has resisted and outlived efforts by seven U.S. presidents to force or induce him to be reasonable and accommodating, remains unabashedly defiant, and in today's world, the impotence of the strong is his greatest guarantee of all.

Notes

1. The literature covering Cuba's foreign-policy motivations, behavior, and objectives is quite rich and polemical. Curiously enough, analysis of U.S.-Cuban relations dropped off when Havana's campaigns in Africa started, and it has taken the crisis in Central America to refocus scholarly interest on the subject. Among numerous sources dealing with Cuba's external relations, the following, as well as others mentioned in subsequent footnotes, are representative. *Caribbean Review,* vol. 9, no. 1 (Winter 1980): the entire issue is devoted to "The New Cuban Presence in the Caribbean"; William J. Durch, "The Cuban Military in Africa and the Middle East: From Algeria to Angola," *Studies in Comparative Communism,* vol. 11 (Spring-Summer 1978), pp. 34–74; H. Michael Erisman,

"Cuba's Long March: The Struggle for Third World Leadership," *SECOLAS Annals,* vol. 11 (March 1980), pp. 42–46; Enrique A. Baloyra, "The Madness of the Method: The United States and Cuba in the Seventies," in *Latin America, the United States and the Inter-American System,* eds. John D. Martz and Lars Schoultz (Boulder, Colo.: Westview Press, 1980); Carla Anne Robbins, *The Cuban Threat* (New York: McGraw-Hill, forthcoming); Tad Szulc, "Confronting the Cuban Nemesis," *New York Times Magazine* (April 5, 1981), pp. 36–39+.

2. *A New Inter-American Policy for the Eighties* (Washington, D.C.: Council for Inter-American Security, 1980). Quoted in L. Francis Bouchey, "Reagan Policy: Global Chess or Local Crap Shooting," *Caribbean Review,* vol. 11, no. 2 (Spring 1982), p. 22.

3. See essays by William M. LeoGrande, "Foreign Policy: The Limits of Success" and Edward Gonzalez, "U.S. Policy: Objectives and Options," in *Cuba, Internal and International Affairs,* ed. Jorge I. Dominguez (Beverly Hills: Sage Publications, 1982). See also W. Raymond Duncan, "Cuba," in *Latin American Foreign Policies,* eds. Harold E. Davis and Larman C. Wilson (Baltimore: The Johns Hopkins University Press, 1975).

4. See Wolfgang Grabendorff, "Cuba's Involvement in Africa: An Interpretation of Objectives, Reactions and Limitations," in *Latin American Foreign Policies,* eds. Elizabeth G. Ferris and Jennie K. Lincoln (Boulder, Colo.: Westview Press, 1981); or Mohammed Ayoob, "The Horn of Africa," in *Conflict and Intervention in The Third World,* ed. Mohammed Ayoob (New York: St. Martin's Press, 1980).

5. Alfred Stepan, "The United States and Latin America: Vital Interests and the Instruments of Power," *Foreign Affairs, America and the World, 1979,* vol. 58, no. 3 (1980), p. 686.

6. Edward Gonzalez, "Complexities of Cuban Foreign Policy," *Problems of Communism,* vol. 26 (November/December 1977), pp. 1–15.

7. Carlos Alberto Montaner, *Secret Report on the Cuban Revolution,* trans. E. Zayas Bazan (New Brunswick, N.J.: Transaction Books, 1981), p. 261.

8. Fidel Castro, "Speech on the Twenty-fifth Anniversary of Moncada, July 1978," in *Fidel Castro Speeches* (New York: Pathfinder Press, 1981), p. 53.

9. Ernesto F. Betancourt, "Exporting the Revolution to Latin America," in *Revolutionary Change in Cuba,* ed. Carmelo Mesa-Lago (Pittsburgh: University of Pittsburgh Press, 1971). For a good compendium of Guevara's doctrines, see Donald C. Hodges, *The Legacy of Ché Guevara* (London: Thames and Hudson, 1977).

10. Quoted in "The Basis of Cuba's Foreign Policy: Cuba Will Always Carry Out Revolutionary Internationalism," *Intercontinental Press* (July 1982), pp. 498–499.

11. Edward Gonzalez, "Institutionalization, Political Elites, and Foreign Policies," in *Cuba in the World,* eds. Cole Blasier and Carmelo Mesa-Lago (Pittsburgh: University of Pittsburgh Press, 1979), pp. 3–36.

12. Ibid., p. 18.

13. The complexities of the crisis and some of its implications are discussed in Martin C. Needler, "Hegemonic Tolerance: International Competition in the

Caribbean and Latin America," *Caribbean Review,* vol. 11, no. 2 (Spring 1982), pp. 32–33, 56. Also, see Richard Feinberg, "Central America: No Easy Answers," *Foreign Affairs,* vol. 59, no. 5 (Summer 1981), pp. 1121–1146. For an assessment of the Communist threat to the region, see Robert Wesson (ed.), *Communism in Central America and the Caribbean* (Stanford: Hoover Institution Press, 1982), especially the essays by William LeoGrande and Nelson Goodsell.

14. *Granma Resumen Semanal,* vol. 17, no. 17 (1982), p. 8.

15. U.S. Department of State, Bureau of Public Affairs, *Caribbean Basin Initiative,* Current Policy No. 370 (1982).

16. For a balanced discussion of the internal and foreign policies of the Sandinista regime, see John A. Booth, *The End and the Beginning: The Nicaraguan Revolution* (Boulder, Colo.: Westview Press, 1982).

17. In *Castro Speeches* (note 8 above), p. 326.

18. Federico G. Gil, "The Future of United States–Latin American Relations," *SECOLAS Annals* (March 1976), p. 11.

19. William LeoGrande, "Cuba Policy Recycled," *Foreign Policy,* No. 46 (Spring 1982), p. 115.

20. Barry M. Blechman and William J. Durch, "Bay of Pigs + 20," *Washington Quarterly,* vol. 4, no. 4 (Autumn 1981), p. 87.

21. Jorge I. Dominguez, "Cuban Foreign Policy," *Foreign Affairs,* vol. 57, no. 1 (Fall 1978), p. 107.

22. Jorge I. Dominguez, "Cuba in the 1980's," *Problems of Communism,* vol. 30 (March–April 1981), p. 50.

23. Ernesto Betancourt and Wilson Dizard, III, "Castro and the Bankers" (Washington, D.C.: The Cuban-American National Foundation Inc., 1982), p. 14.

24. Cubans in the island are often referred to as *insulares.* For interpretations of the Mariel exodus and data regarding Cuban entrants, see Juan Clark et al., "The 1980 Mariel Exodus: An Assessment and Prospect" (Washington, D.C.: Council for Inter-American Security, 1981); and Barry Sklar, "Cuban Exodus— 1980, The Context" (Washington, D.C.: The Library of Congress, 1980).

25. Jorge I. Dominguez, "Domestic Bread and Foreign Circuses," in *Cuban Communism, Fourth Edition,* ed. Irving L. Horowitz (New Brunswick, N.J.: Transaction Books, 1981), p. 467.

26. "Red Carpet for Foreign Capital," *Latin America Weekly Report,* vol. 82, no. 14 (April 1982), pp. 9–10; "Havana Pleads for a Truce," *Latin America Weekly Report,* vol. 82, no. 36 (September 1982), pp. 9–10; "Cuba's Inside Story: The Economic Plight," *Latin American Times Special Report* (July 1982), pp. 17–24.

27. See speech by Ramiro Valdés on October 8, 1982, *Granma Resumen Semanal,* vol. 17, no. 43 (October 1982); see speech by Fidel Castro on July 26, 1982, *Granma Resumen Semanal,* vol. 17, nos. 31–32 (August 1982).

28. U.S. Congress, Joint Economic Committee, *East-West Trade: The Prospects to 1985,* "Cuba Faces the Economic Realities of the 1980's," Joint Committee Print (Washington, D.C.: Government Printing Office, 1982), p. 135.

29. Maurice Halperin, *The Taming of Fidel Castro* (Berkeley: University of California Press, 1981), p. 331. See also notes on p. 329.

30. Irving L. Horowitz, "The Cuba Lobby" in *Cuban Communism* (note 25 above), p. 521.

31. Wayne S. Smith, "Dateline Havana: Myopic Diplomacy," *Foreign Policy*, No. 48 (Fall 1982), p. 163.

32. Following President Reagan's speech to Cuban exiles in Miami in May 1983, Havana responded forcefully, calling the president (among other things) "Adolfo Reagan" and refuting various charges he had made against the Cuban government. See the editorial "Histeria Imperialista," *Granma Resumen Semenal,* vol. 18, no. 22 (May 29, 1983) pp. 1–2.

6
The Evolution of U.S. Policy Toward El Salvador: The Politics of Repression

John A. Booth

Introduction

The advent of the Reagan administration appeared bound to transform the Salvadoran insurrection into a confrontation between the United States and the Soviet bloc, with Washington reasserting its Cold War policy of containing Communism. As President Reagan himself has said:

> The situation here is, you might say, our front yard, it isn't just El Salvador. What we're doing . . . is to try to halt the infiltration into the Americas by terrorists, by outside interference, and those who aren't just aiming at El Salvador but, I think, are aiming at the whole of Central and possibly later South America—and, I'm sure, eventually North America. [We are] trying to stop this from being exported in here, backed by the Soviet Union and Cuba. . . .[1]

Certainly strong evidence of the importance that the White House attached to blocking an insurgent victory was the dramatic increase in overall U.S. assistance to El Salvador's government in the early 1980s.

Coming as it did only six years after the U.S. humiliation in Vietnam and on the very heels of the Iranian hostage crisis, the drama of the Central American showdown obscured several key issues, paradoxes, and problems. Despite some important differences in style, Reagan's policy in El Salvador was mainly a continuation of President Carter's stance. Paradoxically, however, before 1979 previous U.S. administrations—including Carter's—had manifested a degree of concern about Salvadoran politics that, by standards for the region as a whole, barely exceeded the perfunctory. Moreover, the great increase in both concrete involvement in and symbolic attention paid to the country came at a time when the capacity of the United States to implement an active strategy in the region had sunk to a post–World War II low.

This chapter traces the historical evolution of U.S. relations with El Salvador against the background of the origins and development of the Salvadoran insurrection and of shifting U.S. international roles and capabilities. In order to account for the apparent paradoxes in its recent positions, Washington's interests in Central America—both objective and subjective—as well as certain features of the foreign-policymaking process are explored.

Origin and Development of the Salvadoran Insurrection

The political/economic roots of the contemporary Salvadoran crisis can be found in the last century. Following the introduction of coffee in the mid-1800s, the bigger landowners sought to take advantage of its great profit-making potential by acquiring more acreage. These growers supported laws to break up Indian communal lands (1881–82), which they then acquired. They also promoted antivagrancy legislation, which forced peasants to work on the coffee plantations and used private armies to assure compliance. The subsequent rapid expansion of the landowners' wealth and political power permitted the emergent coffee oligarchy to dominate Salvadoran politics unchallenged until 1931.

Labor and peasant organizations began to develop after 1911 and by 1930 had become widespread as the effects of the Great Depression hit the working classes. These groups helped to elect populist Arturo Araujo president in 1931, but his mild reformism and increasing proletarian unrest led the army to oust him later that year. Amid rising instability, General Maximiliano Hernandez Martinez assumed the presidency. When the peasant-labor movement led by Augustin Farabundo Marti rebelled against the new regime in early 1932, Martinez massacred 30,000 workers, peasants, and Indians in crushing the revolt. He then ruled as dictator until 1944, implementing certain economic programs and a modernization of the finance and banking systems that very much benefited the coffee oligarchy.

The end of World War II brought revived reform agitation from El Salvador's labor movement and progressive middle-sector elements. At the urging of the United States, Martinez resigned in 1944. An interim regime tried to implement democratic changes, but was overthrown in 1945 by former Martinez cohorts. In 1948 a coup by unhappy junior officers inaugurated a new era of military rule based on a dominant official party (patterned on the Mexican model) known first as the Partido Revolucionario de Unificación Democrática (PRUD, 1950–60) and later as the Partido de Conciliación Nacional (PCN, 1961 onward). The PRUD-PCN commitment to generating economic development through infrastructure building cemented the army's alliance with the civilian oligarchy and largely ignored a growing array of social problems. After 1950 numerous political parties from across the ideological spectrum developed to oppose the PRUD-PCN and the alliance between armed forces and economic elites (Baloyra calls it the "reactionary coalition"[2]) that prevails in El Salvador to this day.

> In order to remain competitive, maximize its profits, and survive periods of low export prices, the Salvadoran oligarchy relied on low agricultural wages. In addition, it remained adamantly opposed to any attempt to change a very unequal system of land tenure which enabled it to monopolize the profits of the export trade and to use these to control the financial sector as well.[3]

In 1961 El Salvador joined the Central American Common Market (CACM), which spurred regional economic integration, foreign investment, and rapid industrialization. As in Nicaragua and Guatemala, the CACM's programs tended to promote greater inequality by increasing the profits flowing to the already rich. Salvadoran industrialization involved capital-intensive, highly mechanized production of consumer goods that boosted the country's overall economic output (see Table 6.1), but failed to absorb the rapidly growing labor supply. Moreover, a 1965 agricultural minimum-wage law quickly increased the number of landless peasants and further concentrated land ownership by undermining traditional tenancy patterns. Much of the nation's best acreage was soon converted from subsistence-level cultivation by tenants to speculative production of such export crops as cotton. El Salvador thus entered the 1970s with an ever greater concentration of wealth, increased rural and urban lower-class unemployment, and decreased agricultural self-sufficiency among the peasantry.

After a decade of industrialization and rapid economic growth, the 1973 OPEC embargo and the subsequent rapid escalation of oil prices initiated a protracted wave of inflationary increments in the cost of living. From 1963 through 1972 El Salvador's consumer price index had average annual increases of less than 2 percent, but from 1973 to 1979 it zoomed to 12.8 percent (see Table 6.1). The effect of this high inflation rate on working-class wages was a steep drop in real income in 1974–75 with a slight recovery in 1976 followed by a further sharp

TABLE 6.1
Selected Political and Economic Indicators
   for El Salvador

Year	Rise in Consumer Price Index[a]	Real Working-Class Wage Index[b]	Gross Domestic Product Growth[c]	Growth Per Capita[d]	Number of Industrial Disputes[e]	Approximate Deaths from Political Violence[f]
1963	0.9%	90				
1964	1.8	--				
1965	1.4[g]	--				
1966	-0.9	--				
1967	1.8	105				
1968	1.8	---				
1969	3.2[g]	---				
1970	2.6	96				
1971	0.3	94			12	
1972	1.7	98			23	
1973	6.4	100			6	
1974	16.9	92	6.4%	3.5%	73	
1975	19.1	90	5.6	2.5	14	
1976	7.0	95	4.0	1.0	2	
1977	11.9	88	5.9	2.8	19	
1978	13.3	87	4.4	1.4	29	180
1979	15.0	--	-3.1	-5.9	75[h]	6,000
1980	40.0[i]	--	-15.0[i]	---	100[h]	10,000
1981						12,500

Sources: James W. Wilkie and Stephen Haber, Statistical Abstract of Latin America, Volume 21 (Los Angeles: University of California Latin American Center Publications, 1981); James Dunkerley, The Long War: Dictatorship and Revolution in El Salvador (London: Junction, 1982); Tommie Sue Montgomery, Revolution in El Salvador: Origins and Evolution (Boulder: Westview Press, 1982); and John A. Booth, "Regional Crisis in Central America: The Socioeconomic and Political Roots of Rebellion" (Paper presented at the 1982 International Congress of Americanists in Manchester, England).

[a] From Wilkie and Haber, Table 210.
[b] From Booth, Table 2.
[c,d] From Wilkie and Haber, Table 210.
[e] From Wilkie and Haber, Table 1400.
[f] Rough estimates based on Socorro Jurídico figures cited
    in Montgomery and in Dunkerley.
[g] Estimate based on average inflation rate for other Central
    American nations for the same year.
[h] Rough estimate based on number of unions supporting
    general strikes, from Dunkerley and Montgomery.
[i] Cited in Dunkerley.

decline (see Table 6.1). Concurrently wealth became further concentrated in fewer hands as trends established in the 1960s continued. The coffee oligarchy expanded its hold over the agricultural sector and then, by heavily investing those profits, increased its control of Salvadoran industry. In short, while the poor grew poorer during the mid-1970s, the capitalist elite grew both relatively and absolutely wealthier.

This pattern finally broke in 1979 as the country's economy was disrupted by the Nicaraguan revolution and burgeoning domestic unrest. As shown in Table 6.1, the expansion of the Gross Domestic Product (GDP) for the previous five years had averaged 5.3 percent annually, but in 1979 it actually declined by 5.9 percent as investment dropped sharply. These reverses, which were due to capital flight motivated by the Sandinista victory and growing instability in El Salvador itself, caused further unemployment and worsened the impact of the recession on the working classes.[4]

Popular mobilizations supporting calls for better pay and agrarian reform began to swell in the mid-1970s as real income plummeted. The number of industrial disputes rose dramatically in 1974, declined in 1975–76 as wages improved briefly, and then again escalated rapidly in 1977–78 as inflation ate away at living standards. Although official data since 1978 are not yet available, other evidence suggests that 1979 and 1980 brought even more labor unrest, with industrial unions growing in membership and several national confederations becoming more militant. Catholic community organizations known as Christian base communities (CEBs) spread widely through urban and rural poor neighborhoods in the late 1960s and early 1970s. These groups soon became vehicles for making political and economic demands as well as for self-help activism and for catechism. New peasant organizations, so feared by the coffee oligarchs, also developed during this period and began to agitate for higher agricultural wages and land reform.

The Salvadoran authorities responded harshly to this spreading discontent. President Arturo Armando Molina (1972–77) employed public-security forces against striking workers and peasants, political opponents, and student demonstrators. Right-wing paramilitary groups and death squads such as the Organización Democrática Nacionalista (ORDEN) and the Fuerzas Armadas de Liberación Nacional—Guerra de Exterminación (FALANGE), most of which were organized by elements of the Salvadoran oligarchy,[5] began to terrorize political dissidents. Under President Carlos Humberto Romero (1977–79) the repression escalated rapidly. Death squads and the military, often unable to identify or locate the small guerrilla bands that had appeared in the early and mid-1970s, instead attacked opposition party leaders, students, union members, activist clergy, the CEBs, and peasants. Disappearances became commonplace; massacres of entire villages began to occur with alarming frequency. By 1979 the rate of killings had reached almost 700 per month, with independent observers attributing 80 percent of these deaths to the security forces and rightist death squads. The right-wing violence caused the once apolitical Archbishop Oscar Arnulfo Romero y Galdamez to begin to support the popular movements and to denounce the regime's excesses. The repression also radicalized many persons who had initially become politically, but peacefully active for limited reformist goals. Many union and community betterment group members became revolutionaries, convinced that no solution to their problems other than a resort to arms would work.

Government/paramilitary brutality became so intense and popular mobilization so widespread that—in a pattern common in Salvadoran politics—a moderately progressive faction within the armed forces overthrew President Romero on October 15, 1979. The conspirators hoped to prevent a revolution and its potential damage to the military's corporate interests by promoting social and economic reforms. Although the centrist Partido Demócrata Cristiano (PDC) and the left-center Movimiento Nacional Revolucionaria (MNR) took part in the junta, by January 10, 1980 the MNR and PDC leaders had quit the coalition in protest over the failure to control political terrorism. Thus a process of progressive marginalization of the new regime's moderates began that within months had given military conservatives and the oligarchy control of the government. Despite some progressive initiatives (bank nationalization and a sweeping agrarian reform plan) under the moderate junta in 1979–80, no reduction in rightist violence occurred. As centrist groups became frustrated and alienated from the authorities, they began joining the more radical opposition and the movement soon bloomed into a broad revolutionary front, the Coordinadora Revolucionaria de Masas (CRM). Around the time of Archbishop Romero's March 24, 1982 assassination, the five existing guerrilla organizations, their ranks rapidly multiplying, merged into the Frente Farabundo Martí para la Liberación Nacional (FMLN), while other dissident elements created the Frente Democrático Revolucionario (FDR) as the political arm of the newly unified rebel opposition.

In 1980 the paramilitary right reorganized and stepped up its terror campaign, the armed forces began to fight the guerrillas more system-atically, and the government began to repudiate some of the prior reforms, especially in the agrarian sector. But the FMLN also stepped up its activities, and by mid-1980 it appeared inevitable to most observers that the besieged regime would soon fall. New aid from the Carter and then the Reagan administrations, however, provided an indefinite re-prieve.

During 1981 the war escalated. The civil government, headed by José Napoleon Duarte of the PDC, struggled to carry out its programs against bitter and increasingly successful obstruction by the oligarchy. Duarte had no control over the armed forces, which continued their own terror and butchery against civilians and also permitted continued paramilitary violence. Under pressure from the United States to maintain at least a semblance of reform, the government called for the election on March 28, 1982, of a constituent assembly to draft a new constitution.

A lull in the hostilities during early 1982 permitted a campaign in which the FDR refused to participate for fear of physical extermination, thus leaving the field open to several extreme right-wing parties to challenge the PDC for control of the state. A substantial turnout, widely interpreted as the Salvadoran people's expression of hope for a peaceful solution to the murderous conflict gripping their country, saw the leading PDC (with 40 percent of the vote) fail to win a majority in the new Assembly, where ultimately a rightist coalition elected Roberto D'Aubisson to head the body. D'Aubisson, former head of a secret police agency and strongly suspected of taking part in several assassinations of opposition figures (including Archbishop Romero), led the radical Alianza Republicana Nacional (ARENA). The Assembly also chose businessman Alvaro Magaña as El Salvador's interim president.

Within weeks of its election, the Assembly abandoned the heart of the agrarian reform program (particularly those provisions affecting the coffee plantations) while the armed forces and paramilitary right reescalated their political terrorism back to the previous high levels (approximately 1,000 victims per month). The FMLN-FDR, surprised by the high electoral turnout, nevertheless regrouped and in September 1982 launched a very effective offensive that the 31,000 government troops, now buttressed with U.S. weapons, training, equipment, and advice, had little success in countering. Indeed by early 1983 the regime was in crisis due to severe fissures within the armed forces and the Constituent Assembly's right-wing coalition as well as between the government and the military.

The Evolution of U.S. Policy Toward El Salvador

The political, economic, and military roles and capabilities of the United States in the international system have evolved substantially since 1900, reshaping in the process Washington's interests in, and policies toward, Latin America. For much of the twentieth century the U.S. posture regarding El Salvador, though not fairly characterized as indifferent, had never greatly preoccupied U.S. officials. El Salvador has most often been handled within the larger framework of U.S. policy for the region as a whole and has seldom aroused much specific attention because of its diminutive size, its lack of access to the Atlantic coast, its unsuitability for transisthmian transit, and its distance from Panama. Thus the massive concern focused on the country in the last few years seems all the more dramatic.

1900–1940

Prior to World War I the United States became a leading industrial nation, displaced Britain as the major military power in the Western hemisphere, and actively sought to promote its security and financial interests through a policy of political and economic intervention in the Caribbean and Central America. A series of administrations acquired new Caribbean territories, assured U.S. economic and political hegemony within the hemisphere via the development of the Panama Canal and several military expeditions, and increasingly controlled European and Asian access to Latin America. But Washington's heavy-handedness in the Basin eventually caused its relations with Latin America to deteriorate so badly that by the late 1920s presidents Hoover and Roosevelt felt that some movement toward a rapprochement was necessary and thus scaled down overt U.S. interventionism. This restraint became more pronounced in the 1930s as Germany and Japan became growing security concerns for Washington.

In sharp contrast to several nearby countries, El Salvador's relationship to the United States involved neither military nor fiscal intervention. U.S. private investment there rose from $1.8 million in 1908 to $24.8 million in 1929, while British investments declined during the same period to less than $9 million. In 1929 about one-eighth of all U.S. capital in Central America was in El Salvador.[6] Washington briefly sent three warships into Salvadoran waters during the abortive revolt of 1932, but landed no troops. Initially (in 1931) the United States refused to extend diplomatic recognition to the regime of General Martinez, but the Roosevelt administration finally did so in 1934. Basically, then, aside from private U.S. investments, the country was largely left to its own devices during this era.

1940–1959

World War II prostrated Europe while leaving the United States at the pinnacle of world economic, political, and military power. In the Western Hemisphere mobilization for the war effort had increased the dependency of Latin American nations upon Washington and had sorely damaged many of their economies. But despite hemispheric expectations of aid and pleas for it, the United States decided to focus its postwar attention upon Japan and Europe because of its rapidly developing conflict with Moscow. With its influence in Latin America at a historical peak, Washington incorporated the region into its alliance system in a determined effort to contain the expansion of Soviet Communism.

El Salvador's President Martinez had strongly sympathized with Fascism before the war. Indeed before 1940 his army was trained by German officers. The outbreak of hostilities, however, led Martinez to change sides and to support the Allies. Consequently he established military links with the U.S. armed forces and strengthened his country's economic ties to the United States. Although the Great Depression had cut deeply into U.S. investments in El Salvador, the nation's trade relations with the United States had become much tighter. For example, the proportion of its coffee exports destined for the U.S. market rose from under 20 percent in 1930 to over 80 percent in 1944.[7] As the war began to wind down, popular pressure for Martinez to resign grew intense, and finally in 1944 Washington helped to persuade him to step aside. Later, however, the U.S. diplomatic mission, reflecting the containment mentality that had led Washington to prefer conservative authoritarian regimes over reformist democracies such as that developing in neighboring Guatemala, supported the 1948 coup by Salvadoran officers that established the current system of military-oligarchic rule.[8]

1959-1978

During the 1960s the bipolar international system began to undergo important changes, though the decade began with the Cold War at its height and the tensions generated by this struggle had a significant impact on U.S. policy toward Latin America. Cuba's 1959 revolution moved it into the Soviet bloc, which spurred Washington to intensify its efforts to contain Communism in the Western Hemisphere. Kennedy's Alliance for Progress, which facilitated the formation of the Central American Common Market and the Andean Group, was one response during the 1960s to Fidelista radicalism. Cuban-inspired insurgencies in some Latin countries and its active promotion of insurrection in others led to greatly increased U.S. hemispheric military assistance programs. Washington's overt efforts to maintain the region's anticommunist cohesion included sponsoring both the Bay of Pigs (1961) and Dominican Republic (1965) invasions as well as encouraging the overthrow of Chile's socialist government in 1973. Ironically these policies— especially the Alliance's attempts at generating economic development and the Pentagon's security aid for anticommunist regimes—helped set into motion in several Central American nations profound alterations that would contribute to the region's crisis in the late 1970s.

Both a recession and optimism about the possibilities for ousting military rulers (as per the Cuban experience) led to a period of unrest in El Salvador during 1959–60. A reformist junta ousted President José María Lemus in 1960, but in January 1961 it in turn was toppled by a conservative countercoup in which the United States embassy took an active role.[9] Meanwhile the Alliance and the CACM were stimulating a considerable influx of overseas capital into El Salvador. Foreign investment, some 60 percent of it from the United States, rose from $43 million (with less than 2 percent in manufacturing) in 1960 to $115 million (with about 40 percent in manufacturing) by 1969.[10] During the 1960s Washington lent El Salvador over $100 million for development programs. Also, as part of its military response to the Cuban-Soviet challenge in Latin America, the United States in 1964 organized, along with Guatemala, Honduras, Nicaragua, and El Salvador, the Central American Defense Council (CONDECA). CONDECA linked its members' armed forces into an integrated operational system under the U.S. Army's Panama-based Southern Command and promoted assistance, training, and equipment standardization. El Salvador experienced a brief rise in its military aid after CONDECA's formation, but such help eventually dropped to its previous low levels after 1966 and did not rise again until the Nixon administration assumed office (see Table 6.2).

The Alliance for Progress was supposed to insure that some of the new prosperity it produced trickled down to the Latin American working classes, thereby undermining socialism's appeal. Its programs did spur rapid economic growth in the CACM countries, but experts today concur that they failed to contribute to political stability by encouraging controlled reform or by improving the overall lot of the poor. For instance, Baloyra states that "the United States was not able to make much headway through the Alliance for Progress in El Salvador, nor was it able to sell socioeconomic reforms to the oligarchy."[11] Dunkerley adds that "no major transformation took place; the outcome . . . for the vast bulk of the population was a restructuring and acceleration of impoverishment."[12] Finally, Montgomery argues that for El Salvador "the traditional developmentalist assumption that wealth generated through industrialization or modernization will 'trickle down' . . . is groundless."[13] Indeed the worsening maldistribution of income, rising unemployment, and a recession led to growing unrest in the late 1960s. When tensions between El Salvador and Honduras over their highly unequal balance of trade (favorable to El Salvador) and some 300,000 Salvadoran squatters in Honduras intensified in 1969, El Salvador invaded Honduras in a short but bloody war intended to divert popular attention away from its domestic problems. Washington, hoping to

TABLE 6.2
United States Military and Economic Assistance
to El Salvador, 1946-1983 (millions of dollars)

Year	Economic Aid	Military Aid	Total Aid
1946-1952			
Annual Average	0.3	0.0	0.3
1953-1961			
Annual Average	1.2	0.01	1.21
1962-1966			
Annual Average	15.8	1.1	16.9
1967	4.5	0.3	4.8
1968	9.4	0.5	9.9
1969	13.0	0.4	13.4
1970	12.6	0.6	13.2
1971	4.7	0.4	5.1
1972	8.4	0.4	8.8
1973	3.5	0.5	4.0
1974	10.2	1.3	11.5
1975	3.9	5.5	9.4
1976	6.0	1.0	7.0
1977	8.1	0.6	8.7
1978	10.9	0.0	10.9
1979	11.4	0.0	11.4
1980	58.3	5.9	64.2
1981	114.0	35.5	149.5
1982	204.5	81.0	285.5
1983	164.9	61.3	226.2

Sources: U.S. Department of State, cited in Jenny
Pearce, Under the Eagle: U.S. Intervention in
Central America and the Caribbean (London: Latin
America Project, 1982 ed.), pp. 244, 259; and G. Pope
Atkins, Latin America in the International Political
System (New York: Free Press, 1977), Tables C, D,
and E.

salvage CONDECA, helped to resolve the conflict by pressuring San Salvador to end its attack.

Military assistance to El Salvador under the Nixon administration remained low for several years, but then jumped in 1974 and 1975 as the Pentagon stepped up security aid throughout most of Latin America following the Chilean coup in 1973. However, in contrast to the Salvadoran case, the overall level of hemispheric assistance (military and economic combined) under the Nixon and Ford administrations remained relatively constant (see Table 6.2).

Even though Washington maintained an aggressive containment posture during the 1960s, the global system was undergoing changes that added new poles of power to the international arena and ultimately weakened both the U.S. and Russian blocs. China's break with Moscow preceded other political fissures in the Soviet sphere. NATO solidarity was shaken by France's withdrawal and the Greek-Turkish dispute over Cyprus. The Nonaligned Movement grew as former Third World client states of both superpowers began to act with increasing independence. In the economic realm, the United States was adversely affected as control over key energy resources shifted to oil-exporting developing nations, its self-sufficiency in raw materials declined, rising energy costs and the Vietnam war disrupted the country, strong trade competitors emerged in Asia and Europe, and domestic productivity deteriorated.

First détente under presidents Nixon and Ford and then Carter's recognition of Third World needs along with his emphasis on human rights and arms control policies represented U.S. efforts to minimize the impact in the international realm of its weakened alliances and its diminished capabilities.

> The Nixon-Ford-Kissinger regime conceived its first task, after honorable extrication from the [Vietnam] war, as bringing American power into balance with vital armed interests at a reduced level of national effort and a lessened risk of armed intervention. It sought to shore up containment at a level of involvement that would be acceptable to the American public and consistent with constraints on unilateral American power that had emerged during the last two decades. . . . President Carter, . . . without really abandoning the overriding objective of containment, . . . set out to implement it in a manner congenial to American geopolitical retrenchment and moral resurgence—by downplaying the "inordinate fear of communism" that had led the country "to embrace any dictator who joined us in our fear. . . ."[14]

Jimmy Carter became president in 1977 just as internal tensions in El Salvador were again building rapidly and human rights violations were increasing. Carter, seeking to repair damage to U.S.–Latin American relations from Washington's involvement in the 1973 overthrow of the Chilean government, openly pressed San Salvador for an improvement in its human rights performance. For example, he vetoed a $90 million Inter-American Development Bank loan for human rights reasons. The incoming Romero regime took umbrage at such U.S. "interference" in its internal affairs and subsequently refused U.S. military assistance in 1978 and 1979.

1978 to the Present

Carter, however, soon had come to terms with a continued Soviet military buildup, increased international turbulence, and growing domestic economic woes that had enlarged the "interest-power gap" that he had inherited from his predecessors. "Reacting against this trend on pragmatic and domestic political grounds, the administration began after only a year to modify, abandon, or reverse major components of its original grand design."[15] In Central America the White House had, of course, initially restricted security assistance and arms sales to El Salvador, Nicaragua, and Guatemala because of their serious human rights violations. But this stance encouraged opposition forces, especially in Nicaragua, where internal economic and political strains further fueled the insurrection led by the Sandinistas. The Somoza regime collapsed in July 1979, and the radical FSLN emerged dominant within the new government. Embarrassed by its inability to keep the Marxist Sandinistas from power and by the Iranian revolution and hostage crisis—and with a presidential election looming—the Carter administration began to toughen its stand on the growing opposition movement in El Salvador.

Since Carter had negotiated the gradual turnover of the Canal to Panamanian control and needed Congressional approval of the rather unpopular treaty and enabling legislation, he did not want El Salvador to add to Nicaragua's destabilization of the Central American scene. Thus, despite San Salvador's 1977–78 refusal of military assistance, discussions between U.S. envoys and President Romero brought a lifting of martial law and an increase in U.S. economic assistance. As the Nicaraguan rebels moved toward victory in mid-1979, Washington became more tolerant of the ballooning human rights abuses by the Salvadoran military and paramilitary forces. Total U.S. aid to El Salvador in 1980 jumped 600 percent over the 1979 figure to $64.2 million (including $5.9 million in 1980 military assistance). In short, from relatively early in Carter's tenure, "as the violations of human rights became ever more frequent in incidence and horrible in method, U.S.

'standards' became correspondingly more flexible [in order not] to prejudice U.S. support for the Salvadoran armed forces."[16]

Yet because Romero would not or could not control human rights abuses, the Carter administration apparently became involved in plotting to overthrow him.[17] Although the conspiracy that succeeded in ousting Romero on October 15, 1979, was not the one that it was backing, Washington enthusiastically endorsed the new government and began pushing for a reduction in human rights violations and for social reforms. Believing its own fantasy that "given its status as a superpower and the resources at its command, the United States could dictate the outcome of a crisis like that in El Salvador,"[18] Washington vastly stepped up its intervention in pursuit of two contradictory goals—"the inauguration of a democratic regime and the denial to the left of any important role in the process."[19] As Baloyra convincingly demonstrates, San Salvador's inability to curtail violence and move effectively toward meaningful social reforms rapidly alienated the centrist and moderate leftist opposition (which was soon forced by repression into the FMLN-FDR camp), thus dooming the U.S.-backed October 15 junta to isolation from any significant popular or organizational base. Moreover, Washington's efforts to forge a stable ruling coalition between the reactionary military/oligarchic elements and the Duarte faction of the PDC were bound to fail because of the well-entrenched and growing distrust (if not hatred) between them.

The Reagan administration has not basically changed the general direction of U.S. policy on El Salvador, but rather has merely altered the emphasis on some of its aspects. For instance, Reagan markedly increased the level of U.S. military and economic aid to the country, but this was in fact merely a continuation of a trend begun by Carter. Likewise, although Reagan and Secretary of State Haig heavily stressed confronting the Soviet Union and Cuba in the Caribbean and downplayed the human rights issue, Carter had also been strongly committed to containment and had by his term's end diluted his human rights standards beyond recognition.

President Reagan's advisors on hemispheric affairs did, however, produce some innovations concerning El Salvador. Specifically, because they regarded Duarte and his PDC with much less sympathy than had Carter, Reaganites began to work more closely with and to support more vigorously various right-wing parties. This reorientation led to the disarticulation of the socioeconomic reform proposals that the Christian Democrats and Carter had put forward as soon as the rightist coalition won control of the assembly after the March 1982 elections. The Reagan team has also been more prone to regionalize Caribbean

Basin conflicts by pushing El Salvador, Costa Rica, and Honduras into the anti-Sandinista CADC, encouraging Costa Rican hostility toward Managua, and pressuring Honduras to become involved in fighting the Salvadoran rebels. Reagan also orchestrated a multilateral destabilization campaign, including both diplomatic and economic pressure and illegal covert activities, against Nicaragua's Sandinista government. Overall, however, the major differences between the policies of the Carter and the Reagan administrations have been ones of style and degree rather than substance.

Certainly the consequences of Washington's support for the post-1979 Salvadoran regimes have been great.

> The principal reason for the extended nature of the war was the capacity of the junta to hold its piecemeal military apparatus together . . . to ward off guerrilla offensives and impose a repression. . . . It could only have achieved this, or indeed survived for more than a few weeks, with the resolute support of the US. . . . First Carter and then Reagan, who followed the same line but with a much more concerted bellicosity, poured in money, equipment, and men to hold the line. At no stage has this been a discrete operation; it is a function of the return of the Cold War. . . .[20]

U.S. Interests in El Salvador

Given the growing U.S. attention to and intervention in El Salvador since 1978, we must explore the perceived stakes involved in Central America and the Salvadoran conflict. From the shifts in Washington's position, one might reasonably assume that the basic conception of its interests in the region have changed drastically since the late 1970s.

Dominguez makes a useful distinction between *objective* and *subjective* foreign interests.[21] The former are concrete; they "arise from explicit external conditions that happen to matter to the United States" and are, in principle, "observable and verifiable by many people." Subjective concerns, on the other hand, are "substantively unrelated to specific target countries" and are "imputed by the United States on external phenomena."[22] Observers may even differ over whether they actually exist. Another way to make the same dichotomy would be to typify objective interests as materialistic and subjective interests as intangible. Both kinds have influenced Washington's Central American policy since the last century, but their relative significance has changed considerably over time.

Most experts agree with Dominguez that at present "the objective interests of the United States in Central America outside of Panama are very modest—so modest, indeed, that U.S. interests in Central America should be defined almost exclusively as subjective."[23] In the mid-nineteenth century, however, the area's importance was much more substantive because it was a key transit route between the eastern and western U.S. coasts. Later the construction of the Panama Canal greatly enhanced this status. Since 1945, however, the advent of a two-ocean U.S. fleet and nuclear weapons borne by intercontinental bombers and missiles, the development of great aircraft carriers and oil tankers that cannot pass through the Panamanian locks, and a sharp decline in US. shipping through the canal have sharply reduced the significance of the transisthmian waterway and of Central America in general to the economic and military security of the United States.

Why then, in the absence of truly great objective interests, has Washington become so heavily involved in the area? The answer lies in certain *subjective* concerns that have loomed very large for recent administrations. In Carter's early years, for instance, democracy and human rights received a somewhat higher priority than such previously emphasized matters as maintaining political order, minimizing Marxist-Leninist influence, and the defense of Washington's regional hegemony. We have seen, however, how Carter became much less enamored with human rights after 1979 and resurrected more traditional policies. Similarly, the Reagan team has been preoccupied with preventing Moscow from gaining further footholds in the Caribbean Basin, assuring continuing U.S. dominance there, and preventing instability and "terrorism."

Highlighting the importance he attached to Central America, President Reagan declared: "Make no mistake, the well-being and security of our neighbors in this region are in our own *vital interest*" (emphasis added).[24] In March 1981 Secretary of State Haig told Congress that "the outcome of the situation [in El Salvador] is in the *vital interest* of the American people and must be so dealt with. . . . I know the American people will support what is prudent and necessary providing that they think . . . that we are going to succeed and not flounder as in Vietnam" (emphasis added).[25] He also stated that "we will not remain passive in the face of this communist challenge,"[26] and to the direct question, "Do you rule out the use of combat troops in El Salvador without qualification," he unequivocally stated, "No."[27] Despite repeated denials in 1981–82 that Washington had any concrete or immediate plans to send front-line units to El Salvador or elsewhere in Central America, such remarks clearly implied that containing Communism and maintaining U.S. hegemony in the area constituted vital issues—that is, interests critical to the survival of the United States and therefore worth fighting for.

U.S. Subjective Interests in El Salvador

The Carter Administration

The Carter administration's penchant for promoting human rights and social reform in the Third World was not inconsistent with the postwar tradition of seeking to contain Communism, but rather was a sophisticated version of that policy. The views of Carter and such close foreign affairs consultants as National Security Advisor Zbigniew Brzezinski and Secretary of State Cyrus Vance had been shaped by thinkers connected to institutions like the Atlantic Council, the Council on Foreign Relations, and the Council of the Americas. These organizations, largely funded by U.S.-based multinational corporations, have often "provided personnel for government, and acted as a major forum for contacts and discussion between big business, the media, and the universities."[28] In 1973 the Council on Foreign Relations, seeking to retool the world economic order and U.S. foreign policy in a manner compatible with the interests of international capitalism, established the Trilateral Commission under Brzezinski's directorship. Including in its ranks U.S., Japanese, and European commercial and political leaders, the commission "sought a broad global strategy for the management of interdependence, the promotion of liberal trade policies, and . . . reflected the major concerns of the giant multinational corporations . . . which seek above all a stable, secure environment in which to operate."[29] Brzezinski criticized the Nixon-Kissinger world view for "overemphasis on East-West relations to the neglect of the North-South dimension"[30] and saw the emergent Third World bloc as a potential threat because it controlled access to raw materials whose exploitation is critical to the industrialized capitalist powers. The trilateral perspective stressed the need for the West to recognize the legitimacy of the demands and aspirations of the developing nations as pivotal to stimulating global economic stability.

Jimmy Carter, also a trilateralist, drafted Brzezinski, Vance, and many others from the commission to serve in key foreign-policy posts. Together they helped to shape his administration's focus on human rights and on responding positively to calls for a more just international order as a means to contain Moscow. Brzezinski summarized this strategy's relevance to Central America as follows: "American longer range interests would be harmed by continuing indifference to the mounting desire in Central America for greater social justice and national dignity, as our indifference will only make it easier for Castro's Cuba to exploit that desire."[31] Human rights concerns were thus seen as being instrumental in circumscribing pro-Soviet socialist influence. Accordingly the White House supported some limitation on military assistance programs for human rights reasons, but also sought to retain various loopholes. For instance, the administration lobbied successfully for modifications to the Foreign Assistance Act that set restriction thresholds and aid levels requiring prior congressional approval at amounts well above the normal Pentagon disbursements to many Third World nations.[32] This ploy allowed the containment-oriented military assistance cake to be coated with altruistic icing, thereby helping the administration to capitalize on sympathy for human rights while preserving some of its security-aid flexibility.

Although apparently sincere in desiring an end to Somoza's reign, Carter tried hard to block the Sandinistas from coming to power by delaying the dictator's departure while Washington sought to forge a workable center-right government of national reconciliation. But Somoza's refusal to negotiate in good faith and the continued brutality of his National Guard ruined this scenario. In fact, the stalling tactic exacerbated the situation and gave the FSLN time to establish firm leadership over the insurrection. The administration, in Dunkerley's view, made such errors because its low-quality diplomats in Managua were incapable of appreciating the depth of the opposition to the Somoza dynasty and the Sandinistas' popularity:

> The attitudes and actions of the U.S. towards the Nicaraguan revolution were in part the result of the residual incompetence and lack of integration in a massive diplomatic and intelligence network. . . . Because Central America was in the "backyard" it had merited relatively little serious political analysis; the quality of the senior diplomatic personnel posted there was far from impressive. Before the summer of 1978 the U.S. Embassy in Managua had never even made contact with the FSLN to assess its political positions.[33]

With its policy falling apart during the Somoza regime's last days, Carter unsuccessfully urged the OAS to send an inter-American peace-keeping force to the country. When it did not materialize, Somoza finally fled.

The Sandinista victory sent alarm bells clanging in Washington. Mistaking its intelligence and analytical shortcomings in Nicaragua as simply tactical errors, the White House redefined its Central American interests and its preferred methods to achieve them:

It [the FSLN triumph] revived the question of Cuba, underlined the strategic importance of the Panama Canal, and highlighted the weaknesses of Washington's client regimes in the rest of the region. One response to this . . . was the revival of the domino theory and a distinct aversion to negotiations with the radical forces on the ground that Nicaragua now lay within the sphere of Soviet-Cuban influence.[34]

The Nicaraguan crisis so traumatized the Carter team that it elevated containment in Central America to a higher priority than improving human rights. As the U.S. adopted a strategy of minimizing its losses in Managua by remaining relatively friendly and helpful to the new Sandinista regime, it concluded that El Salvador was on the brink of repeating the Nicaraguan experience and set out to prevent such an occurrence. Brzezinski summed up Washington's new hardline stance by declaring, "The United States could never permit another Nicaragua, even if preventing it meant employing the most reprehensible measures."[35]

The Reaganites' strident Cold War rhetoric in the 1979–80 presidential campaign tended to obscure much of Carter's rightward shift in Central America. Within weeks of the Sandinista victory his administration had begun to work to forestall "another Nicaragua" by taking a much more active role in El Salvador's rapidly developing civil strife. Between July and October 1979 U.S. emissaries tried vainly to forge a PDC-oligarchy coalition to replace Romero and preempt the insurgents' appeal. Given the apparently progressive character of the junta that came into power on October 15, and because its leaders shared Washington's fear of the left, the Carter administration quickly endorsed the new regime. The United States thus

lumped together all the organizations of the Left, ignoring or overlooking differences in their ideologies and tactics, as well as linkages to "middle class" organizations that continued to divide them. . . . Concerned with the rapidly deteriorating situation, . . . [neither the United States nor the junta dealt] with the issue of participation of the popular organizations in the new order that they were advocating.[36]

This U.S. strategy of marginalizing the left—which had already failed in Nicaragua—was put into effect in El Salvador and immediately began destroying any remaining moderate political ground. The Carter White House continued to struggle to create and hold what it called a "center" consisting of the PDC's Duarte faction and the oligarchy. This plan unraveled, however, because of the extremism of the oligarchy, which employed terror not only against the left but also against its putative allies in the coalition (the PDC, government workers, and even U.S. advisors) and did everything possible to undermine proposed reforms. Only constant U.S. diplomatic pressure and greatly stepped-up military aid in 1980 kept the rebels from winning during the U.S. presidential campaign.

The Reagan Administration

The crucible of Reagan's Central American policy was the president-elect's transition team. Several people working on the region had close ties to New Right organizations and to individuals such as Jesse Helms, who in January 1981 would chair the Latin American Subcommittee of the Senate Foreign Relations Committee in the new Congress. Transition team members came from such conservative think tanks as Georgetown University's Center for Strategic and International Studies (CSIS), Stanford University's Hoover Institution, the American Enterprise Institute (AEI), and the Heritage Foundation as well as from lobbies like the Coalition for Peace through Strength (CPS), the American Security Council (ASC), and the Council for Inter-American Security (CIAS).[37] Their attitudes were exemplified by Jeane Kirkpatrick (CSIS), who said, "The doctrine of social change had been embraced like a religious dogma by the Carter administration. Now the problem is that progress often turns out to look a lot like Cubans and Russians."[38] Roger Fontaine (AEI/CSIS) spoke of the need to "act a good deal more aggressively in preserving what's left of, and preserving what opportunities are left for, democracy, particularly in Central America. . . . You are going to have to give these countries—El Salvador, being one, Guatemala another—a good deal more economic . . . and military advisers [and] . . . military training. . . . I think this controversy between lethal and non-lethal aid is absurd. You don't fight terrorists and guerrillas with non-lethal aid."[39] Kirkpatrick later became UN ambassador and Fontaine the Latin American specialist on the National Security Council.

President Reagan did not involve himself deeply in shaping Central American policy during his first year in office. In his stead, Secretary of State Haig, who, as a Kissinger disciple and a Council of Foreign Relations associate, was initially perceived as the administration's leading foreign affairs liberal, moved to the forefront and ultimately adopted a stance similar to that of the New Right, moving to alter Carter's positions that were criticized as insufficiently tough. Baloyra argues that the impact of such U.S. conservatives was

> that they consciously or unwittingly helped to legitimize the actions and programs of the more violent rightist element in El Salvador. These

conservatives wanted not only to "draw a line" in El Salvador but to dictate a geopolitical approach to the problem, which could only result in a regionalization of the conflict. These elements did not appear as interested in a peaceful solution as they did in . . . "getting tough" with Nicaragua and Cuba.[40]

Throughout their first year the Reaganites pushed this intransigent stance. But when the verbal and material escalation orchestrated by Haig produced vociferous and broadly based criticism within the United States, the president himself stepped in to moderate Washington's harsh rhetoric. From then on the administration, now perceiving that its options for action in El Salvador were at least partially constrained by public opinion, began to downplay its militaristic image. For instance, in order to pursue containment without further arousing the U.S. peace movement and skeptical Congressmen, the White Hosue strongly promoted the March 1982 Salvadoran elections. A modicum of success in lowering the level of violence briefly in early 1982 helped keep U.S. aid flowing and the regime propped up.

Washington's style mellowed still further when George Schultz replaced Haig in 1982. Reports from within the State Department began to circulate in late 1982 that the new secretary was exercising more control over Central American policy. Schultz did not remove, but apparently did restrain the New Right elements who had by then come to be referred to by some State Department dissidents as the "war party." For example, after months of rumors that Washington would send combat units to Central America in December 1982 and despite an evident weakening of the Salvadoran regime and its armed forces, no such intervention occurred and U.S. spokesmen began to insist that under no foreseeable circumstances would troops be deployed.[41]

Conclusion

As of early 1983, the FMLN has been engaged in a highly successful six-month offensive that has given it more control over towns and territory, numerous small victories over government forces, and significant amounts of captured weapons. Thus, even with a roughly 50 percent buildup of the Salvadoran military and $81 million in U.S. security aid in fiscal year 1983, both the Defense Department and San Salvador were calling for increased assistance in 1984. The Pentagon was also recommending that more U.S. military advisors be dispatched. On the political front the Salvadoran regime, which had been reorganized in 1982 and acquired an aura of legality through the elections, seemed weaker in 1983 than when Reagan took office.

Shortrun prospects in 1983 for Washington's Salvadoran policy included many unpalatable possibilities. Additional U.S. aid was needed merely to hold the guerrillas at bay, and even with such help the FMLN-FDR appeared closer to victory than ever. For the government to have a chance to win would probably require the use of substantial foreign combat forces. The political climate in the United States was highly unfavorable to such intervention by the Pentagon. Honduras might have been able to supply some troops, but Guatemala was tied down with its own war and no other obvious candidate from the region had appeared. It seemed quite likely, therefore, that the Salvadoran conflict might well drag on through the remainder of Reagan's first term, with perhaps greater U.S. financing, while the FMLN-FDR continued to gain strength.

Several consequences may be expected from an extension of the fighting. Continued U.S. support for the reactionary coalition would surely impede progress toward discussions that might forge a workable solution to the political crisis and to the pressing need for economic and social reforms. Meanwhile the country's economy could continue to decline due to the war of attrition being waged by the guerrillas and disinvestment by the private sector, which means that unemployment would become steadily worse and its by-products, disease and famine, would become even more common. The longer Washington prolongs the conflict, the worse would be future U.S.-Salvadoran relations should the FMLN-FDR emerge triumphant either through a military victory or a negotiated settlement.

The Reagan policy of regionalizing the Salvadoran struggle, along with the possibility of other crises in Central America and elsewhere in the Third World, poses potentially debilitating problems for Washington. Moreover, the administration is pursuing increased confrontation with Moscow in both the Central American and global arenas with the United States controlling far fewer of the resources (i.e., military and economic power, diplomatic and moral leverage) necessary for such an undertaking than at any time since World War II. Therefore Washington's goal of reestablishing its regional hegemony through repression of reform in Central America is both a high-risk gamble for the United States and a promise of death for the many who would inevitably be caught in the crossfire.

Notes

1. Quoted in Marvin E. Gettleman et al., *El Salvador: Central America in the Cold War* (New York: Grove Press, 1981), p. 267.

2. See Enrique A. Baloyra, *El Salvador in Transition* (Chapel Hill: University of North Carolina Press, 1982).

3. Ibid., p. 2.

4. See John A. Booth, "Toward Explaining Regional Crisis in Central America: The Socioeconomic and Political Roots of Rebellion." (Paper presented to the 44th International Congress of Americanists in Manchester, England, September 6–10, 1982).

5. Baloyra, *El Salvador* (note 2 above), pp. 83–116; Tommie Sue Montgomery, *Revolution in El Salvador: Origins and Evolution* (Boulder, Colo.: Westview, 1982), passim; and James Dunkerley, *The Long War: Dictatorship and Revolution in El Salvador* (London: Junction, 1982), passim.

6. Edelberto Torres Rivas, *Interpretación del desarrollo social centroamericano* (San José, Costa Rica: Editorial Universitaria Centroamericana, 1971), pp. 299–302; Rafael Menjivar (ed.), *La inversión extranjera en Centroamérica* (San José, Costa Rica: Editorial Universitaria Centroamericana, 1974), pp. 14–15; Jenny Pearce, *Under the Eagle: U.S. Intervention in Central America and the Caribbean* (London: Latin America Bureau, 1982 ed.), p. 18.

7. Pearce, *Under the Eagle* (note 6 above), p. 26; Torres Rivas, *Interpretación* (note 6 above), p. 291.

8. Baloyra, *El Salvador* (note 2 above), p. 75.

9. Ibid., pp. 40–43.

10. Dunkerley, *The Long War* (note 5 above), p. 51.

11. Baloyra, *El Salvador* (note 2 above), p. 75.

12. Dunkerley, *The Long War* (note 5 above), p. 48.

13. Montgomery, *Revolution* (note 5 above), p. 94.

14. Robert E. Osgood, "The Revitalization of Containment," *Foreign Affairs,* vol. 60, no. 3 (1982), pp. 468–469.

15. Ibid., p. 469.

16. Dunkerley, *The Long War* (note 5 above), p. 112.

17. Montgomery, *Revolution* (note 5 above), pp. 7–25.

18. Baloyra, *El Salvador* (note 2 above), p. 76.

19. Ibid., p. 77.

20. Dunkerley, *The Long War* (note 5 above), p. 163.

21. Jorge Dominguez, *U.S. Interests and Policies in Central America* (Washington, D.C.: American Enterprise Institute, 1982), pp. 4–5.

22. Ibid.

23. Ibid., p. 13.

24. Quoted in Robert A. Pastor, "Our Real Interests in Central America," *Atlantic Monthly* (July 1982), p. 30.

25. Ibid., p. 34.

26. Gettleman et al., *El Salvador* (note 1 above), p. 217.

27. Ibid., p. 220.

28. Pearce, *Under the Eagle* (note 6 above), p. 104.

29. Ibid., p. 105.

30. Ibid.

31. Ibid., p. 116.

32. Ibid., p. 120.
33. Dunkerley, *The Long War* (note 5 above), p. 121.
34. Ibid.
35. Ibid., p. 162.
36. Baloyra, *El Salvador* (note 2 above), p. 86.
37. Pearce, *Under the Eagle* (note 6 above), pp. 165–180.
38. Ibid., p. 173.
39. Ibid., pp. 172–173.
40. Baloyra, *El Salvador* (note 2 above), p. 124.
41. Author's interviews and conversations in Central America (November 22–29, 1982).

7

The Politics of Asymmetrical Interdependence: U.S.-Mexican Relations in the 1980s

Bruce M. Bagley

Introduction

During the late 1970s and 1980s, fueled by Mexico's oil boom, U.S.-Mexican interdependence increased qualitatively. The Mexican economy surged into high gear under President José López Portillo's (1976–82) expansionary economic program, and Mexican imports from the United States rose steeply. By 1981 Mexico had become the United States' third largest trading partner, and in 1982 it replaced Saudi Arabia as the United States' chief supplier of imported oil. U.S. direct private investment in Mexico rose to almost $8 billion, and U.S. banks held over $25 billion of Mexico's $80-billion foreign debt. During Mexico's severe financial crisis in 1982 Washington played a leading role in organizing the international bail-out that prevented an economic collapse. Moreover, millions of tourists cross the border in both directions each year, and more than a million undocumented Mexican workers enter the United States annually in search of higher wages, and between 3 and 5 million reside there illegally. Nowhere in the world is the interrelationship between a developed and developing country more extensive, and the two societies promise to become even more interdependent in coming decades.[1] This relationship is, however, decidedly asymmetrical, given the United States' clear economic, technological, and military superiority. Consequently the Mexicans understandably continue to fear domination by, and dependence on, their more powerful and industrialized northern neighbor.

The unevenness in such interdependence undeniably confers an overall advantage on the United States, but it by no means guarantees that Washington will be able to secure favorable outcomes in all bilateral issue areas. Contrary to common *dependentista* expectations, rather than intensifying U.S. control, growing interdependence has often increased Mexico's relative autonomy. In practice complex interdependence has meant that the United States is more constrained in using its power than in the past; the interconnections between the two nations are so pervasive that unilateral U.S. actions against Mexico inevitably damage Washington's interests as well. For instance, employing military force against Mexico—invoked at various times in the nineteenth and early twentieth centuries—has become largely inapplicable in the contemporary context. U.S. restrictions on trade, investment, and credits are awkward and generally self-defeating, hurting the U.S. business community almost as much as the Mexican. Similarly, sealing the border would deny U.S. employers cheap Mexican labor while creating sociopolitical tensions in Mexico that Washington definitely does not want to confront. Finally, despite some people's desire to punish Mexico for its independent foreign policy in Central America and the Caribbean by imposing sanctions on unrelated socioeconomic questions, it is politically difficult, if not impossible, to do so because so many domestic U.S. constituencies stand to be injured in the process.

Mexico, on the other hand, has not been similarly inhibited from playing linkage politics in its dealings with the United States. For example, López Portillo's standard response to Washington's complaints about undocumented Mexican immigration was to insist that the problem could be best solved by granting greater access to U.S. markets. Such concessions would, in his view, permit Mexico to provide jobs for its own people and thereby eliminate the fundamental cause of northern migration. In general, because Mexico's interests are less complex (i.e., less global) than those of its superpower neighbor, linkage strategies have been seen by Mexican leaders as relatively inexpensive and effective mechanisms for maximizing their bargaining power with Washington.

Growing interdependence has not functioned to harmonize Mexican-U.S. relations. Instead disagreements and tensions on many bilateral, regional, and international issues have become more profound and pervasive than at any time in recent memory. This chapter seeks to determine why these two countries, despite their growing interdependence, currently find themselves so often at odds. It also explores how their association is likely to evolve over the remainder of the 1980s and attempts to identify the major policy options open to them in their dealings with each other and the larger international system.

The structural problems inherent in asymmetrical interdependence have been exacerbated by the Reagan administration's unwillingness to abandon U.S. hegemonic pretensions over Mexico and the Caribbean Basin, despite Washington's growing inability to maintain the basic rules governing interstate relations in the region."[2] This decline in U.S. power has been attributed to such factors as the Vietnam syndrome and a failure of national will; Soviet-Cuban expansionism in Central America; and negative long-term economic trends like the impact of the 1973 and 1979 energy crises, chronic inflation, cyclical recession, declining productivity, and increased competition from Western Europe, Japan, and several Third World nations. But no matter which explanation or combination thereof is accepted, they all suggest that the United States is no longer in a position to assert hegemonic power in the hemisphere. The dissolution of the *pax americana* has been nowhere more evident, nor potentially threatening to Mexico, than in the Caribbean Basin. Given its proximity to this increasingly turbulent area, Mexico has been strongly motivated to exert greater influence there to protect its own national interests.

Awareness of the confluence of variables that has given Mexico the capability, the opportunity, and the inclination to assume an expanded regional role (especially in Central America) does not, however, explain why its leaders have chosen to use their resources and leverage as they have. To develop such an analysis, which is critical to formulating a viable U.S. policy toward Mexico and the Basin, requires an understanding of how the Mexicans interpret their own national interests within the present global context and how they evaluate the costs involved in pursuing the various options open to them. Similarly, the mere declaration that Mexico has risen to the status of a middle power says little about the constraints placed on its foreign policy by the interplay of domestic and international factors. To clarify those considerations—and thus the proper U.S. response to Mexican initiatives—demands an understanding of the domestic roots of Mexico's foreign policy and an examination of its status within the international system. Also, the "petrolization" of the Mexican economy resulting from the oil boom of the late 1970s calls for exploring the limits imposed by the world petroleum market. Finally, Mexico's 1982 financial collapse highlights the importance of probing its relationship to the global economic system.

Mexican Versus U.S. National Interests

In Washington policymaking circles, Republican as well as Democratic, the basic assumption underlying most analyses of U.S.-Mexican relations is that the two countries' national interests are essentially identical, at least on the big issues. This commonality is presumed to be grounded in factors such as geographical proximity (a 2,000-mile undefended border), economic complementarity (capitalist, market-oriented systems characterized by a high degree of interdependence), political compatibility (both prodemocratic and anticommunist), and similar security concerns. Flowing directly from this premise have been policy recommendations like the North American Common Market idea, advocated by Republican candidate Ronald Reagan during the 1980 presidential campaign, and calls for greater U.S.-Mexican coordination in the Caribbean Basin made by Reagan's Secretary of State Alexander Haig in May 1981.

The cool reception that these proposals received in Mexico City caused perplexity and consternation in Washington. Likewise, Mexico's refusal to join the General Agreement on Trade and Tariffs (GATT) in 1980, its continuing diplomatic ties with Cuba, its support for the Nicaraguan revolution, and its August 1981 joint declaration with France recognizing the FMLN-FDR opposition in El Salvador as a representative political force have also confused and exasperated U.S. policymakers.

Perhaps the most frequent response in Washington has been to explain Mexico's failure to identify its interests with those of the United States in primarily psychological terms. Thus one often hears the argument that Mexican foreign policy is the product of an immature and emotional anti-Americanism or that it reflects the need of Mexican politicians to reaffirm their *macho* images before Mexcian public opinion. A second, increasingly common line has been to portray Mexican policymakers as misguided, mistaken, naive, ignorant of the full extent of Cuban-Soviet subversion in the hemisphere, and insensitive to the dangers that Communist infiltration represents to the stability of Mexico itself. The thread that runs throughout these comments is an unwillingness to entertain the possibility that Mexico's national interests may, at least in some cases, differ markedly from those of the United States.

As in Washington, in Mexico there is no universally accepted definition of the nation's vital interests, much less agreement concerning which strategies might be most likely to secure them. Nevertheless there does appear to be a relatively high degree of consensus on at least three elements.[3] First, in terms of national security, there is a generalized perception that the principal threat to Mexico is not Soviet-Cuban subversion, but rather the United States itself. This view is clearly rooted in the country's historic vulnerability to its dominant northern neighbor. The loss of roughly one-half of its territory to an expansionist United States in the mid-nineteenth century led Mexico to adopt the essentially defensive principles of nonintervention, self-determination, and the peaceful resolution of international disputes that have characterized its foreign policy ever since. In its most paranoid contemporary version, the primary Mexican preoccupation is that a severe disruption of world petroleum supplies might trigger a U.S. move south designed to guarantee U.S. access to vital energy sources during the crisis. Even if they discard the likelihood of any direct intervention, many Mexican analysts express fears that growing U.S. dependence on Mexico could lead to a loss of Mexican national autonomy and extreme political pressures from Washington.

Beyond the basic questions of national security and territorial integrity, Mexican elites perceive economic development to be their paramount national interest. Indeed, high growth rates have been an essential element in the maintenance of elite consensus and the "peace of the PRI" (Institutional Revolutionary Party) throughout the post–World War II period, for they have allowed the system the latitude needed to co-opt and demobilize key sectors of Mexican society without resorting to highly conflictual redistributive measures or extreme repression of the southern cone variety.

Since the United States is Mexico's main trading partner, its largest foreign investor, and its major international creditor, it is clearly crucial to the country's modernization. But while most North American analysts now routinely classify the bilateral relationship as a form of interdependence from which both states profit,[4] many Mexicans continue to characterize it as a dependent one (or at best an asymmetrical form of interdependence) and insist on diversifying their country's international ties.[5] The Mexicans are obviously aware that cooperation with the United States is critical to their development, but they are also wary of Yankee imperialism and are intent upon asserting control over their own economy and natural resources.

As in the case of national security, Mexican perceptions of the country's national interests in the area of economic development vary from those of the United States, and these differences contain important policy implications. In the first place, economic nationalism leads Mexicans to be suspicious of entering into a formal North American common market; they fear that they would be relegated permanently to the position of raw-material supplier to the industrial north. Long-term integration with the United States and Canada will come, if at all, only after an extensive period of experimentation with more limited sectoral-level programs that guarantee Mexico's own industrial expansion. Economic nationalism also translates into a series of complex restrictions on foreign investment. Such limitations are obvious with regard to the state-owned petroleum sector, where direct external investment has been banned altogether since 1938, and in the secondary petrochemical field, where foreign investment cannot exceed 40 percent in any given firm; but the limitations exist virtually everywhere. Nationalism has also sparked a protectionist streak in Mexican trade policies and a statist orientation in its approach to economic development, both tendencies running counter to the dominant ideological preferences in the United States, especially those of the Reagan administration.

A third major area in which Mexican perceptions of their national interests differ from stock U.S. assumptions of compatibility is in the realm of domestic political stability. The Reagan administration has consistently argued that Mexico is potentially the final domino in a falling Central American chain set off by Cuban-Soviet subversion in Nicaragua. Mexico, however, rejects this East-West definition of the Central American crisis and emphasizes instead the economic inequalities, social injustices, and political repression that have spawned broadbased opposition movements in countries like Nicaragua, El Salvador, and Guatemala. Moreover, the López Portillo administration never accepted the idea that Mexico is likely to become a target for groups based in Central America (either now or in the future), as many U.S. conservatives have claimed.

Mexican reasoning on the question of the nation's internal stability runs counter to Reaganite logic at several crucial points. First, Mexican policymakers see any effort to prop up the illegitimate regimes of El Salvador and Guatemala through military aid as not only doomed to fail, but also as bound to involve tremendous human suffering, population displacement, and economic disruption throughout the region. The civil war in El Salvador alone has already generated hordes of displaced persons, thousands of whom are now in Mexico. In addition, rising levels of conflict and violence in Guatemala have resulted in people flooding into southern Mexico.[6] Rather than a solution to the Central American crisis, López Portillo viewed the Reagan military approach as directly destabilizing Mexico, for as long as the violence goes on in Central America, the country will continue to be beset with economic and political refugees that it can ill afford to receive. From this perspective Reagan's militarization of Central America will only prolong the inevitable at great cost to the entire region in general and to Mexico specifically.

Second, López Portillo was convinced that by befriending leftist forces and governments in the Basin, Mexico could purchase a kind of insurance policy against the export of radicalism. The argument is that if the region's radical revolutionary regimes are economically indebted to Mexico and in need of continued assistance, it is unlikely that they will permit hostile acts to be launched from their territory. López

Portillo also believed that the chances for moderating the subsequent behavior of these governments would be greater if a cooperative strategy is pursued. The Reagan administration has viewed this approach as nothing less than appeasement.

Finally, the Mexican authorities are aware that their country, unlike virtually any other in Latin America, has an institutionalized political left—made up mostly of intellectuals, journalists, students, some union leaders, and radical parties—which it must take into account, particularly in the area of foreign policy.[7] Although Washington seems unaware of it, for any Mexican president to align himself with Reagan's hardline stance in Central America and the Caribbean would provoke intense internal opposition. Mexico's sympathetic attitude toward the Sandinistas in Nicaragua and the Frente Democrático Revolucionario in El Salvador is partly due to the strength of the limited but vociferous sectors of public opinion in favor of these groups. López Portillo, as did his predecessors, used a progressive foreign policy to defuse domestic opposition to PRI rule, and President Miguel de la Madrid Hurtado has found himself constrained to maintain similar attitudes for the same reasons. There is, of course, room for maneuver, for Mexican presidents enjoy great autonomy in foreign affairs. But any major reversal of Mexico's stance on Central America would undoubtedly arouse stinging domestic criticism.

U.S.-Mexican Relations and the International Economy

Despite more or less serious bilateral disputes over natural-gas pricing, petroleum export levels, oil spills, GATT, protectionism, illegal immigrants, fishing rights, and Central American policy during the late 1970s and early 1980s, the volume of trade, investment, and credits flowing between the United States and Mexico increased steadily. On the strength of Mexico's petroleum sales abroad, which accounted for 75 percent of its total exports in 1981, and its imports of machinery, high-technology goods, steel, and grain, bilateral commerce is likely to expand even further during the 1980s once the current recession ends and economic expansion begins again.[8]

There are, however, major problems that threaten severe disruption if they are not quickly confronted and successfully resolved. Signs of growing weakness and instability in the Mexican economy began to appear in 1981, and the situation reached crisis proportions during the first half of 1982. At the height of the euphoria about the oil boom of 1978–80, the López Portillo administration had set ambitious growth targets of 8 percent or more a year, promised jobs to Mexico's rapidly expanding work force, and increased public spending in virtually all sectors from health and education through road building, port development, and the expansion of private industry and agriculture. Most of this activity was financed through foreign borrowing, with private commercial banks rushing in and accepting low profit margins on their loans in order to retain a share of the booming market. But rapid development overheated the Mexican economy and kicked inflation up to 30 percent in 1981. As the world recession slowed price increases in the United States and other industrial countries, Mexico's balance-of-payments situation began to deteriorate significantly. The softening of world oil prices from June 1981 onward was especially injurious because of the nation's growing dependence on petroleum exports. Thus Mexico's 1981 trade balance with the United States ran about $3 billion in the red, while the current accounts deficit ballooned from $6.7 billion to $11.7 billion in 1981.[9]

In an effort to keep its share of the declining world oil market and thereby maintain the vital flow of petroleum export revenues needed to finance growth, in June 1981 the PEMEX Chief Jorge Diaz Serrano ordered a $4-a-barrel cut in oil prices. In the nationalist furor unleashed by the price reduction, Diaz Serrano lost his job (as well as his chance for the presidency). His successor, Julio Rodolfo Moctezuma Cid, then attempted to roll back at least part of the cut. Rather than restoring the original levels, however, these efforts to push prices back up set off a spate of contract cancellations by key buyers in France, the United States, and elsewhere that lowered the nation's export revenues by almost 50 percent over the second half of 1981 and severely undermined international confidence in the Mexican economy.[10]

Meanwhile foreign bankers were still willing to lend to Mexico, but on terms that proved increasingly expensive and carried shorter and shorter repayment periods. In 1980 only 4 percent of the nation's public debt involved short-term financing. But by the latter half of 1981 the proportion had risen to 12 percent, and in the first quarter of 1982 it reached 13 percent. Nevertheless the López Portillo regime persisted in its costly projects, using foreign borrowing to underwrite public spending that increased by 21 percent over 1981 in real terms. Consequently the public sector debt skyrocketed from 7.3 percent of gross domestic product in 1980 to 12.5 percent in 1981 and an estimated 15 percent in 1982. By August 1982 the nation's total foreign debt stood at $80 billion ($60 billion in the public sector and $20 billion in the private sector), among the largest in the Third World.[11]

Faced with a rapidly deteriorating Mexican economy, many shaken bankers in the United States and Europe proved unwilling to renew even short-term government loans. Indeed over the first half of 1982, a consortium of international banks tried to put together a $2.5-billion loan package for Mexico, but encountered serious problems with many of the smaller members of the syndicate. The larger institutions were finally forced to assume most of the burden themselves. With their foreign reserves dangerously depleted and international credit increasingly difficult to obtain, in August 1982 the Mexicans were forced to freeze dollar deposits, float the peso again (having previously done so in February 1982), impose a two-tiered preferential dollar exchange rate, request a rollover of their short-term loans for ninety days, and appeal to the international community for a bail-out.[12]

Confronted with turmoil in its southern neighbor's economy, the Reagan administration took the lead in organizing international assistance for Mexico. Given the extensive interdependence between the two countries, Washington literally had no other choice. A complete collapse in Mexico would have had profoundly negative repercussions throughout the entire Western financial system. By the end of August 1982, a $1.85 billion line of credit to the Bank of Mexico was announced by the Bank for International Settlements (BIS) in Basel, Switzerland. The U.S. Federal Reserve agreed to provide $925 million of the total, with the central banks of eleven other major industrial nations offering to put up the other half. Spain, the second largest customer for Mexican oil after the United States, offered to lend as much as $175 million. In addition, U.S. commercial banks extended $1 billion in crop-export loans to Mexico, guaranteed by the U.S. Commodity Credit Corporation, while the U.S. government advanced $1 billion in payments for future sales of Mexican crude to the Special Petroleum Reserve. Finally the commercial banks, under considerable prompting from the U.S. Federal Reserve, agreed to extend Mexico new credits in the range of $500 million to $1 billion and to accept a moratorium on principal repayments totalling about $10 billion for three months. They did, however, make their assistance contingent upon the successful conclusion of a Mexican deal with the International Monetary Fund,[13] and such an agreement was signed in late December 1982. Implementing this austerity package will almost certainly generate significant discontent among the masses and lead Mexican policymakers to blame their difficulties on the international financial system and the industrial powers that control it, especially the United States.

Under these circumstances strains in U.S.-Mexican relations were bound to become more severe. Flights of capital from Mexico into the United States prompted some harsh rhetoric from President López Portillo and precipitated the imposition of highly complex and restrictive exchange controls that were quite unpopular with U.S. citizens. The decision to increase deliveries to the U.S. Special Petroleum Reserve heightened Mexican fears of dependency on the United States and elicited nationalist criticism that Washington was taking advantage of Mexico's weakness to get oil at depressed prices. López Portillo's draconian nationalization of his country's banks on September 1, 1982, alarmed many commercial bankers in and outside of Mexico as well as key advisers in the Reagan administration. There was also considerable resentment in the United States of Mexico's failure to accept IMF conditionality more promptly.[14]

Yet despite the growing strains, neither Mexico nor Washington is likely to adopt policies that would seriously threaten their relationship. Nor can they afford to allow differences in other areas—such as fisheries, Central American policy, or border migration—to endanger the overall framework of bilateral economic ties, because both countries would suffer unacceptable damage. Instead the real question appears to be whether economic distress and the need for emergency assistance from the United States and the international financial community will oblige Mexico to assume a lower profile or otherwise moderate its positions in Central America and the Caribbean.

The United States, Mexico, and the Caribbean Basin Crisis: Divergent Perspectives

Mexico's rise to regional power status and its attendant foreign-policy autonomy forced López Portillo to make some fundamental choices regarding the Basin. Beginning with the 1979 decision to withdraw official recognition from the Somoza dictatorship through its August 1980 joint facility with Venezuela, its August 1981 communique with France on El Salvador, and its 1982 mediation efforts on behalf of Cuba and Nicaragua, Mexico consistently adopted positions at variance with the United States and especially the Reagan administration. The conflicts have been most intense over U.S. hostility toward Nicaragua, Grenada, and Cuba and U.S. military support for the Salvadoran government, but are by no means limited to these issues. For instance, in his fifth State of the Union Address on September 1, 1981, López Portillo harshly condemned the U.S. decision to produce the neutron bomb, lamented the demise of the Second Strategic Arms Limitation Treaty talks (SALT II), and decried the growing arms race between the two superpowers. The Caribbean, however, has been and remains the primary bone of contention.

In July 1981 Secretary of State Alexander Haig invited the foreign ministers of Mexico, Venezuela, and Canada to meet with him in the Bahamas to discuss ways of achieving greater coordination of their aid activities in the crisis-ridden Caribbean Basin. These countries were singled out by Haig because they were the only hemispheric nations with assistance programs in the area amounting to $100 million or more.

By convoking these regional powers—subsequently labeled the Nassau Group—the Reagan administration hoped to achieve several objectives simultaneously. First, smarting from criticism that his tendency to perceive Caribbean affairs in terms of East-West competition was grossly simplistic, President Reagan announced in May 1981 that the United States was moving to address the area's economic deficiencies. The Nassau meeting provided him the opportunity to showcase his "mini-Marshall Plan"—later called the Caribbean Basin Initiative (CBI)—and thereby demonstrate that he was pursuing sophisticated, multifaceted policies toward the region. Also, aware that U.S. resources alone were insufficient to meet the Basin's pressing needs, the White House apparently hoped that the Nassau Group would increase the flow of aid without Washington having to foot the entire bill. Finally, the administration viewed the Nassau Group as a potential vehicle for rallying hemispheric solidarity against Soviet-Cuban expansionism. Indeed the mini-Marshall Plan was prompted as a necessary response to socio-economic problems that "Cuba and others seek to exploit through terrorism and subversion."[15]

While all three nations agreed to send delegations to Nassau, their initial reactions to Washington's proposals varied widely. The Venezuelans were enthusiastic; the Canadians were willing to listen, but were noncommittal; and the Mexicans decided to attend, but expressed grave reservations about the direction that the program might take, especially given what they viewed as Reagan's obsession with Cold War warrioring. From the outset the Mexicans demanded guarantees that the plan would not contain any military element; that it would not be used as a political instrument to fight against Cuba, the Soviet Union, or Communism; and that no country in the region (i.e., Cuba, Nicaragua, or Grenada) would be automatically excluded.

Following the conference, Mexican Foreign Minister Jorge Castañeda made it clear that his government had not agreed to accept or to participate in Reagan's scheme, but only to study it further. Moreover, he stressed that Mexico would maintain its cordial relations with Nicaragua and Cuba. Both Venezuela and Canada welcomed the initiative as a positive step and promised to explore possibilities for future cooperation, although Ottawa was wary of the plan's political thrust. Meanwhile Washington embarked on a series of bilateral consultations with Caribbean and Central American regimes to get a better idea of their needs and priorities. The result was the CBI, which was launched by President Reagan in a speech before the Organization of American States in February 1982.

In general, the CBI was favorably received by the intended recipients. Both Mexico and Venezuela, however, pointed out that its $350 million in emergency aid for fiscal year 1982 was too little for such a large nation like the United States to give, especially since they (both much smaller and poorer countries) had each committed roughly the same amount in regional aid. Some critics also noted that the lion's share of the emergency assistance was going to El Salvador and that the plan excluded Cuba, Nicaragua, and Grenada. The $350 million was quickly disbursed, but the Reagan administration proved unable to secure Congressional passage of the CBI's trade and investment provisions in 1982, and the measure died.

Washington's inability to elicit greater support from its Latin Allies in the Nassau Group derived from its unwillingness to abandon its hegemonic aspirations in the Caribbean Basin. This situation was exacerbated by Reagan's unilateral actions there during 1981–82 and a growing sense in Mexico, Venezuela, Colombia, and other countries that his hardline approach was itself a major cause of tension. Also, friction with each of these regional powers further limited the possibilities for cooperation.

Frustrated leaders in Mexico have watched in alarm as the levels of conflict in Central America have risen steadily. They fear that without negotiations, the area will inevitably sink deeper into chaos. Certainly the Salvadoran civil war has ground grimly on despite the March 1982 elections there and substantial Pentagon assistance. U.S.-sponsored covert actions have bled the Sandinistas and obliged them to adopt an increasingly repressive political/economic model at home and to align with Cuba and the Soviet Union abroad. While not driving the Sandinistas from power, Reagan's policies have heightened tensions between Nicaragua and Honduras and run the risk of precipitating open hostilities between them. The administration has also been financing a military buildup in Honduras that threatens to bring the armed forces back to power. It is doubtful that Guatemala's U.S.-backed regime led by General Rios Montt will be able to pacify the country or create a stable political system. More likely is an intensification of the civil war there and, inevitably, a growing refugee problem for adjoining Mexico.

The widespread perception in Mexico that Reagan's policies simply were not working was compounded by events elsewhere in Latin America during 1982. In retrospect the Falklands/Malvinas war was a watershed episode that clearly alienated Mexico and many other Latin American countries from the United States. Also, Washington's less-than-enthusiastic response to pleas for an expansion of IMF and World Bank lending capacity during 1981 and most of 1982 was particularly inept, given that it had to retreat from that position in late 1982 due to acute financial crises in Mexico, Brazil, and Argentina. Finally, the continuing international recession increased the area's already severe structural problems and heightened economic tensions with the United States.

The Reagan administration's reaction to its difficulties with the Nassau Group and particularly to Mexico's "unhelpful" attitude has been to try to create other subregional forums wherein Mexico would play little or no role. Accordingly the White House promoted the establishment of the Central American Democratic Community (CADC) composed of such relatively malleable countries as Costa Rica, Honduras, and El Salvador. Venezuela and Colombia, along with the Dominican Republic, Jamaica, and the United States, participated as observers at the organization's first meeting in February 1982 where the upcoming March 1982 Salvadoran elections were endorsed. But the Falklands/Malvinas war, U.S. pressure to admit the Rios Montt regime, and criticism from nonmembers like Mexico and Nicaragua led to the CADC's virtual dissolution in late 1982.

In contrast to Washington's hardline approach, the Mexicans have consistently sought to defuse the explosive situation in Central America by seeking negotiated settlements. Contrary to the claims of many North American conservatives, López Portillo was not trying to install radical, Marxist-Leninist governments in the Basin. In fact, his policies were designed to modify the virulence of the Sandinista revolution and the leftist insurgency in El Salvador and to prevent the regionalization of Caribbean conflicts. Mexico's preferred outcome throughout the area is either pluralist democracies or "left-wing PRIs" (that is, regimes similar to Mexico's one-party-dominant system that would be moderately revolutionary, moderately pluralist, not aligned with either superpower, and tolerant of mixed economies). Confronted with the choice between right-wing governments like the Somoza dictatorship in Nicaragua, D'Aubuisson in El Salvador, or Lucas Garcia in Guatemala, the Mexicans have consistently favored discussions with the leftist opposition and power-sharing formulas over the perpetuation of repressive systems. Such policies are not adopted lightly nor are they the result of momentary flashes of anti-Americanism or sudden surges of machismo. Among the limited alternatives available the Mexicans have opted for those that they believe will facilitate long-term stability in the region at the least cost to themselves.

Following the Falklands/Malvinas war, Venezuela joined Mexico in launching a Central American peace probe. On September 15, 1982, the two countries sent identical diplomatic notes to Honduras, Nicaragua, and the United States calling on them to negotiate their outstanding differences. Subsequently Panama endorsed this proposal, and a bipartisan group of 106 members of the U.S. House of Representatives urged President Reagan to respond positively to it.

Of course Washington's willingness to cooperate in these or any other discussions regarding Central America remains the key to their ultimate success, as the Mexicans are well aware. But indications are that President Reagan will not enter into such talks unless Nicaragua first meets his preconditions. In response to the Mexican-Venezuelan suggestion, he announced that he had sent letters to both López Portillo and Venezuelan President Luis Herrera Campins expressing his "great interest" in their "very constructive" recommendations for a negotiated settlement of the Nicaraguan-Honduran problem. But in subsequent clarifications State Department officials made it abundantly clear that the United States felt the Mexican-Venezuelan plan dealt with "only one aspect of the regional problem." They also declared that the White House preferred the verifiable and reciprocal accord outlawing arms trafficking, subversion, and foreign military and security advisors in the entire area recommended by a group of Caribbean Basin countries in San José, Costa Rica, just two weeks after the Mexican-Venezuelan proposal.[16]

Reagan's objection to the Mexican-Venezuelan plan was that it did not address the problem of Nicaraguan subversion in Central America or Cuban and Soviet bloc backing for such activities. His advisors also contended that the joint proposal did not address the Sandinista's growing totalitarianism; that is, their refusal to permit moderate opposition leaders to participate in the governance of the country. The administration's endorsement of the San José alternative was justified on the grounds that "any meaningful attempts to address the problems of Central America must be within a regional context that achieves 'democratic pluralism' and an 'end to support for terrorist and insurgent' groups in other countries of the region."[17]

Neither Reagan's noncommittal response to the Mexican-Venezuelan proposal nor his government's endorsement of the San José plan represented any real change in Washington's basic approach to the region or its determination to turn back what it views as a wave of Communist-inspired subversion in Central America. Reagan did not reject the Mexican-Venezuelan plan out-of-hand because he was under increasing pressure, both domestic and international, to adopt a more flexible attitude toward negotiated settlements. He was also anxious to keep channels of communication open with President-elect de la Madrid prior to their first meeting on October 8, 1982, in the hope that he could divert the incoming Mexican president's foreign policy away from support for Nicaragua and for leftist insurgents elsewhere in Central America. Washington still maintains that the door is open to negotiations with Managua, but only if the Sandinistas first alter their unacceptable behavior within and outside Nicaragua's borders. The Sandinistas have repeatedly replied that they are willing to discuss all outstanding issues with the United States, but without preconditions on either side.

Given this impasse, the Reagan administration is unlikely to agree to talks with the Sandinistas any time soon. (The Hondurans, after consulting Washington, have also refused to negotiate their differences directly with Managua.)[18] Much more probable is an intensification of the war of attrition currently being conducted against Nicaragua by opposition groups based in Honduras. Covert CIA support for these anti-Sandinista forces is common knowledge, and while the extent of Honduran governmental involvement in these destabilization efforts remains unclear, some degree of complicity is apparent because the *contras* continue to operate from Honduran soil unimpeded and no arrests or captures have taken place.

Ultimately the Reagan administration would like to force the Sandinistas to accept negotiations on U.S. terms or to overthrow them altogether. Washington will probably continue to endorse diplomatic solutions publicly, for politically it cannot afford to do otherwise. But little progress can be expected unless either the United States or Managua radically alters its position. Without such discussions present Reagan policies clearly heighten the possibility of a war between Honduras and Nicaragua that could spread throughout the region.

Faced with open-ended escalation of the violence in Central America and what they perceived as a misguided and intransigent Reagan administration, the Mexicans have distanced themselves from Washington and have promoted Latin cooperation in a search for negotiated settlements to the Basin's conflicts. In this context, the January 1983 meeting in Contadora, Panama, to which Mexico, Venezuela, Colombia, and Panama (but *not* the United States) were invited, was symbolically important despite its failure to produce any concrete formulas for regional peace.

Although Assistant Secretary of State Thomas Enders declared that Washington was not at all upset about being so ignored, such developments cannot be viewed with equanimity in the Reagan White House. Yet the joint Mexican-Venezuelan proposal of September 1982, the Contadora meeting in January 1983, and Costa Rica's call in March 1983 for a peace conference that specifically excluded the United States all suggest that an exclusionary trend may be emerging. Enders went to some lengths to deny that interpretation, stating that Washington was "pleased to see the countries of the region taking responsibilities for the grave problems of the region." An aide added that "we see this as a logical continuation of the San José talks begun at the meeting in Costa Rica last October 4 [1982]."[19] But clearly these initiatives contain implicit challenges to U.S. hegemony in the Basin. Certainly if a Latin American summit would recommend a Mexican-style settlement in Central America, there is little reason to believe that the Reagan administration would agree to go along with it. Consequently Washington would become even more isolated within the hemisphere, and the chances for a serious rupture in its relations with Mexico and a number of other Latin American countries would be enhanced.

Upon her return from a trip through Central America in February 1983, UN Ambassador Jeane Kirkpatrick submitted a sober assessment of the situation in El Salvador and the rest of the region and urged Reagan to launch a major economic aid program there similar to the European-oriented Marshall Plan, which she characterized as "a response to a regional problem that was simultaneously economic, social and military. That was a highly successful use of American strength."[20] Clearly she felt that the United States must reassert its power—its hegemony—in the Basin to prevent the spread of Russian-Cuban influence and Marxist-Leninist regimes and to protect Washington's global posture. "Ultimately," she said, "I am concerned about the potential strategic threat to the United States that a strong Soviet military presence in the Caribbean and Central America would constitute, and what it does to our ability to act elsewhere in the world."[21] A few weeks after her alarming report and only twelve hours after Pope John Paul had concluded an eight-day Caribbean tour in which he called for "dialogue, not violence," Reagan sent a request to Congress for expanded military aid for El Salvador.

The Mexicans, along with Venezuela and Colombia, have continued to seek Latin American solutions to Latin American problems and have declared their willingness to share responsibility for guaranteeing stability in the region. But because Washington seriously doubts their capacity to safeguard U.S. interests, it has remained unwilling to entrust to them "the effort to stop the advance of Communism" in the Caribbean Basin.[22]

Conclusion

During the last few months of López Portillo's tenure, U.S.-Mexican relations reached one of their tensest points in post–World War II history. Mexico's economic collapse prompted mutual recriminations, with López Portillo bitterly denouncing the international economic system, the world banking community, and the Reagan administration's policies (i.e., high interest rates and recession) for reducing his nation's growth potential while the White House pushed Mexico to accept an IMF austerity program. Although de la Madrid has eased some of these strains by proceeding with the IMF plan, and Washington has provided substantial assistance, the probability of future U.S.-Mexican crises nevertheless remains high.

With the continuing slide in world petroleum prices, Mexico's economic problems will get worse even if there is a mild U.S. recovery. The U.S. government and U.S. banks as well as the multilateral lending institutions will have to provide billions more in order to keep Mexico from defaulting on its foreign debt. Beyond rescheduling the $20 billion in short-term loans that it now owes them, the international banks working with Mexico have been under pressure from the IMF to lend the country $5 billion in new money to complement the IMF's $4-billion emergency package. As the price for doing so, the 530 banks involved (including 170 U.S. institutions) have demanded premium interest rates and stiff special fees totaling more than $800 million: $600 million on the old loans and $200 million on the new ones. Although such profiteering increases the chances for ultimate bankruptcy, no other practical alternative is presently available to Mexicio.

While Washington has given the Mexicans badly needed economic assistance, they have not been especially grateful for it because they believe that the United States has primarily been defending its own interests, striking in the process sweetheart deals on Mexican oil for its Special Petroleum Reserve and on Mexican grain purchases from U.S. farmers. Such sentiments have been reinforced by intense disagreement with Reagan's hard-line approach to Central America and the Caribbean. Indeed the fear, resentment, and frustrations that these foreign policy differences have aroused in Mexico have prevented Washington from reaping much credit for its economic aid. Unless the Reagan administration modifies its position by accepting negotiations in El Salvador and opening a sincere dialogue with Nicaragua, the conflicts in the Basin are almost certain to intensify and thereby further strain U.S.-Mexican relations.

There is, however, little that Mexico can do to alter Washington's Caribbean posture. Internal economic problems will inevitably limit the resources that President de la Madrid will be able to dedicate to foreign policy objectives without severely shortchanging domestic priorities. Mexico's relative economic and military weakness vis-à-vis the U.S. and the overwhelming importance of its bilateral relationship with its northern neighbor leave it without much leverage. The Mexicans can continue to offer their services as mediators and attempt to influence the Reagan administration by enlisting the support of other Latin American nations behind proposals for negotiated settlements, but without a major shift in Washington, the prospects for a successful political solution in Central America are zero.

Notes

1. Following Robert Keohane and Joseph Nye, dependence is defined here as "the state of being determined or significantly affected by external forces." Conversely, interdependence means "mutual dependence"; it refers to situations characterized by "reciprocal effects" among countries or among actors in different countries. Interdependent relations always involve costs because interdependence inevitably restricts autonomy. Nothing, however, guarantees that interdependent relationships will be mutually beneficial. Indeed less dependent actors can often use the interdependent relationship as a source of power. For a discussion of these concepts, see Robert Keohane and Joseph Nye, *Power and Interdependence: World Politics in Transition* (Boston: Little, Brown and Company, 1977), pp. 8–11.

2. Ibid., p. 44.

3. It is important to recognize that not all groups in Mexico share these common assumptions. Ties with U.S. interests make many Mexican businessmen more pro-U.S. than their political counterparts (as does their fear of Communism). Thus far their dissenting voices have not been heard very loudly in Mexican foreign-policy circles, although some observers believe that they may force President de la Madrid to moderate his support for Nicaragua. Other analysts maintain that elements of the Mexican armed forces also depart from the consensus because of their growing anxiety about possible spillover effects from the Central American conflict (especially those in Guatemala and El Salvador).

4. For analyses of U.S.-Mexican relations from the "interdependence" perspective, see David F. Ronfelt and Caesar Sereseres, "The Management of U.S.-Mexican Interdependence: Drift Toward Failure?" (Santa Monica: Rand Corporation, 1978), p. 72; Gale W. McGee, "A U.S. Perspective" in Richard D. Erb and Stanley R. Ross (eds.), *U.S. Policies Toward Mexico: Perceptions And Perspectives* (Washington, D.C.: American Enterprise Institute, 1979), pp. 40–45; and Robert H. McBride, "The United States and Mexico: The Shape of the Relationship" in Robert H. McBride (ed.), *Mexico and the United States* (Englewood Cliffs, N.J.: Prentice-Hall, 1981), pp. 1–30.

5. Mexican dependency is examined by Carlos Rico, "Las relaciones México-Norteamericanas y los significados de la interdependencia," *Foro Internacional,* vol. 20, no. 2 (October–December 1978), pp. 342–362; and Rosario Green, "Mexico's Economic Dependence," in Susan Kaufman Purcell (ed.), *Mexico-United States Relations. Proceedings of the American Academy of Political Science,* vol. 34, no. 1 (1981), pp. 104–114.

6. *New York Times* (September 26, 1982), p. A4, reported the flight of more than 40,000 Guatemalan refugees into Mexico over the preceding twelve months. On the refugee problem in Guatemala, see *New York Times* (September 12, 1982), p. E3; (September 15, 1982), p. A2; and (October 6, 1982), p. A2.

7. On the linkage between domestic politics and foreign policy, see Olga Pellicer de Brody, *México y la Revolución Cubana* (Mexico City: El Colegio de México, 1972); Olga Pellicer de Brody, "Tercermundismo del capitalismo mexicano: Ideología e realidad," *Cuadernos Políticos,* no. 3 (1975), pp. 52–59;

and Yoram Shapira, "La política exterior de México bajo el regimen de Echeverría: Retrospectiva," *Foro Internacional,* vol. 19, no. 1 (July–September 1978), pp. 62–91.

8. *Washington Post* (August 29, 1982), p. A14.

9. Ibid. See also *New York Times* (September 12, 1982), p. F26.

10. Ibid., p. F26.

11. *Washington Post* (August 29, 1982), p. A14.

12. *Wall Street Journal* (April 2, 1982), p. 27; (August 9, 1982), p. 17; and (September 28, 1982), p. 30; *New York Times* (October 10, 1982), pp. F1, F28; *Washington Post* (August 21, 1982), pp. A1, A4; and (August 29, 1982), pp. A1, A14.

13. *Wall Street Journal* (August 20, 1982), p. 22; (August 24, 1982), p. 35; and (August 30, 1982), pp. D1, D5.

14. To signal its concern over the Mexican economic crisis and the failure of the López Portillo administration to reach an agreement with the IMF, in mid-September 1982 President Reagan sent National Security Advisor William Clark to Mexico to see if de la Madrid would go along with the belt-tightening measures demanded by the International Monetary Fund and other lenders [*Wall Street Journal* (September 16, 1982), p. 35].

15. U.S. State Department, "Background On The Caribbean Basin Initiative," Special Report No. 97, p. 1.

16. *New York Times* (October 7, 1982), p. A7.

17. *Latin American Weekly Report* (October 15, 1982), p. 2.

18. President Suazo Cordova responded that he was too busy to attend a meeting with Nicaragua's Daniel Ortega set for October 13, 1982 in Caracas, "raising the question whether he now opposed the idea of direct negotiations" [*New York Times* (October 10, 1982), p. A6]. In subsequent conversations held in the United Nations under the auspices of Secretary General Javier Perez de Cuellar, the foreign ministers of Honduras (Edgardo Paz Barnica) and Nicaragua (Miguel D'Escoto Brockman) agreed that their respective defense ministers would hold direct talks in an effort to settle their outstanding disputes, but this meeting resolved nothing. It was also reported that Honduran President Cordova had agreed conditionally to meet with Sandinista leader Ortega if the "foreign ministers from the four countries [Mexico, Venezuela, Nicaragua, and Honduras], the rest of Central America and the leading Caribbean countries agree first on an agenda" [*New York Times* (October 12, 1982), p. A4]. Such conditions were, of course, a delaying tactic.

19. *New York Times* (March 6, 1983), p. A12.

20. Ibid., pp. A1, A11.

21. "Reagan Sounds the Alarm," *Newsweek* (March 14, 1983), p. 22.

22. *New York Times* (March 13, 1983), p. E4.

8

The Politics of Developmentalism: U.S. Policy Toward Jamaica

Jacqueline Anne Braveboy-Wagner

The election of President Reagan marked an important change in Washington's foreign policy, resulting in a more polarized view of the world. This change has had ramifications for U.S. political and economic relationships with the Third World in general and with the Caribbean in particular. This chapter focuses on the characteristics of recent U.S. developmental policy, with particular attention to Jamaica, the island nation singled out by President Reagan to be the showpiece of modernization in the Caribbean.

The United States and the Third World

Beginning in the late 1970s and especially after the inauguration of President Reagan, U.S. foreign policy became more security-conscious and anti-Soviet. Under the Carter administration there had been some flexibility toward the developing nations rooted in a recognition that their nationalism, though often garbed in the guise of socialism, did not equal Communism, that their prime concern was with economic development and self-reliance after hundreds of years of colonial and neocolonial domination, that this necessitated experimenting with different strategies, culling from the experience of both East and West, and that global interdependence was such that the United States could not afford to ignore these concerns.

In the spirit of accommodation, the Carter administration's policy seemed to be one of "affirmative involvement and support for the independence and diversity of developing nations."[1] It gave substantial aid for reconstruction and development to a Sandinist-dominated Nicaraguan regime—one important example of its departure from the traditional U.S. stance of helping only friendly Third World regimes (particularly in Latin America). Moreover, though always recalcitrant, the Carter White House made certain concessions to southern nations such as concluding commodity agreements (on a case-by-case basis) and participating in an Integrated Programme for Commodities, both of which were strongly desired by Third World states in order to stabilize their crucial export trade. Washington also extended more credit and aid to less developed countries (LDCs) through increased developmental assistance, relaxed quotas, and supplementary financing arrangements within multilateral institutions.

At the same time it must be added that the differences between the various U.S. administrations in the development field have been those of degree, not kind. For instance, under Nixon the Generalized System of Preferences (GSP), which gave special treatment to selected LDCs and products, was negotiated. Also, President Ford entered the North-South dialogue after realizing that southern unity was not as ephemeral as originally thought and that the United States was becoming isolated in its opposition even among northern nations. Similarly President Carter did not really abandon the basic principles that have long guided U.S. foreign policy (i.e., support for pluralistic democracy and for the liberal economic model). Indeed his economic program was not necessarily sympathetic to the Third World; for example, quotas were imposed on sugar and other commodities with adverse affects on producer nations. Also, like President Reagan, Carter strongly opposed the global economic negotiations being pushed by the Third World on the grounds that such talks could subvert the role of the existing multilateral institutions dominated by the United States. Finally, the Reagan administration has already reversed its negative stand on quota increases and agreed to a 50 percent increase in the resources of the International Monetary Fund (IMF).

In short, there has been remarkable continuity in U.S. policy on these matters. However, what has changed across time is Washington's relationship with the Soviet Union and the degree to which administrations are willing to use both financial and military resources to counter perceived Russian influence and promote U.S. aims in the Third World. Political questions have inevitably been linked to developmental policy, affecting the level and type of aid offered to LDCs and the degree of U.S. tolerance for Third World experimentation with noncapitalist strategies of modernization.

Although the Carter administration initially exhibited considerable flexibility regarding the developing nations, by the late 1970s the Soviet invasion of Afghanistan and perceived Cuban intervention in the Ca-

ribbean and Central America had moved Carter toward a more rigid
posture involving increased emphasis on military assistance. Reagan
has expanded this policy. For the Third World this has meant a return
to decreased choice in developmental experimentation, at least if U.S.
economic aid, which is much greater in absolute terms than that of
other nations, is to be expected. In fact, an actively supportive foreign
policy is now a definite prerequisite for such U.S. help. But what
distinguishes Reagan's policy is the degree to which it has returned to
the Cold War practice of linking liberal democracy to development and
development to emulation of the U.S. model of free enterprise. Washington's ends are served by Third World Development if it is based
on the ideals of private enterprise (local and foreign), free trade, and
external assistance that serves primarily to stimulate trade and investment, which in turn generates income for development. This Westernized
(U.S.) paradigm is concerned with expansion in production. The benefits
of such growth are assumed to trickle down to the poor, with minimal
state intervention needed domestically or internationally. Rostow's five
well-known stages of development show how the process is supposed
to work:

1. *Traditional Society*—characterized by pre-Newtonian science
and technology with a very high proportion of resources devoted
to agriculture.
2. *The Precondition for Take-off*—characterized by the translation of scientific discovery into technological progress and, in
the non-Western world, by the intrusion of more advanced societies.
3. *The Take-off*—the resistance to growth is finally overcome
with increases in investment, industrial expansion, and commer-
cialization of agriculture.
4. *The Drive Towards Maturity*—when output regularly outstrips
the increase in population.
5. *The Age of Mass Consumption*—when leading sectors shift
towards durable consumer goods and services.[2]

Apart from stressing technological growth and market relations, the
scheme is internationally diffusionist, proposing that modernization
spreads from developed to developing societies and, within Third World
countries, from the modern to the traditional sectors. Development is
seen as requiring the stimulus of certain material inputs, mainly capital
and technology, from the advanced industrial nations, as transmitted
through foreign investment and assistance.[3] Such a model is diametrically
opposed to the "dependency" school of thought popular in the Third

World, which stresses the distortions created by too much reliance on foreign aid and investment, by the inequalities of the international trading system that favors northern manufactured products, and by strategies that do not specifically address problems of social inequality.[4]

Dependency viewpoints have been reflected in Third World moves to diversify trading partners and aid donors; control the operations of transnational corporations; increase commodity power, including cartelization and producer-consumer associations; and expand the access of LDC manufactures to markets in developed countries. Furthermore, the simplified view of the role of aid implied in the Rostow model is out of touch with a world in which recession, inflation, and high energy prices have caused massive borrowing by Third World nations to meet ever-growing current account deficits. In other words, the links between aid and trade have been obscured by the problems of excessively high debt service and inability to repay loans on time. The Reagan administration has recognized these problems to some extent by agreeing to expand the resources of the IMF, but its basic orientation has remained unchanged. Thus it has emphasized:

1. *The Primacy of the Market in Development.* According to a report by the staff of the Overseas Development Council, Reagan has been committed to "a strong emphasis on the present and potential role of private enterprise and market forces in relations with the Third World. This position is linked to the administration's frequently articulated belief that the United States experience is a relevant model for successful Third World development."[5] Before the 1980 election, Reagan stated that "a strong America and the spirit of our free enterprise system have a great deal to offer the poor, less developed nations of the world. . . . Investment from the private sector is the key to development."[6] Thus at the important Cancun summit of twenty-two northern and southern leaders and later, he put forward a view stressing that "more than [by receiving] aid and government intervention . . . nearly all of the countries that have succeeded in their development over the past 30 years have done so on the strength of market-oriented policies and vigorous participation in the international economy. Aid must be complemented by trade and investment."[7] At Cancun, Treasury Secretary Donald Regan also noted that "trade is what the [Third World] needs. In two years our trade with non-OPEC, less developed nations is equal to the aid that's been given by the various institutions in 36 years."[8] Finally, the administration's diffusionist views are reflected in Reagan's belief that "the answer to the problems of the developing countries lies in the recovery of the developed economies. 'Stay the course' has therefore become the message to the Third World as well as to the American people."[9]

2. *Preference for Bilateralism.* The Reagan administration has exhibited a "clear preference for bilateral development assistance programs over those of the multilateral institutions in which the United States has been a leader since World War II."[10] Bilateralism has, of course, always been the preferred mechanism for U.S. official aid, accounting for over 90 percent of assistance in the 1960s and varying between 61 and 87 percent in the 1970s,[11] and Reagan has accentuated that proclivity, spurred on by his heightened concern for security matters. Bilateral aid has always been useful as a vehicle to obtain political ends. In the 1950s and 1960s, it was seen as means of countering Communist influence in the Third World and promoting democracy, stability, development, and friendship. Although these goals proved beyond reach, such assistance has remained tied to strategic aims. Thus Israel and Egypt alone have in recent years accounted for almost half of all U.S. aid. Even President Carter used assistance politically to encourage democracy and human rights (except in strategically located countries). Economic aid has also remained tied to U.S. business interests, with the 1962 Hickenlooper amendment barring help to countries that nationalize U.S. industries without compensation.

3. *Downgrading of Multilateral Institutions.* Along with increased bilateralism has come reduced multilateralism. Carter generally supported appropriate increases in the resources available to international institutions in order to help LDCs out of their severe economic difficulties. But Reagan reduced contributions to such organizations, perceiving them as "out of control" and perhaps even acting outside the interests of the United States. In fact, his administration cracked down on both the World Bank and the IMF against extending what it considers unnecessary credit. In addition to these major institutions, subsidiary organizations have suffered. A particular case has been the International Fund for Agricultural Development (IFAD), created in 1977 and financed by both OPEC and the West. President Carter authorized substantial funding for the fund's first two years, but subsequently the new Reagan administration called for halving the U.S. contribution.

Overall, Reagan's view has been that other developed nations and OPEC countries should pick up the slack caused by U.S. cutbacks. However, reduction has not always been the case. Recognizing that the major problems that LDCs are having with debt repayment have repercussions for the world economy, Washington approved an increase in the IMF's resources. Treasury Secretary Regan has even called for a new institution capable of responding quickly to the needs of nations in such difficulties. Also, Washington has clearly favored increasing the multilateral resources available to countries with which it shares a common interest. Thus the administration has pressured the IMF to grant loans on easier terms to nations like Jamaica and Brazil. Such favoritism has been extremely important given the cutbacks in private loans to LDCs: IMF agreement to lend to a country generally guarantees that private banks will also be supportive. Finally, the U.S. would like to strengthen, not reduce, the operations of the International Finance Corporation (IFC), a position perfectly in accord with Reagan's views on private enterprise. The IFC is the World Bank's affiliate that helps to raise loan and equity capital and normally assists private investors in establishing themselves in member states.

The United States and the Caribbean Basin

The Latin American/Caribbean region, situated as it is in the U.S. sphere of influence, has special strategic and political importance to Washington as well as economic significance. In the mid-1970s, 81 percent of U.S. foreign investment was in Latin America,[12] and one policymaker noted in 1979 that

Latin America is the source of one out of every six barrels of oil we import. Our exports to the area have tripled since 1967 to almost $20 billion annually. We now sell more machinery, consumer goods and chemicals to Latin America than to the rest of the Third World combined. Three nations—Mexico, Brazil, and Venezuela—are among our top dozen trading partners.[13]

The Caribbean Basin has been described over and over again in the last few years as vital to the United States both for economic and political reasons. Investment there amounts to a relatively small $10 billion and, except for bauxite and oil, the region provides few crucial commodities. But as President Reagan noted, "nearly half of our trade, two-thirds of our imported oil and over half of our imported strategic minerals pass through the Panama Canal or the Gulf of Mexico."[14]

Given all the above, it is somewhat puzzling that Washington has devoted so little energy to hemispheric developmental concerns. For example, compared with other Third World regions, Latin America ranks last in bilateral economic and military aid.[15] To a large extent the low and declining level of bilateral assistance has been attributed to the fact that the area overall is at a higher stage of modernization than Afro-Asia and is therefore more dependent on trade and investment opportunities and on private and multilateral financing for development. But this certainly does not apply to all hemispheric countries, especially those in the Caribbean Basin, and also ignores the uneven progress that characterizes even the most advanced nations such as Brazil and

Mexico. Moreover, the United States in the past has not instituted special measures aimed at liberalizing commerce with the region nor has it granted these states special trade financing.

The lack of attention that the United States has paid to Latin America is related to the fact that the area has generally been under firm U.S. control and has been relatively tranquil compared, for instance, to the Middle East, even though its stability has often masked oppression. U.S. policy has therefore centered on ad hoc measures. When the hemisphere shows signs of becoming agitated or yielding to left-wing pressures, a plan for increased assistance tends to be quickly formulated with either a bilateral or regional emphasis. Such was, of course, the Alliance for Progress, drawn up after the Cuban Revolution. But détente with the Soviet Union, along with Havana's isolation and preoccupation with domestic affairs, soon removed fears of Cuban intervention, and Washington lapsed again into a policy of benign neglect.

The Cuban problem, and hence the need for a new ad hoc program, surfaced again during the 1960s in the Basin, helped along by the pullout of the stabilizing British presence and the advent of black nationalism in the island Caribbean, and by rebellion against decades of U.S.-supported repression in Central America. We will deal specifically with the English-speaking Caribbean here.

When the so-called "Big Four" countries (Jamaica, Trinidad and Tobago, Guyana, and Barbados) gained their independence between 1962 and 1966, this at first presented no problems for Washington since the countries chose to adopt a pro-Western stance and a capitalist developmental strategy. Their decision amounted to a rejection of Third World (Afro-Asian) neutrality and ideological experimentation in favor of retaining the institutions and ideas left by British colonialism. The choice also rested strongly on geopolitical considerations. Small and economically dependent, emerging in a tight bipolar world, and under the intimidating shadow of the United States, these nations were not in a position to experiment. Added to this was the fact that, because of the gradual and peaceful nature of the transition to independence (except in Guyana), the cultural and psychological dependency inculcated by England prevented the development of the type of deep resentment against the colonizers (or neocolonialists) that produce ideological and nationalistic militancy.[16] Thus economic and political dependence on the British led naturally enough to dependence on the nearer United States.

The open-economy strategy based on private enterprise was followed not only because it was one of the legacies of colonialism, but also because it appeared to have produced remarkable results in nearby Puerto Rico, then the U.S. showpiece in the Caribbean. The failure of the model in both Puerto Rico (which ended with a so-called food-stamp economy and high emigration to the mainland) and in other areas of the Caribbean led to modifications in the 1970s. In Guyana, Jamaica, and Grenada the failure led to major changes in developmental policy. In essence, it was realized that uncontrolled capitalism generated, among other things, foreign domination of Third World economies and excessive dependence on external forces with a subsequent subrogation of political power; decapitalization by foreign private enterprise; an increase in imports with adverse affects on the balance of payments; the decline of agriculture with the growth of industry and urbanization; rising unemployment as people moved to the cities while capital-intensive industries and those with limited opportunity for expansion failed to produce enough jobs; more urban crime; and a widening of the gap between the elites and the masses, city and countryside, and workers and management.

To those who were interested, Cuba offered a socialist-oriented strategy as opposed to the capitalist model that was seen to have aggravated inequity in the Third World, if not the West.[17] It was true that its closed, state-economy approach had generated heavy dependence on the Soviet Union, a large and inefficient bureaucracy, and consumer shortages due to the emphasis on heavy industry and had failed to insulate the island against the problems caused by falling world prices of agricultural commodities, especially sugar. Also, the Sino-Guevarist focus on labor mobilization and moral incentives had produced, on the one hand, overemphasis on high production targets for sugar (targets that inevitably failed to be met) and, on the other, the growth of inefficiency, poor work habits, and antisocial behavior. But Cuba could offer relative technological advancement, broad successes in health, education, and housing, relief from unemployment, experience in agricultural collectivization and moderation of distorted patterns of land tenure, and the example of the social and political rewards of a mobilized society. Thus Havana's assistance was sought and received by several Caribbean governments, which, however, generally found a mixed-economy model more compatible with their needs.

The Carter administration reacted to the increased Cuban visibility in the English-speaking Caribbean and Central America by ceasing its attempts to find an accommodation with Havana and by establishing a stronger military/economic presence in the Basin. However, as Table 8.1 shows, Washington put more emphasis on official developmental assistance than on direct economic support (i.e., quickly disbursed and relatively unreviewed loans and grants for short-term economic emergencies that generally benefit the private sector). Reagan inherited the Cuban problem and also responded by increasing aid to the region,

TABLE 8.1
U.S. Aid To The Caribbean Basin*
   (millions of dollars)

	1980	1981	1982	1983
Developmental Assistance	225.0	168.4	211.1	217.6
(percent of total)	(66.6)	(35.8)	(21.2)	(28.2)
Direct Economic Support	15.2	143.4	490.0	326.0
Food Aid	83.7	108.7	123.1	120.9
Military Assistance	13.8	50.5	172.1	106.2
Total	337.7	471.0	996.3	770.7

*Loans and grants to Caribbean Basin nations. The figures
for 1982 come from the budget and include the CBI request.
The 1983 figures refer to requests.

Source: Reproduced from the New York Times
February 28, 1982), p. 1E. Original source is the State
Department. Percentages have been added.

but with strong emphasis on direct support programs. Development
assistance was reduced proportionately.

In his Caribbean Basin Initiative, Reagan asked for and received
emergency aid of $350 million in 1982 for economically hard-hit
countries, with most going to the private sector. El Salvador was the
main beneficiary, while Jamaica received $50 million and the Eastern
Caribbean was originally granted only $10 million. Congress subsequently
reduced El Salvador's share, allowing the difference to be distributed
among other countries (including an increase of $5 million to the Eastern
Caribbean). President Reagan noted that the money was needed to
enable countries to "put themselves in a starting position from which
they can begin to earn their own way. But this aid will encourage
private-sector activities, not displace them."[18] Although he targeted the
assistance toward meeting balance-of-payments problems and providing
credits for the private sector, Congress modified this, taking steps to
ensure that part of the funds would underwrite traditional development
projects in health, education, and infrastructure.[19]

In keeping with his private-enterprise emphasis, Reagan also presented
an innovative plan allowing duty-free entry into the United States for
twelve years for all products from the Basin except textiles and apparel,
which would, however, have more liberal quota arrangements. Although

he noted that 87 percent of the region's exports already enter the U.S. market free under the Generalized System of Preferences (GSP), he felt that they cover only the "limited range of existing products," not the "wide variety of potential products" the Caribbean people are capable of producing.[20] Goods could qualify for duty-free treatment only if 25 percent of the value is added in the area (as opposed to the 35 percent required under previous rules). Moreover, a domestic industry or company must prove it has suffered serious injury before imports from the Basin can be restricted, a significant loosening of the previous protection procedures. These recommendations ran into trouble in a protectionist Congress pressed by various labor interests. Consequently footware, handbags, petroleum products, leather apparel, and tuna fish were added to the list exempted from free-trade treatment by the time the measure was passed in the House. Sugar's eligibility was also limited according to U.S. market conditions in order to protect the domestic price-support program.

The duty-free provisions are intended, of course, to stimulate investment in the Basin. Before receiving duty-free treatment, countries are required to have bilateral discussions with the United States on their self-help measures and to gain Washington's approval. A second incentive is a 10 percent tax credit for any new investment made in the Caribbean by a U.S. company. Also, technical assistance and training is to be offered to help the private sector in Basin countries to benefit from the opportunities of the program, including "investment, promotion, export marketing and technology transfer efforts, as well as programs to facilitate adjustments to greater competition and production in agriculture and industry."[21] Finally, Reagan proposed to work with Mexico, Canada, and Venezuela to coordinate development efforts and to encourage assistance from Europe, Japan, other Asian allies, and multilateral development institutions.

A comprehensive discussion of the advantages and disadvantages of the plan would be far removed from the subject of this chapter, but it should be noted that the CBI has been attacked in both the United States and the Caribbean. The complaints in the United States have centered on the free-trade provisions, the contention being that thousands of jobs would be transferred out of the country. In the Basin and to some extent in the United States as well, there has been criticism of the program's heavy trade and investment orientation, the major charges being that commodity stabilization is more important, that most countries do not have the infrastructure necessary to attract investment and therefore public aid and public-sector involvement is more needed, and that local operations will be displaced by foreign companies. The low level of aid offered has also been denounced, as has the exemption of two of the region's most important and most economically troubled products—sugar and textiles—from duty-free status. There has also been trepidation that the plan's bilateral nature will give Washington too much decisionmaking control over the economic future of recipient countries. Finally, Caribbean leaders have expressed discontent about the lack of attention to the problems of individual countries, the lumping together of Central America and the Caribbean, the CBI's military aspects, and the exclusion for political reasons of Grenada and Nicaragua.[22]

Despite the criticisms the Reagan administration has been determined to make the CBI and related projects work to demonstrate the virtues of private enterprise and market relations, with Jamaica having been singled out as the centerpiece. In his address to the nation on the subject, Reagan noted approvingly that "after a decade of falling income and exceptionally high unemployment, Jamaica's new leadership is reducing bureaucracy, dismantling unworkable controls and attracting new investment. Continued outside assistance will be needed to tide Jamaica over until market forces generate large increases in output and employment, but Jamaica is making freedom work."[23]

Jamaican Developmental History and Relations with the United States

Selecting Jamaica as the CBI showpiece was entirely fortuitous, but certainly appropriate considering that it is among the most strategically and economically important Caribbean Basin countries to Washington. It is geographically close to both the United States and Cuba and could therefore serve as a fine counterpoint to the Marxist model that Cuba represents. It supplies approximately 76.5 percent of all bauxite used in the United States. And the United States is already Jamaica's largest trading partner.

The island also has solid democratic credentials, an important complement to the liberal economic model. Despite disturbances that produced a state of emergency during the elections of 1976 and political violence that claimed from 500 to 600 lives during the 1980 election campaign (not to mention rumors of a "military solution" prior to the voting), the democratic system has survived and with it a tradition of orderly transfers of power between the two main parties that is quite rare in the Third World. Reagan's 1980 triumph coincided fortuitously with the victory of the ideologically compatible Edward Seaga in Jamaica after a decade of socialist experimentation. Here, then, was a great opportunity for Washington to emphasize the contrast between the economic bankruptcy that Seaga inherited and the progress that ideally would be generated by the return to capitalist development.

As did other countries in the region, Jamaica chose an open economy after independence in 1962, and like them it later discovered the negative aspects of the model—the growth of dependence, urbanization, a widening of the gap between the masses and the elite, unemployment, the decline of agriculture as the bauxite industry grew, and the problem of uncontrolled exploitation by multinational corporations. But in 1962 these drawbacks were not foreseen. The basic development strategy then espoused by the ruling Jamaica Labour Party (JLP) was also approved by the opposition People's National Party (PNP), although the latter was more oriented toward social justice and state control. The JLP had its base in the peasantry and proletariat and concerned itself primarily with income distribution and workers' rights. On the other hand, the PNP had originated as a middle-class movement with a program centered on the constitutional and anticolonial struggle. Both, however, soon expanded their constituencies. The JLP, with its status-quo and procapitalist bent, gained the support of big business and of the upper class, while the PNP, the party of change, gained the support of the "informed and politicized sectors of the working class and small peasantry"[24] by espousing Fabian-type democratic socialism. Yet both organizations ended up dominated by the professional middle class.

Nevertheless the differences between the two parties had clearly sharpened by the 1970s. In its last years in office, the JLP had to face a rising tide of mass discontent and black nationalism. The PNP, led by Michael Manley, was able to harness some of this discontent by preaching egalitarianism and socialism and by identifying with the sufferers in the urban ghettos. In turn the PNP was radicalized by its new members—militant, urban, unemployed youths committed to black nationalism and a Third World/Africanist perspective. Indeed a 1977 poll found that more than 30 percent of PNP hard-core activists supported a Communist approach to the country's problems.[25] The level of anti-imperialist, anti-U.S. rhetoric being put out by the PNP leadership was high enough and its programs "socialist" enough that President Reagan could hail Seaga's victory in 1980 as bringing back Jamaica from "Communist rule."[26]

Under Manley the PNP's programs focused on increased political mobilization, more state involvement in the economy, and greater attention to immediate social problems. The PNP first antagonized the United States and the six foreign bauxite corporations operating in the island by its imposition of a production levy, its demand for participation in the industry, and its leading role in the creation of a bauxite cartel, the International Bauxite Association. The negative reaction of the companies and the world recession combined eventually to reduce Jamaica's bauxite revenues, although the levy yielded more than $900 million in the 1970s. The PNP also enlisted Cuba's help in building a large number of small dams to combat summer droughts, in constructing schools, in improving health care, and in modernizing agricultural and fishing techniques. The government nationalized public utilities, transportation, and several manufacturing enterprises; bought eight of the twelve big sugar estates; established collectives in agriculture; created a public works employment program; and tried to improve housing, notably by creating a National Housing Trust to finance an expansion program. Viewed separately, none of these moves was particularly radical. Indeed nearby capitalist-oriented Trinidad and Tobago adopted similar policies. But the level of societal mobilization and the accompanying foreign policy of militant nonalignment and Third World solidarity, tinged with a pro-Soviet, pro-Cuban stance, alarmed the United States.

Within Jamaica, political polarization and violence were increasing. In addition, the world recession was adversely affecting the tourist industry and prices for sugar and bauxite on the international market, oil costs were increasing and strong price competition in bauxite was coming from Australia—all of which led to severe balance-of-payments difficulties. Hurricanes and floods contributed to problems in agriculture. Socialist rhetoric and instability frightened away investors and caused the middle and upper classes to send their capital abroad. Imports were limited and production dropped, creating serious shortages. International loans (public and private) were not very forthcoming, given Jamaica's low credit rating; when the IMF did extend aid between 1977 and 1979, it insisted that the government institute an austerity plan that led to more price increases and import restrictions, reduction in buying power and real incomes, and growth in unemployment. The denouement of this economic nightmare is well known: Kingston rejected the terms of another proposed IMF loan in 1980 and found itself virtually bankrupt despite some help from Europe and Third World sources in Latin America and the Middle East. Worried and beleaguered Jamaicans then voted Manley and the PNP out of power in the early elections held in October 1980.

The U.S. role during this period is relevant to understanding the zeal with which it greeted the Seaga government. Initially Washington appeared to have been willing to give Kingston the benefit of the doubt as far as its developmental and foreign policies were concerned. For example, in 1976 the deputy assistant secretary for inter-American affairs vigorously denied reports that the United States was attempting to destabilize the Manley regime and asserted that the Jamaican democratic system is profoundly non-Communist, and the Jamaican government is still geared almost completely to trade with non-Communist countries. Its government faces serious social and economic problems, but we hope and trust that it will manage to deal effectively with these, at the same time preserving an open political system and close and friendly relations with the United States.[27]

The Carter administration's advent made relations easier, especially because it coincided with the rise of moderates within the PNP. Kingston accepted an IMF loan that it had initially rejected and appointed a more temperate new finance minister. Washington and the multilateral institutions dominated by it reciprocated with appropriate loans. But relations took a turn for the worse as conditions deteriorated in Jamaica and the United States exhibited rising concern about Cuba's involvement in the Basin. Thus in 1980 Washington's aid amounted to only $2.7 million in grants for small projects in agriculture, health, education, and population control. Also, the U.S.-dominated IMF refused to modify its stringent conditions for a Jamaican loan, which resulted in refusals by commercial banks to lend the island more money.

Seaga's triumph in the 1980 election was welcome news to the incoming Reagan administration because his procapitalist approach to development dovetailed nicely with the president's philosophy. Enhancing the relationship even more in Washington's eyes was the fact that Seaga quickly broke relations with Cuba, accusing Havana of meddling in the elections. (Whether either the United States or Cuba was actively involved in trying to influence the voting outcome remains unclear.) Despite Seaga's statement that he would pursue a balanced foreign policy, his visits in the next two years were only to such pro-Western countries as Venezuela, Australia, the Philippines, South Korea, Puerto Rico, Canada, and Antigua (along with several visits to the United States). This orientation helped him secure much-needed aid, including $700 million from the IMF's Extended Fund Facility for 1981–84 on terms that did not include devaluation or laying off workers in the private sector; $133.1 million from the World Bank in 1981–82, a threefold increase over the previous fiscal year, which made Jamaica the largest recipient of World Bank lending for fiscal year 1982; a pledge of $350 million from the World Bank–led Caribbean Group for Cooperation in Development for specific recovery projects; a loan of over $70 million from a syndicate of foreign banks; project loans from the Inter-American Development Bank and loans to Jamaican companies from the U.S. Overseas Private Investment Corporation (OPIC); refinancing of current debts from foreign banks; loans and credit lines from Venezuela, Great Britain, Sweden, Canada, and the U.S. Import/

Export Bank; and $112 million from the U.S. Agency for International Development (AID) for the fiscal year 1982, making Jamaica the second highest recipient of U.S. aid per capita after Israel.[28]

Also, Kingston established a National Investment Promotion Committee to facilitate local and foreign investment and joint ventures. Counterpart private-sector associations were organized in the United States, Britain, West Germany, Venezuela, Puerto Rico, and Canada to work for capital investment and transfer of technology to the island. The U.S. group, the U.S. Business Committee on Jamaica, is chaired by David Rockefeller and numbers among its twenty-five members such giants as Exxon Corporation, Chase Manhattan Bank, Eastern Airlines, the Atlantic Richfield Company, and the Bank of America. The committee reportedly enjoys unusual government support and access to President Reagan and senior officials. It soon concluded that pure private investment in the more traditional sense would not do the trick by itself, especially in the short run, and thus has pushed for Federal assistance to cooperating corporations. In an important recent case the General Services Administration, at President Reagan's behest, authorized the purchase of $67-million worth of Jamaican bauxite for the U.S. strategic stockpile, even though bauxite ranks low on its list of needed materials. Moreover OPIC, again with presidential encouragement, exceeded its limit on insurance by guaranteeing a $50-million loan against political risk such as war or expropriation to Kaiser, Reynolds, and Anaconda Aluminum Company to help them expand a jointly owned bauxite venture in Jamaica.[29]

The high level of aid and the willingness to take special measures underscores the importance the Reagan administration has assigned to Jamaican recovery and economic growth. In response Kingston has agreed on a development strategy that includes: reforms in the country's tax structure; deregulation and reduction of state ownership of companies (many of which are, in any case, inefficient); measures to increase agricultural production, including special assistance to the sugar cooperatives, reconstruction in the banana industry, and strengthening of extension services and marketing facilities; greater incentives in favor of exports and the gradual lifting of protection to some industries; loosening of import controls; credits to local businessmen; and promotion of private investment in the bauxite industry and in tourism.[30]

It is too soon to tell whether Jamaica will experience real recovery, despite some expansion of the Gross Domestic Product (GDP) and a decline in inflation. The prime minister predicted a 4 percent increase in the economy in 1982 (following a 2 percent gain in 1981), but this estimate proved too optimistic. In any event a high growth rate does not say much about a country's development. As Third World specialists have so often pointed out, income measures ignore the distribution of benefits and provide little insight into the structural characteristics of the economy. In the 1960s, for example, Jamaica's economy grew by 4.6 percent a year according to World Bank figures, but did so, as already noted, at the cost of increased economic dependence, agricultural deterioration, high urbanization, and unemployment. There are signs that the old model of an open economy (with some modifications toward state control) will be no more of a panacea in the 1980s than it was in the 1960s, especially given existing world recessionary conditions. Most importantly, the limits to bilateralism are more visible today, and there is a much clearer need for a global approach to the problems of Jamaican/Third World development.

Unlike the 1960s, which saw more money flowing into the extractive sector and banking, opportunities in the 1980s are oriented toward manufacturing. But companies are hesitant to invest in an area where labor and infrastructural conditions are not of the best and, perhaps more crucial, are unwilling to expand into risky or unnecessary ventures during a recession. The result has been less of an investment boom than either Jamaica or the United States anticipated. The *New York Times* reported that in the twelve months ending March 31, 1982, only eighteen new U.S. investments totaling $10 million had been made (despite the goal of attracting almost $700 million in three years). Six other commitments totaling $32 million had been approved but were not yet operative.[31] In fact, as a result of the low response, Jamaica reduced its requirements from local ownership from 51 percent, a JLP policy set in the 1960s, to 48 percent. Without adequate investment Jamaica's export thrust will suffer.

In the trade area the deficit has been widening, which to some extent has to be expected given increased imports in food and raw materials (which were in short supply during the last years of the Manley administration). But exports have not grown enough, the sugar and banana industries remain depressed, and bauxite production has been cut back (although the sale to the U.S. strategic stockpile was expected to bring mining levels in 1982 almost up to those of 1981). The trade deficit went up to $195.8 million in the first half of 1982, compared to $136.9 million during the same period in 1981. But tourism has revived, and a new regulation requiring visitors to pay in U.S. dollars for all but minor purchases and stipulating that Jamaican dollars must not be brought in or taken out of the island is expected to forestall black-market currency transactions and generate foreign exchange. The government has borrowed heavily to finance the recovery and the balance-of-payments deficits. This has raised concern about the size of the foreign debt, which stood at $1.3 billion in December 1982. International reserves remain negative, as all borrowing has been used to service the economy.

Even within a capitalistic framework social growth needs special attention. Thus Seaga has retained many features of the previous administration's policy. For example, the special works program has been modified but not eliminated, and the literacy agency established by the PNP (JAMAL) is continuing, with efforts redirected at illiteracy prevention and compulsory education at the primary-school level. But the major concerns of the man in the street during 1982 were the cost of living and unemployment. The latter, which rose to over 31 percent under Manley, was still above 25 percent, and the cost of living remained high. New U.S. investment created only 1,000 jobs at most, while about 250,000 people were estimated to be out of work. Certainly the mechanics of the marketplace are not solving these problems. In fact, as one researcher notes, "Mr. Seaga has not successfully addressed the economy's underlying structural problems. Tangible progress is usually equated with goods on the shelves, but most of the populace remains removed from modern capitalist enterprise, relying instead on peasant production, domestic jobs, street vending, begging and crime."[32] In other words the bulk of the population probably will not benefit from capitalist growth, if the example of the 1960s is taken.

The vulnerability of small economies, especially in a world recession, is an unavoidable fact of life. The problems confronting Kingston are similar to those being faced by numerous developing nations, and many of these difficulties are related to structural inequalities in the international economic system itself. For example, Jamaica has been trying since the 1960s to improve its agricultural performance. Neither the policies of the JLP nor those of the PNP have so far proved successful. This is because, like so many other LDCs, Jamaica depends for export revenue on a few traditional crops whose prices are subject to wide fluctuations on the world market, depending on supply and demand factors, many of which are beyond its control. Improvements in this area, then, can only be achieved by international commodity agreements that would prevent such instability. The price of sugar, for example, has gone from a high of 30 cents a pound in 1974 (up in that year from 7 cents) to well below ten cents (and still falling) in 1982. Similar problems affect the export of raw materials, despite greater national control among the LDCs of the operations of the multinationals and of efforts at cartelization.

The issue of developmental financing is also best tackled at the global level. This is a very difficult time for the newly industrializing countries, which have taken out loans to finance current account deficits and modernization programs and then have been unable to repay on time, thus creating enormous problems for the international economy. Kingston has been borrowing heavily and may find itself in the same bind. At this point it would probably have to face the same austerity planning that has been forced on such countries as Brazil and Mexico, possibly with political repercussions. Also, with Third World countries defaulting on their debts, U.S. investors have become exceedingly cautious in considering overseas ventures. Since Jamaica is so dependent on foreign assistance and a possible candidate for default, U.S. companies may hesitate to get involved there.

In any case, economic dependency opens the way to excessive political influence from the outside. Kingston's cozy relations with Washington could be problematic if Seaga, who does not want to mortgage the island's future, decides to pursue a path that the United States dislikes. The close ties also entail liabilities for Washington, whose concentration on Jamaica is not necessarily healthy for its larger Basin policy. Extending the island special treatment shows a lack of awareness of the subtleties of Caribbean politics. Gordon K. Lewis once noted that "the psychological isolationism of the Jamaica public mind and its corollary, the smug self-satisfaction and conviction of superiority . . . are to others, the least attractive facets of the Jamaican character."[33] Despite participation in the Caribbean community, Kingston's tendency has always been toward relative detachment from other countries of the region, which it has viewed as less advanced. This has been accompanied by a focus on the United States. It is logical to assume that the current renewed emphasis on Jamaica's U.S. connection would reinforce this isolationist sentiment and heighten its neighbors' latent hostility. The problem is all the greater because the area has become politically pluralist with the presence of socialist Grenada. Polarization, intensified by policies of exclusion and favoritism from abroad, is hardly conducive to Caribbean unity. Yet such unity is needed for the stability and development that the United States should and does desire.

Finally, whatever the current developmental bent of Jamaica (or the majority of the Caribbean nations), change is always highly probable and may lead, as in the past in Jamaica and Guyana, to experimentation that may not exactly conform to U.S. ideals. There is no reason to expect that the Jamaican tradition of democratic transition between JLP and PNP governments (generally a two-term turnover) has come to an end. With the PNP reorganizing to eliminate its ties with the Communists and to modify its rhetoric, it will surely be returned to power if the material advancement promised by Seaga is not forthcoming. While there is nothing wrong with a U.S. policy that supports a friendly capitalist Jamaica, the inability to see ahead could unnecessarily hamper good relations between Washington and Kingston and between the JLP and the PNP in the future. More realistic and farsighted American planning could avoid this.

Notes

1. Statement made by Secretary of State Cyrus Vance, quoted in Viron Vaky, Assistant Secretary of State for Inter-American Affairs, *State Department Bulletin* (April 1979), p. 57.

2. Walt W. Rostow, *The Stages of Economic Growth: A Non-Communist Manifesto* (Cambridge, Mass.: Cambridge University Press, 1960), pp. 4–11.

3. Susanne J. Bodenheimer, *The Ideology of Developmentalism: American Political Science's Paradigm Surrogate for Latin American Studies* (Beverly Hills: Sage Publications, 1971), p. 24.

4. Among dependency writers who exhibit widely differing orientations, see Ronald H. Chilcote and Joel C. Edelstein (eds.), *Latin America: The Struggle with Dependency and Beyond* (New York: John Wiley and Sons, 1974); Andre Gundar Frank, *Capitalism and Underdevelopment in Latin America: Historical Case Studies of Chile and Brazil* (New York: Monthly Review Press, 1969); and the policy-oriented Raul Prebisch, *Towards a Dynamic Development Policy for Latin America* (New York: United Nations, 1963).

5. Roger D. Hansen et al., *U.S. Foreign Policy and the Third World, Agenda 1982* (New York: Praeger Publishers, 1982), p. x.

6. Chau T. Phan, *World Politics, 81/82* (Guilford, Conn.: Dushkin Publishing Group, 1981), p. 13.

7. President Reagan repeated the views he expressed at Cancun in his address on the Caribbean Basin Initiative. See *New York Times* (February 25, 1982), p. A14.

8. *Newsweek* (October 26, 1982), p. 44.

9. Alan Riding, *New York Times* (December 6, 1982), p. D9.

10. Hansen et al., *U.S. Foreign Policy* (note 5 above), p. x.

11. Ibid., pp. 236, 239.

12. Martin M. McLaughlin et al., *The United States and World Development, Agenda 1979* (New York: Praeger Publishers, 1979), p. 263.

13. *State Department Bulletin* (April 1979), p. 56.

14. *New York Times* (February 25, 1982), p. A14.

15. Hansen et al., *U.S. Foreign Policy* (note 5 above), p. 243. The assessment is based on figures for fiscal years 1980 and 1981.

16. For an analysis of the changes that have taken place in the English-speaking Caribbean since 1962, see Jacqueline Braveboy-Wagner, "Changes in the English-Speaking Caribbean: An International Systems Perspective with Implications for the United States," *Caribbean Monthly Bulletin* (October 1981), pp. 50–64.

17. Although in the developed states there is a positive correlation between income distribution and GNP indicators (suggesting that wealth does trickle down), this is not the case in developing societies where the economic and social structures that facilitate such "trickle-down" are not operative.

18. *New York Times* (February 25, 1982), p. A14.

19. *New York Times* (May 20, 1982), p. A20.

20. *New York Times* (February 25, 1982), p. A14.

21. Ibid.

22. See, for example, Alan Riding, "Caribbeans Weigh New Offer Against Experience," *New York Times* (February 28, 1982); Robert Henriques Girling, "CBI: A Basket To Carry Water?" *Caribbean Contact* (November 1982); Coletta Youngers, "A Closer Look at the CBI," *Caribbean Contact* (October 1982); and Jacqueline Braveboy-Wagner, "We're Missing the Boat in Denying Aid to Grenada," *Los Angeles Times* (April 8, 1982).

23. *New York Times* (February 25, 1982), p. A14.

24. Carl Stone, *Democracy and Clientelism in Jamaica* (New Brunswick, N.J.: Transaction Books, 1980), p. 116.

25. Ibid., p. 187.

26. This was probably also a reference to reported links between the PNP and a small Marxist party (the Workers Party of Jamaica) that was played up by Seaga during the 1980 general elections. On the subsequent break between the two parties, see *Caribbean Contact* (October 1982), p. 16.

27. *State Department Bulletin* (July 5, 1976), p. 52.

28. H. V. Hodson, *Annual Register of Events* (1981), pp. 91–92; and *Caribbean Contact* (May 1982), p. 9; (December 1982), p. 5.

29. *New York Times* (November 12, 1982), p. D7.

30. Hodson, *Annual Register of Events* (1981), p. 92; World Bank, *World Development Report* (1981), p. 73.

31. *New York Times* (April 28, 1982), p. D7.

32. *New York Times* (September 8, 1982), p. A26.

33. Gordon K. Lewis, *The Growth of the Modern West Indies* (London: MacGibbon and Kee, 1968), p. 186.

Conclusion

The Insular Caribbean as a Crucial Test for U.S. Policy

Abraham F. Lowenthal

Introduction

As preceding chapters have pointed out, recent events in the island Caribbean (along with concern about the possible impact on the region of a "ripple effect" generated by revolutionary and counterrevolutionary violence in Nicaragua and El Salvador) have prompted a fresh spate of worries, rhetoric, and action in Washington. Because these developments have occurred within the context of intensified superpower rivalry in the Third World, they have lent added importance to U.S. relations with countries on its "third border." Indeed the archipelago, like mainland Latin America during the Alliance for Progress era, has emerged as a crucial testing ground for Washington's ability to respond constructively and effectively to instability in small, nonindustrial societies. Consequently this concluding chapter will examine in detail the policy options available to the United States in the insular Caribbean.

President Jimmy Carter, impelled by a concern for both human rights and the modernization of Third World nations, determined at the outset of his administration that the island Caribbean and its problems merited high-level attention. Secretary of State Cyrus Vance, UN Ambassador Andrew Young, and Mrs. Carter all visited the area, and Under Secretary of State Philip Habib led an important mission there in 1979. The number of U.S. government officials assigned to the region was expanded.

Reprinted, with some revisions, by permission of the author and the publishers, from *The Wilson Quarterly* (Spring 1982), pp. 113–141, and including excerpts from Abraham Lowenthal, "Misplaced Emphasis," reprinted with permission from *Foreign Policy*, vol. 47 (Summer 1982), copyright 1982 by the Carnegie Endowment for International Peace.

The State Department, for the first time, appointed a deputy assistant secretary specifically charged with overseeing U.S.-Caribbean relations.

Later, in the wake of Washington's "discovery" in mid-1979 that a Soviet combat brigade was stationed in Castro's Cuba, a Caribbean Contingency Joint Task Force was established.[1] The Navy staged a series of maneuvers and marine amphibious exercises (including a well-publicized "assault" near the U.S. base at Guantanamo Bay in Cuba), and U.S. warships made 125 calls to twenty-nine Caribbean ports during 1980 alone. The Voice of America established a powerful new transmitter in Antigua capable of beaming medium-wave broadcasts throughout the archipelago.

In all, the Carter administration nearly doubled U.S. economic assistance to the Caribbean (from $96 million in 1977 to $184 million in 1981). Washington also took the lead in 1977 in establishing the Caribbean Group for Economic Cooperation and Development—a consortium of thirty-one aid-giving and recipient governments and sixteen financial institutions such as the International Monetary Fund. The consortium has channeled more than $300 million to the Caribbean since 1978. To supplement all this activity, Carter helped to launch, with considerable fanfare, a "private-sector entity" called Caribbean/Central American Action, which was supported by fifty-one U.S. corporations and staffed in part by Foreign Service personnel on leave, to work on improving U.S. ties with these regions.

President Reagan has demonstrated as much if not more interest in U.S.-Caribbean relations. His first official visitor was Jamaica's new prime minister, Edward Seaga; even in his austere 1982 budget, aid to the Caribbean surpassed $200 million. He also held lengthy discussions about the region with President José López Portillo of Mexico, Prime Minister Pierre Trudeau of Canada, and other world leaders and allowed suggestions of a "mini-Marshall Plan" to filter into the press (although the idea was eventually modified beyond recognition).

The resurgence of attention provides an opportunity for a new look. How is the Caribbean evolving? What are the real U.S. interests in the region and how are they changing? What are the different ways in which U.S. aims might be promoted and the likely risks and benefits of each? To what extent is it feasible or desirable to fashion special policies toward the Caribean? What kind of approach might work?

Caribbean Economics

The economic organization of the Caribbean runs the gamut from the tax havens of the Bahamas, reportedly the largest single Eurocurrency market outside London, to Cuba's brand of socialism (where free-market transactions are beginning to be permitted again), with all manner of hybrids in between.

In the Dominican Republic, because dictator Rafael Trujillo's vast personal fiefdom passed to government ownership after his assassination in 1961, a big share of the economy is now in the public sector; the government tries through generous incentives to encourage private investment, domestic and foreign. Jamaica and Guyana, whose leaders chose to build various forms of socialist-oriented "mixed" economies, are now concerned about how to reattract and stimulate private investment. Grenada, whose principal exports are bananas and nutmeg and whose main economic potential lies in tourism, is apparently opting for Cuban-style "socialism" in a ministate where no form of economic organization can much alter the obvious constraints on growth: scant resources, a small island, a tiny population.

Economic productivity ranges from the abysmal showing by Haiti— "the land of unlimited impossibilities," whose chief local growth industry may be the smuggling of refugees to the United States (at up to $1,500 a head)—to the uneven but impressive performances of Martinique and Guadeloupe, the Bahamas, Puerto Rico, Trinidad and Tobago, and Barbados. The region includes four out of the six countries with the lowest GNP per capita in the Western Hemisphere (Haiti, Dominica, Grenada, and Guyana). But it also boasts eight territories with GNP per capita among the highest (Martinique, Trinidad and Tobago, the Netherlands Antilles, Guadeloupe, Puerto Rico, Suriname, the Bahamas, and Barbados). Trinidad and Tobago has been lucky. It is the only Caribbean nation to have struck oil and today produces 200,000 barrels per day.

Although per-capita incomes in the region are high by Third World standards, bitter poverty is still widespread. Two-thirds of Haiti's rural population were reported in 1978 to have annual incomes below $40; 50 percent of Haiti's children under five suffer from protein-calorie malnutrition, with 17 percent classified as gravely undernourished. Seventy-five percent of preschool children in the Dominican Republic suffer from malnutrition, 4 percent severely. One-third of Jamaica's people have annual incomes under $200, barely enough to cover a tourist's stay for a single night at one of Montego Bay's fancy hotels. In the slums of West Kingston, writes Trinidadian V. S. Naipaul, "hovels of board and cupboard and canvas and tin lie choked together on damp rubbish dumps behind which the sun sets in mocking splendour."

Overall, the island economies are in deep trouble. Caribbean shares of world production of sugar and of bauxite are falling, and even absolute levels are declining in many cases. The region's share of world tourism revenues is also dropping. At the same time higher prices for oil and other imports burden economies in the Caribbean as elsewhere in the Third World.[2] Although the Dominican Republic's significant progress counters regional trends, it too has been hard hit by the price of oil. In 1973, for instance, it earned almost twice as much from sugar exports as it spent on oil imports; by 1979, oil imports cost about $75 million more than the country's total income from sugar.

Most islands have few known resources beyond the sun and sea, and this fact will never change, for "the pencil of God has no eraser"— as an old Haitian proverb puts it. Those places with a broader resource base—Jamaica, for example, with its bauxite and the Dominican Republic with its nickel and gold—have seldom been able to exploit these assets fully. All of the islands have limited domestic markets, insubstantial local savings, and inadequate financing capacity. Agriculture is weak and declining through most of the region. "King Sugar" is now, at best, a princely pretender, its dominance undercut during the twentieth century by large cane growers in Louisiana and Brazil and by the thriving European sugar-beet industry. Most of the islands have deliberately sought to diversify their economies, moving toward manufacturing (Puerto Rico), textiles (Barbados), petroleum refining (Aruba and Curaçao), financial services (the Cayman Islands), mining (many places), and tourism (everywhere). As elsewhere, people have moved off the farm and into the towns. The result: food production per capita—of pineapples, bananas, beans—has fallen during the past fifteen years in Jamaica, Guyana, Haiti, and Trinidad and Tobago. The region as a whole now imports more than $1 billion worth of food annually, costing the equivalent of at least 10 percent of total exports.

While agriculture is declining, so is the push toward industrialization. The burst of industrialization-by-invitation begun during the 1960s has run out of steam. Most of the islands have found that it is easier to "take off" than stay aloft. Constrained by small size, they cannot generate enough power, in the form of capital, local markets, and so on, to sustain altitude. And capital must generally be imported, so many of the profits—from the making of watches or socks, the retreading of tires, the refining of oil—are therefore exported. Few Caribbean islands show any growth since the mid-1970s in the share of GNP accounted for by manufacturing. Industrial stagnation combined with a rural exodus and populations that are growing by 2 and 3 percent a year (versus 0.7 percent in the United States) have produced unemployment rates exceeding 30 percent in some countries—even according to *official* statistics.

All of the Caribbean countries (even Haiti, which has been independent since 1804) bear the mark of centuries of colonial rule and of plantation societies. Ninety percent of the region's population are descendants of the four million slaves imported from West Africa beginning in 1506. The history of the Caribbean has always been largely shaped, and even written, from outside. As William Demas, president of the Caribbean Development Bank, has written, "The [Caribbean] countries have a common historical legacy: the sugar plantation, slavery, indentured labor, monocultural economies producing what they did not consume and consuming what they did not produce . . . and perhaps the longest period of external political dependence in any part of the Third World."

Caribbean Politics

Most Caribbean societies are still not well integrated internally. Many, indeed, are more fragmented socially and politically now than they were a generation ago. The Dominican Republic's civil war in 1965; Trinidad's 1970 Black Power uprising; Bermuda's 1977 race riots; the 1980 general strike in Martinique; Jamaica's recurrent urban violence— all exemplify this trend, as did also the 10,800 Cubans who sought asylum within the garden walls of the Peruvian embassy in Havana in April 1980 and the subsequent sealift that brought 125,000 into the United States.

The islands are even less well integrated "horizontally"—with one another, that is. Although a broader sense of identity is slowly emerging, enhanced by the creation of certain regional institutions such as the University of the West Indies, local efforts to forge a "common market" have come to naught. The West Indies Federation of ten territories established in 1958 lasted only until 1961 because it could not survive interisland rivalries, especially between Jamaica and Trinidad. The eastern Caribbean, the last portion of the Americas to shed colonial rule, is shattering into ministates so small as to raise the possibility that one or another could be taken over by international criminal elements.[3] Interchange between the Commonwealth Caribbean islands and the Spanish-, Dutch-, and French-speaking territories is still minimal.

Politically the area faces contradictory currents. All but four of the fifteen independent countries are formal democracies. "Nowhere else in the world," Jamaica's Edward Seaga has said, "does a conglomeration of parliamentary democracies exist as it does in the Caribbean." But democracy is not always deeply rooted, and an extended period of deceptive political "stability" may be coming to an end. Many long-standing practitioners of "doctor politics"—Lloyd Best's unimprovable phrase to describe the role of scholar-statesmen such as Eric Williams (Trinidad and Tobago), Juan Bosch (Dominican Republic), and Luis Muñoz Marin (Puerto Rico)—are either dead or out of power. Their passing has ushered in an era of uncertainty. Jamaica, once considered highly developed politically, verged on chaos as the 1980 election approached; some 600 persons were killed in preelection violence. In the Dominican Republic the first peaceful transition from one elected President to another came in 1978 only after the Carter administration "jawboned" the local military and thus helped make sure that the ballots were fairly counted. Even Barbadians, who "consider that they and their institutions are perfect," as one nineteenth-century British governor put it, are nervous about the influence of leftist activists on small neighboring islands. Haiti, long ruled by "Papa Doc" Duvalier, is now controlled by his son "Baby Doc"; no one knows when or how this dynasty will end. And in Cuba, where Fidel Castro, at age 54, has directed a highly authoritarian regime for twenty-three years, overt dissidence is increasingly evident.

Indeed polarization seems to be the prevailing trend. Grenada's leftist coup has been matched by a rightward swing (albeit through elections) in the politics of Dominica, St. Vincent, St. Kitts-Nevis, and Antigua and especially by the decisive election in 1980 of Edward Seaga as prime minister in Jamaica after eight years of Michael Manley's "democratic socialism." The prospects for some sort of "pan-Caribbean" consensus grow dim as the islands' politicians move in diverging directions.

On the world scene most Caribbean countries are satellites in search of an orbit, or perhaps of multiple orbits, in the sense of regular and predictable relationships with major powers. The United States acts increasingly as the principal metropole; France and Britain have been slowly withdrawing from the area. Mexico and Venezuela have shown some interest in expanding their relations with the Caribbean, as they demonstrated in mid-1980 by making a joint commitment to sell oil to nine Caribbean and Central American states on extremely favorable terms. The Soviet Union's close relationship with Havana makes the Kremlin a regional actor, although its direct influence has so far been slim outside of Cuba itself, where Moscow underwrites the economy with some $3.4 billion annually and equips the military.[4]

Cuba's situation is not the most extreme case of dependence. Almost all of the island states have special trade and aid agreements with various powers. Martinique, Guadeloupe, and French Guiana, for example, are juridically part of metropolitan France; their citizens participate in French elections and send voting delegates to the National Assembly in Paris. These three territories receive some $570 per capita a year from France, making their economies, in William Demas's words, "the most highly artificial in an area in which there is considerable artificiality." The residents of the Netherlands Antilles receive about $200 per capita, courtesy of The Hague. Washington's subsidy to Puerto

Rico, in the form of transfer payments, amounts to more per capita than the USSR's assistance to Cuba. In all, the islands benefit from more foreign aid per capita than any other group of countries in the world.

The volume of trade with the United States—$12 billion in 1980—reflects one characteristic shared by most of the Caribbean: a high degree of dependence on the U.S. mainland. Not counting Puerto Rico, the United States has more than $4.7 billion in direct private investment in the area. Some 75 percent of the bauxite that the United States imports comes from the Caribbean, as does about $4.5 billion worth of refined petroleum products.

Underlying the Caribbean's contemporary uneasiness is a conflict among goals. All of its people want economic growth, more equity, full employment, political participation, enhanced national autonomy, and more self-respect. These aspirations are not necessarily compatible. Cuba has achieved full employment at the cost of underemployment and severe limits on political freedom. Martinique is prosperous in large part because it is not autonomous. Barbados has grown speedily, but not equitably.

The truth is, no single development strategy in the Caribbean has really worked. As Lloyd Best summed up the postwar experience: "We hoped for economic transformation by borrowing capital, by borrowing management, by borrowing technology, by borrowing this and borrowing that, and by kowtowing before every manner of alien expert we could find." Yet sustained progress has been elusive, and high expectations have turned, here and there, to frustration and violence.

Defining U.S. Interests

What is at stake for the United States in the Caribbean? What are Washington's interests? How are they changing?

Such discussions usually focus on security and economics. Security has usually been defined in terms of keeping hostile political and military influences away from America's "soft underbelly." That was the aim of both the Monroe Doctrine (1823) and the Roosevelt Corollary of 1904.

U.S. military installations dot the archipelago, from the Roosevelt Roads naval base in Puerto Rico to Guantanamo Bay in Cuba. The Caribbean provides access to the Panama Canal, long considered vital to U.S. commerce and defense. The sea lanes on which much U.S. trade depends (including one-half of its imported oil) pass through or near the Caribbean. Washington's economic interest, as traditionally conceived, turns on protecting U.S. commerce in the region as well as access to various local strategic minerals and raw materials. For all these reasons it has long seemed crucial that, if nothing else, the United States maintain what Secretary of State Cordell Hull once called "orderly and stable governments" in the Caribbean.

Many U.S. diplomats continue to think in these terms. They cite the presence of Soviet fleets in the Caribbean (since 1962, twenty-one Soviet naval deployments, vaying in size from two to five ships, have visited the Caribbean); the possible construction of a submarine base capable of handling Russian vessels at Cienfuegos on the southern coast of Cuba; and the KGB's electronic intelligence-gathering installations, also based in Cuba. In addition, they say, U.S. commercial interests in the Caribbean are being threatened by political instability.

Other observers, mostly in academe, ask whether the Caribbean is really still so important to the United States. Changing technology—for example, jet aircraft and long-range missiles—has reduced both the military significance of the area and the feasibility of excluding foreign influence. U.S. naval bases and other outposts there are no longer vital; U.S. power can easily be brought to bear from the mainland. Indeed, most of Washington's remaining military installations in the Caribbean are currently due for phase-out by the mid-1980s, primarily for budgetary reasons. The Panama Canal, although still useful, is no longer *essential* in the old sense. A shrinking share of U.S. trade passes through the canal; many of the world's new oil supertankers are too big to negotiate it, as are almost all of the aircraft carriers around which the Pentagon's fleets are organized.

In practical terms the United States can no longer exert the total control over the region it once enjoyed. From 1898 to 1969 no hostile naval force (aside from German submarines during World War II) entered Caribbean waters, although more recently Soviet ships and submarines have been visiting regularly to "show the flag." The primary means for protecting U.S. strategic interests now lies in great-power agreements, exemplified by the apparent U.S.-Soviet "understandings" of 1962, 1970, and 1979, which, seriatim, are said to have banned from Cuba land-based nuclear missiles, Soviet submarines carrying nuclear missiles, and further deployments of Soviet combat troops.

In economic terms, too, the Caribbean's relative significance for the United States has waned. Before World War II the region accounted for more than 11 percent of total U.S. direct foreign investment and an even higher share of overseas trade. By 1978 the investment ratio (excluding Puerto Rico) had dropped to only 2.5 percent and was considerably less if $2 billion of "paper" assets in the Bahamas is excluded. The share of U.S. petroleum imports coming from or passing through the Caribbean, though still significant, has been declining in recent years as shipments from the Middle East, Nigeria, and Mexico have risen. Bauxite, the area's principal strategic export, is available from many other countries.

There are, however, still good reasons for the Caribbean to remain an important item on Washington's agenda. First, the sovereign nations there constitute a significant bloc in the UN and other international bodies where thus far they have generally supported U.S. policies. For example, the island democracies voted en bloc for the UN resolution condemning Moscow's invasion of Afghanistan and have backed Washington's position on Israel. Should they turn hostile, that could prove to be a major irritant. Imagine, for instance, the trouble that might ensue if the islands went on record in the UN as favoring independence for Puerto Rico.

Second, there is the sheer scale of the human interpenetration between the Caribbean and the United States. Grenada's radical New Jewel Movement is led primarily by men who were influenced, as students in U.S. universities during the 1960s, by the Black Power movement. Jamaica's prime minister, Edward Seaga, was born in Boston and educated at Harvard. People of Caribbean descent are making their presence felt in the United States, as they have been doing ever since the 1920s when the arrival in New York of some 40,000 black West Indians helped touch off what is now called the "Harlem Renaissance." Large, active, and growing Caribbean communities are already a fact of political life in Florida, New York, and New Jersey, just as the Mexican influence grows in the Southwest. Since World War II some 4.5 million Caribbean nationals have left the islands and entered the United States. (Many others have gravitated toward France, Britain, the Netherlands, and Venezuela.) Puerto Rico has exported 40 percent of its total population to the mainland since 1945, primarily to New York, Chicago, and other Northern cities. Over one million Cubans have come to stay since 1960, more than 400,000 Dominicans, at least 300,000 Haitians, and about one million West Indians—all of this over and above the continuing shift of populations from island to island.

These migrations are not unrelated events. They reflect a fundamental, continuous, and probably irreversible response to regional overpopulation and the magnetic attraction that any stronger economy exerts on a weaker one. Haitian peasants flock to the Dominican Republic, where they can earn up to $1.50 for every ton of sugar cane cut, stripped, carried, stacked, and loaded—a princely wage compared to the 30 to 75 cents offered back home. Dominicans, meanwhile, head for more prosperous Puerto Rico. Citizens of all Caribbean countries seek opportunity in the United States, where jobs go begging that native Americans, black or white, will not accept. This flow of people back and forth between the Caribbean and the United States is one of today's most salient U.S.-Caribbean linkages.

Finally, and perhaps most significantly in the long run, the Caribbean has become, by virtue of its proximity to the United States and the increasing international prominence of the region's leaders, a kind of litmus test of the attitudes and policies that Washington will adopt toward Third World countries generally. Thus an intimate relationship exists between the Caribbean and the United States, whether either party likes it or not. What now has to be determined are that relationship's future nature and consequences.

Charting a Policy

In pursuing its ties with the Caribbean, Washington has, in essence, four options to choose from. The first, not now in vogue, is what may be called the "traditional" policy, its chief principle having been well expressed by Assistant Secretary of State Francis Butler Loomis in 1904: "No picture of our future is complete which does not contemplate and comprehend the United States as the dominant power in the Caribbean Sea." This approach combines studied indifference to the islands' underlying economic and social realities with keen sensitivity to potential threats to the military security of the United States. At its crudest, it appears as the "gunboat diplomacy" of the first two decades of this century, repeated again by Lyndon Johnson in Santo Domingo in 1965. This is a deceptively attractive policy because it seems cheap and simple, but it is dangerously shortsighted. It amounts to putting out the fires while doing nothing to remove the flammable material.

A second approach would be for the United States to "disengage" altogether. The assumption here is that the region is economically and strategically irrelevant and would perhaps fare better if left alone. This alternative also has a certain appeal. Given all the other issues with which Washington must deal, it might be tempting to let the Caribbean stew in its own juices, to lavish upon each of these thirty-two struggling entities the "benign neglect" customarily reserved for Burma or Sri Lanka. Realistically, however, such isolationism, particularly with respect to border areas, simply is not feasible for a major power in the modern interdependent world.

A third Caribbean policy—the "activist" strategy—is essentially the one pursued, in different ways, by the Carter and Reagan administrations. Its tenets are two: The United States must retain its special concern for the region's military security and political stability and must, at the same time, increase its economic and technical aid. This scenario, epitomized by the Reagan administration's Caribbean Basin Initiative, calls for beefing up the U.S. presence politically, militarily, economically, and culturally through both the public and private sectors. Its proponents favor adjustments in trade and tariff policy (not just outright injections of money) to facilitate the transfer of capital and technology to the islands. When money changes hands, they think it should be done via *bilateral* agreements to emphasize the American "partnership."

The activists also hope to turn the Caribbean Basin away from Cuba. From its very first days, the Reagan administration moved to counter Havana's diplomatic efforts and tighten restrictions on commerce and exchange. Indeed Secretary of State Alexander Haig threatened repeatedly to "go to the source" to stop Cuban arms shipments to guerrillas in Central America.[5]

The activist policy has some obvious plusses. Focusing more attention, and aid, on the Caribbean gives Washington increased regional leverage. Most of the islands are so small that even limited assistance goes a long way. The timing is also good: Cuba's internal difficulties are growing, while general Caribbean trends are toward greater cooperation with the United States. But the CBI, a centerpiece of the Reagan administration's activism, has left much to be desired. It has been seriously distorted by an East-West focus. Obtaining aid from Washington under the plan depends more on a country's attitudes toward Cuba, U.S. foreign policies, and U.S. private investment than on economic need or development prospects. The insignificant amounts suggested for Haiti and Honduras, the two poorest countries in their respective regions, illustrate this point, as has the administration's obvious intent to exclude from the CBI not only Cuba but also Nicaragua and Grenada. The CBI has reflected Reagan's interest in military security, political loyalty, and advantages for U.S. firms rather than concern for the region's long-term development. Because most Caribbean countries are dependent on the United States, they will speak the language the administration wants to hear, but they are disenchanted by Washington's emphasis and rhetoric.

Among the CBI's other problems is the danger of creating unrealistic expectations. Jamaica's Prime Minister Seaga hopes for a U.S. commitment of $3 billion annually to the region—perhaps ten times what is likely to be forthcoming. Moreover, the preoccupation of the State Department and the White House with Cuba does not sit well with most Caribbean leaders, who perceive Castro as only one of many regional actors rather than as a Cold War instrument. Indeed most of them are not above "playing the Cuba card" to please domestic voters or curry favor in Third World meetings. The U.S. obsession with Havana has diminished the chances of cooperating with Canada, Mexico, and

Venezuela—all of which maintain diplomatic, if not cordial, relations with Castro's government—to develop the Basin.

More generally, the activist approach carries the risk that Washington will become too "interventionist." Even assuming benign intent, active or covert U.S. pursuit of political goals could stifle local initiative or provoke nationalist reactions. And to the extent that U.S. interest in the Caribbean appears to be merely expedient, not really concerned with the region's people but rather only with potential threats to the United States, the chances increase that an active U.S. presence in the region will backfire.

The fourth policy alternative—the one favored, not surprisingly, by many Caribbean leaders—is the adoption by Washington (and others) of a sustained commitment to Caribbean development. Such a posture would emphasize underlying social progress rather than immediate military security; concentrate on the long term rather than the short term; and tolerate diverse political and economic ideologies. Such a "developmentalist" policy would involve large sums of money, channeled primarily multilaterally rather than bilaterally; imaginative efforts to provide "nonaid" concessions; and a scaling down of U.S. efforts to contain or reverse the Cuban revolution. Rather than building up U.S. visibility, Washington would downplay its own role and lay the foundations for a healthier future relationship by focusing on the region's economic stagnation, extreme inequities, malnutrition, illiteracy, and poor social and health services.

This approach responds to a fundamental U.S. interest of having stable, working societies on its third border. It reflects both a moral concern (that one is, to an extent, one's brother's keeper) and a practical realization that festering problems in societies so intertwined with the United States will eventually affect both parties.

Three drawbacks are apparent, however. One is, again, the danger of exaggerated expectations. It is not likely that the high aspirations of Caribbean peoples can all be achieved, even with substantial foreign aid. Some of the obstacles to sustained, equitable growth—meager resources (material and human), insufficient size, extreme vulnerability to bad weather and world market slumps—cannot be wished away.

Second, there is an inevitable tension between accepting any form of economic and social organization—even Cuba's—and reassuring domestic and foreign investors about the region's prospects. Stanching the flow of capital from the Caribbean (not to mention attracting more investment) depends in part on giving businessmen confidence that their role will be valued and their assets protected. The prospect of nationalization or outright expropriation undermines that confidence, to say the least.

Finally, the developmental approach would be hard
Congress is not likely to go along with what would
"no strings" commitment to aid a bewildering cluster of s.
at least not until Americans come to realize that their own
being depends, in some measure, on that of their neighbor.
administration so far has been willing to make that case and it
be that none can.

Toward the Future

U.S. foreign-policy makers should beware of becoming too enamored
with the Caribbean Basin concept (which embraces both the archipelago
and Central America) since the notion has little reality or meaning
outside the United States, where it has a long history as a strategic
concept. From Washington's perspective Central America and the Caribbean are sensitive border regions. Yet there exist important differences
between these two regions. Despite divergent colonial traditions, the
insular territories share social, ethnic, economic, and cultural patterns
as well as historical relationships with the United States and other
Western powers that differ sharply from those in Central America.
Generally the islands are handling social and economic pressures within
a framework of established, functioning political institutions, while
Central America is wracked by civil war. Most are very closely tied to
the United States through extensive economic, cultural, and demographic
interaction. The Central American countries, in contrast, are much
more autonomous, both economically and politically. Tangible U.S.
interests in Central America are scant and hence Washington's leverage
is correspondingly lower than in the Caribbean.

U.S. policies toward the two regions should reflect these differences.
The CBI makes most sense in the archipelago. Lumping Central America
and the island Caribbean together carries the risk that aid will be
channeled mainly to those countries where it can do the least good,
precisely because of insurgent activities.

Unfortunately the very nature of the U.S. political system may make
it impossible to obtain the necessary resources for Caribbean development without emphasizing threats, real or imagined, to U.S. security.
Even those officials who recognize that the Caribbean's problems are
primarily internal, and who understand that long-term economic and
social changes are more important than immediate political loyalty,
tend to believe that anticommunist rhetoric is required to harness
resources. The cost of this approach, however is precisely the kind of
misplaced emphasis found in the CBI. If Congress and the American
people are told that economic assistance is needed for the Caribbean

to prevent Communist inroads, they will not support future aid programs to countries that pursue independent foreign policies and maintain friendly ties with Cuba, even though long-term U.S. interests might best be served by incorporating such states into a comprehensive Caribbean plan.

Washington should recognize and explain to the American public that the key U.S. interest in the Caribbean is related to modernization rather than military security or political loyalty in the narrow Cold War context, and that promoting the islands' economic and social health would be the right thing to do even if Fidel Castro vanished. At the same time Washington should refrain from proclaiming a "special relationship" and from promising "regional preferences" that significantly contradict its basic policies on trade, finance, immigration, and the like. U.S. stakes in the Caribbean are fairly high, but they are even greater elsewhere. On a practical level, history suggests that U.S. interests in the Caribbean, however important they may appear from time to time, will not long sustain the adoption of policies that contravene universal rules. Preferential programs that substantially hurt some other region important to the United States simply will not last. Also, local island leaders are uneasy about the idea of a special relationship because traditionally that has meant singling out the area for rhetorical or military attention: the approach either of Arpege ("Promise her anything . . . ") or of Hallmark Cards ("When you care enough to send the very best"—the Marines).

The Caribbean is too near to take for granted, yet too far, historically and politically, to integrate comfortably into a U.S. "sphere." Thus the challenge for U.S. policymakers is to understand the Caribbean for what it was, for what it is, and for what it could become and to focus on the realistic possibilities that exist for the United States to affect the region positively. Once such lessons are learned, Washington will be much better prepared to deal sympathetically and effectively with other developing states and regions.

Notes

1. The task force, headquartered at Key West, Florida, consists of a modest staff of seventy-five, with representatives from all four services. Its mission: to monitor developments in the Caribbean, conduct training exercises, and devise contingency plans for the use of U.S. forces. It is one component of the U.S. Forces Caribbean Command.

2. Only Trinidad and Tobago is self-sufficient in oil, but many other nations are exploring, including Suriname, Cuba, Barbados, Guyana, Jamaica, the

Dominican Republic. Because Caribbean countries are small, even modest discoveries could be of major importance.

3. In 1980 the FBI arrested ten men in New Orleans who were allegedly planning to overthrow the government of Dominica (population: 77,000), using mercenaries drawn from the ranks of the Ku Klux Klan. The plot was reportedly bankrolled by a Texas millionaire (who hoped to establish a free port in Dominica), supposedly with the blessing of a former Dominican prime minister.

4. Cuba has the best air force in the Caribbean and a modern "gunboat navy." The Soviets have supplied the island with MiG-23 "Floggers" and missile attack boats. Russian pilots reportedly help patrol Cuban skies to free Cubans for duty in Angola, Ethiopia, and elsewhere in Africa.

5. Fidel Castro charged in July 1981 that the United States had also employed germ warfare in Cuba, accounting for a dengue epidemic as well as for the appearance of blue mold tobacco blight and roya rust, which attacks sugar cane. He presented no hard evidence to support his accusations, but one U.S. official's countering observation that Castro is "now as paranoid as he was at the time of the Bay of Pigs" was not unambiguously reassuring.

About the Contributors

H. Michael Erisman is an associate professor of political science at Mercyhurst College in Erie, Pennsylvania. He has written numerous articles, conference papers, and book reviews dealing primarily with Caribbean/Central American affairs, appearing in such journals as *Revista/Review Interamericana, Caribbean Review,* and *Caribbean Studies.* He has contributed a chapter to Barry Levine (ed.), *The New Cuban Presence in the Caribbean* (Westview, 1983) and coedited (with John Martz) *Colossus Challenged: The Struggle for Caribbean Influence* (Westview, 1982). His main fields of interest are U.S. and Cuban foreign policies as well as transnationalism in the Caribbean. He is currently working on a book dealing with Cuban foreign policy.

Bruce M. Bagley is an assistant professor in the School of Advanced International Studies at Johns Hopkins University. His main field of specialization is comparative politics, with particular emphasis on Latin America. He has contributed articles to numerous journals and to books dealing with hemispheric affairs.

Kenneth I. Boodhoo received his doctorate in international affairs from the University of the West Indies (Mona, Jamaica) and is currently an associate professor in the International Relations Department at Florida International University. His major publications, which have focused primarily on the Commonwealth Caribbean, have been published in *Caribbean Review, Caribbean Studies,* and the *Journal of Caribbean Studies.* He contributed a chapter to R. Millet and M. Will (eds.), *The Restless Caribbean* and has two selections in the forthcoming M. Levy (ed.), *Haitian American Issues.*

John A. Booth is an associate professor of political science at the University of Texas in San Antonio. A specialist in political participation in both peaceful and violent forms, his research has focused on Colombia, Costa Rica, Guatemala, and Nicaragua. He is the author of *The End and the Beginning: The Nicaraguan Revolution* (Westview, 1982) and "Political Participation in Latin America: Levels, Structure, Context, Concentration, and Rationality" in the *Latin American Research Review* (1979) as well as other articles, and has coedited *Political Participation in Latin America, Vol. I: Citizen and State* (1978) and *Volume II: Politics and the Poor* (1979).

Jacqueline Anne Braveboy-Wagner received her B.A. and M.A. from the University of the West Indies (Jamaica and Trinidad) and her Ph.D. from the University of Arizona. She is presently an assistant professor of political science at Bowling Green State University. Her main areas of research and publication are Third World affairs, Japan and the Third World, and Caribbean/Latin American politics. She is the author of *The Logic of the Third World* (1983) and *The Venezuela-Guyana Border Dispute* (1983).

Josefina Cintron Tiryakian is a research scholar in the History Department at Duke University. She received her Ph.D. in Latin American history from Harvard University and is a fellow at the Bunting Institute of Radcliffe College. Her writings include articles, book reviews, and conference papers on both Latin American colonial political economy and contemporary U.S.-Caribbean relations, appearing in such journals as *History of Political Economy* and *Hispanic American Historical Review*. She has contributed a chapter to E. C. Frost, M. C. Meyer and J. Z. Vazquez (eds.), *Labor and Laborers through Mexican History* and is presently writing on Puerto Rico and the Caribbean Basin Initiative.

Juan M. del Aguila is an assistant professor of political science at Emory University (Atlanta, Georgia) who specializes in Cuban and Interamerican affairs. He has published "The Limits of Reform Development in Contemporary Costa Rica," *Journal of Interamerican and World Affairs* (1982) and "Cuba's Foreign Policy in the Caribbean and Central America" in *Latin American Foreign Policies* (1981). He is currently working on a book entitled *Cuba: The Dilemmas of a Revolution* (forthcoming, 1984) and is a contributor to the *Latin America and Caribbean Contemporary Record*.

J. Edward Greene, who specializes in comparative Caribbean politics and the Caribbean business environment, is acting director of the Institute of Social and Economic Research at the University of the

West Indies in Jamaica. He is the author of numerous articles, mono-graphs, and books, including *Race vs. Politics* (1974), *The Confused Electorate* (1979, with Jack Harewood and Selwyn Ryan), and *Small Business in Barbados* (1979).

Abraham F. Lowenthal serves as secretary for the Latin American Program (which he helped to establish in 1977) of the Wilson Center at the Smithsonian Institution in Washington, D.C. He has also been the director of studies at the Council on Foreign Relations and has authored and co-authored numerous books and articles on Latin America, including *The Dominican Intervention, The Peruvian Experiment, Armies and Politics in Latin America,* and *Latin America's Emergence.* He is currently writing a book on U.S.–Latin American relations. Lowenthal holds a doctorate from Harvard University.

Index